Effective Grief and Bereavement Support

Effective Grief and Bereavement Support

The Role of Family, Friends, Colleagues,
Schools and Support Professionals

Kari Dyregrov and Atle Dyregrov

Foreword by Magne Raundalen

Jessica Kingsley Publishers
London and Philadelphia

First published in 2008
by Jessica Kingsley Publishers
116 Pentonville Road
London N1 9JB, UK
and
400 Market Street, Suite 400
Philadelphia, PA 19106, USA

www.jkp.com

Library of Congress Cataloging in Publication Data
A CIP catalog record for this book is available from the Library of Congress

British Library Cataloguing in Publication Data
A CIP catalogue record for this book is available from the British Library

ISBN 978 1 84310 667 8

Printed and bound in Great Britain by
Athenaeum Press, Gateshead, Tyne and Wear

Contents

Foreword

When life must go on
Magne Raundalen

This book is a gift to professionals who find themselves confronted with bereaved individuals after a sudden death in the family, whether it is a matter of an infant who suddenly dies, someone who commits suicide, or an accident or illness that abruptly tears aside the thread of life.

This book is a gift to those who wish to extend a helping and supportive hand to a close friend or family member who has suddenly and brutally lost a loved one.

The book is a much yearned for gift because it gives us the knowledge, courage and ability to take action towards becoming better support providers when we find ourselves in the midst of a close, grieving network. For those of us who are professionals, the book is an invaluable resource with regard to understanding the bereaved, understanding how differently and unfathomably a sudden death can affect different individuals here and now, and in the future. In this manner as therapists we can provide better assistance and support for the grief-stricken and simultaneously give advice to a network on call.

How can a single book include all of this? It has been made possible because the authors, sociologist Dr Kari Dyregrov and psychologist Dr Atle Dyregrov, have not cut any corners in terms of giving the book a theoretical and research-based foundation. The reader will be able to take full benefit of their extensive knowledge of the field and where the authors have lacked knowledge, they have personally implemented large, comprehensive studies, in particular studies to illuminate grief reactions and needs on the part of different groups among the bereaved – both now, and in the future. Further, *Effective Grief and Bereavement Support* provides us with new and extensive insights on the attitudes of the surrounding network, the opportunities, the important roles, and its own need for knowledge and support, so that network members can become the best possible helpers. In addition, those who are frequently over-looked, children and young people, are granted broad and well-deserved attention between the covers of the book. It is nothing short of impressive. Yes, more than impressive, because the down-to-earth nature of the studies and the reader-friendly presentation makes this textbook a gift to us all.

And by all of us I do, in fact, mean all.

This book is about all those who must utter the words that life must go on but with altered contents. From being an empty phrase in daily life, for many of those bereaved by sudden death it is more like a heavy burden to be hoisted up a steep incline. For how does one move on when time stands still, when your inner world is in chaos and you find yourself in the deepest of all possible depths? You would almost prefer to remain down for the count. Because days have passed. Weeks and months as well. You know that the years will pass and you feel as if some of those out there in the network are responsible for the countdown. So you must soon now come to the realization that life *must* go on!

This book is about how you, whether a professional or an individual, as part of the network, can help during the initial hours and days after a disaster has become a reality. It can guide you through the first weeks and months, the first year and subsequently, when you need to provide help and support to the survivors of someone close and dear, who has been snatched away. The book gives you concrete warning signals to protect you from personally becoming worn out and depressed from failing to regulate the use of your own energy in your eagerness and desire to help others. All of this has been gathered into one book because the authors have made inquiries of both the affected parties and their networks. They have structured this into a system and they provide a wealth of examples of typical responses.

On the theoretical side you are reminded, in a thorough and pedagogical fashion, that everything you do is communication. This applies to both the words you say and the actions you carry out. This applies to the way in which you choose to refrain from saying things and it applies to what you avoid and neglect to do. In order not to become paralysed at the prospect of such a balanc-ing act, you receive clear advice from the authors to listen and listen some more, and speak less. The saying that there is a reason why God gave man two ears and only one tongue comes immediately to mind. Further, you are reminded that you shall restrain the impulse to quickly offer a multitude of advice because it is so easy to damage the self-image of those who feel as if they are about to lose their footing. More than an eager advisor, they need a supporting arm and a strong shoulder.

At present I have yet to read a more rewarding and convincing analysis of the important significance the social network can have in terms of assisting the grief-stricken to move on in life with their sense of reason and mental health intact. The important function of the network is described as the warm, gentle hand of salvation. The warm, gentle hand prevents and averts blows and scratches when vulnerability and rawness dominate the emotional life. The hand of salvation is the concrete and practical force that at the right moment can rescue the grief-stricken when he or she is in the process of drowning.

The word roadmap is used metaphorically in many contexts. I would say that this book is the most useful roadmap I have ever been offered. Particularly when the landscape in which I am going to move at times appears both inaccessible and dark. The authors of this book have obviously a belief that both you and I, as potential support people for the bereaved after a sudden death, can light up the darkness and simultaneously function as important navigators. With this support, those who have come to a halt can acquire the strength and courage to move on in life.

Preface

It is not easy to know what to say or do if someone close to you suddenly loses a loved one. Nor is it easy for those who are worn down by grief to ask friends to support them on their own terms. Few situations put family or friendship ties so emphatically to the test as a sudden death. On paper it is simple; it is just a matter of being there for the person in question. In reality, it is unfortunately much more difficult. The processes that are initiated can create an abyss between former friends and break up families, but can also lead to ties growing deeper and becoming stronger. Strong feelings come into play in the aftermath of a death and the ties between people are subjected to pressure and strain. While many receive the support that they wish for, the reality is unfortunately that a number of the bereaved feel betrayed by their surroundings, by close family, friends and work colleagues. In these networks there are many who find that their efforts are futile, and they despair over not succeeding in reaching the bereaved in their attempts to provide support. The interaction between the bereaved and their surroundings can be without problems but in many cases becomes full of problems due to the lack of knowledge in those surroundings about grief reactions and the development of grief over time, the fear of making things worse and fear of contacting the grief-stricken. Many bereaved people understand this but are so low on energy that they are not able to do anything about it.

Politicians and professionals in the field often glorify the support that can come from the surroundings of the bereaved following a sudden death. 'It is from our close, social network that we must obtain support when an accident occurs' is a concise expression of that which is often said in eulogies after large-scale accidents that strike suddenly and unexpectedly. This is both important and correct, but those of us whose work in close contact with those who lose their loved ones, with or without forewarning, know that this easily becomes a phrase that we fall back on to express compassion or that we say in hope that the people in the bereaved's surroundings will do their part. In addition, it can conceal an unfortunate evasion of responsibility on the part of the public sector, a convenient assumption, which for many does not correspond with reality.

On behalf of the crisis-stricken and their networks we hope to contribute to promoting the resources and inherent potential of the support and care of fellow human beings. Advice grounded in knowledge and experience to the 'giver' and 'recipient' of social assistance will potentially alleviate the situation of the bereaved, support the network, enrich the relationship between the bereaved and the network, and liberate social resources by enabling the social network to a greater extent to dare to enter into a support role. The advice will to a large degree be based on the experiences of those who have been 'in these shoes' and on countless meetings with bereaved individuals and their social networks through clinical work, bereavement support groups, seminars and research. In addition, we base our work on the wealth of theoretical literature from the field of grief and trauma and on sources of knowledge about communication, social networks and network support.

Through the various chapters, we make a number of references to our own research. In order to avoid the repetition of the details of different projects, we refer to the project names. The methodological frameworks and details for all the projects are then presented in an Appendix.

We who have written this book, sociologist Dr Kari Dyregrov and psychologist Dr Atle Dyregrov, have done our doctorates on topics related to sudden death and grief. Our primary workplace is the Center for Crisis Psychology in Bergen, Norway, where we have extensive research and clinical experience in work with people who have lost loved ones through sudden, unexpected death. The working and research experience also includes crisis-stricken groups in encounters with social networks. We want to extend our gratitude to the many bereaved and their networks, who in taking part in research projects have made an important contribution to this book becoming a reality. All the quotes are from bereaved participating in the research projects as shown in the Appendix. They are direct quotes, but presented with pseudonyms, and permission for their use has been granted from the bereaved. In addition we would like to thank the Unexpected Child Death Society of Norway, who has been an important supporting player and collaborating partner, and the Norwegian Foundation for Health and Rehabilitation, who financed Kari Dyregrov's post-doctoral work and thereby made possible the book project. In addition, the National Institute of Public Health has contributed significantly to the publication of the book.

WHEN YOU BELIEVE
That you will spare me
Not tear open the wound
Be a bit careful.

You hurt me then
And create a distance.

I hunger for words and signs
That show that you understand what lies beneath my surface.
All the time.

Only when you show me that you understand
Can I release my joy and laughter.[1]

---

1   From 'Smerten – den ubudne gjest' ('Pain – the uninvited guest'). Thoughts in a grieving
     process by Inger Marie Aase. SIGMA forlag, 1994. Aase, who has personally experienced
     the sudden and unexpected loss of a child, has given us permission to include this poem.

1

Introduction

People learn to handle most situations in life but when sudden and traumatic events occur, we discover, as does our network, that we are completely incapable of coping.

What is the book about?

The above quote, from a father who lost his 14-year-old son by suicide, indicates the primary intention of this book. This is to contribute to increasing the knowledge about how professionals, and social networks as well, can support the bereaved following a traumatic death. It is otherwise our hope that the bereaved will also find reading the book beneficial. Beyond the contribution of new knowledge to an unexplored field which the book represents, advice to the 'givers' and 'recipients' of social support that is grounded in experience can help alleviate the distress of the bereaved and liberate social resources, by better enabling the surrounding network to dare to enter into a support function.

The book is about the unique and intense encounters that take place between people who have suddenly lost people close to them, and their social network. At a theoretical level it is about social support between closely related partners in situations of crisis, and the many relationships and processes that are initiated in such encounters. An important principle in this context is that such encounters, in the deepest sense, are about interpersonal communication. The point of intersection between expressions of support, personal relationships and the effect of social support is investigated here. At a practical level the book is about providing increased insight and reflection for the 'recipients' and 'givers' of support and care, and it contributes with general advice and hints. The book is based on comprehensive, nationwide research findings from the bereaved of traumatic deaths and research on family and friends who have supported similar bereavement groups.

Our wish is that the book shall liberate potentials and resources that people already possess, enabling the utilization of these in a mutually beneficial manner – particularly in situations where life presents us with adversity. It is our belief that the bereaved and the social network, through a mutual understanding of the dynamics of their interaction, will be able to accept and provide better social support. The latter result can be achieved if the bereaved and their network reach an understanding of what is taking place, by inviting the presence of the other into the support process, and by having confidence in what the other can do. By clarifying the factors that influence cooperation as well as the bereaved individual's support needs, social networks can become more secure with regard to their own support function. In order to create a common understanding of the book's contents, and because some words are, at least in part, scientific terminology specific to the field, we will begin by defining some key terms.

Close bereaved

When we use the term close bereaved we mean people who lose children, a spouse, siblings, grandparents, a partner, etc. In our opinion it is important that the term close bereaved be not only associated with biological proximity but that it should also include 'intimate relationships' – those who personally *experience* having close ties to the deceased. We hereby remind ourselves that best friends or a girlfriend/boyfriend can experience grief that is equally profound as that of the biological family of the deceased and will also potentially be in need of support and care.

Social network

A person's social network is the sum total of the interpersonal relations of significance in his/her life (House and Kahn, 1985). It is a matter of relatively long-term, but often informal, relationships between people. Social networks comprise close or more peripheral family members and friends, colleagues, school friends, neighbours, acquaintances or other bereaved/others in the same situation. One can speak of degrees of intimacy or network 'circles'. Most people will receive support from various 'circles' of network members, ranging from the very closest of friends and family in the 'inner circle' (the intimate networks), through more peripheral individuals and acquaintances, to those with whom one has merely a superficial acquaintance, in the 'outer circle'. Often, but not always, those with whom one has the most frequent and the best type of contact are part of the close social networks, and represent a higher quality and greater quantity of social network support.

Social network support

Social support from social networks (social network support) here entails support and consolation, social stimulation, information, advice, participation in routines and rituals and practical or economic assistance for the bereaved. In correlation with more recent theories in the field, we will refer to network support as something that accelerates mastery or that alleviates distress in the situation following a sudden death (buffer or recovery effect) (Stroebe *et al.*, 2005). Further, it is also a condition that the helper as a rule has an underlying wish to provide assistance in this difficult situation. A central aspect of the book's perspective is that the support takes place in an interaction between the bereaved and the network, rather than a view of the bereaved as support 'recipients' and the networks as support 'givers'. Another important principle is that social support is viewed as being context-dependent, which implies that how social support is experienced and interpreted must be seen in connection with the sociocultural background of the parties involved, and the contexts in which the various acts of support are carried out.

Traumatic death

We use the term traumatic death in reference to child death, and the death of young people and adults that strikes unexpectedly and without warning. Such deaths can be due to accidents, murder, suicide, fire or natural disasters, or can be the sudden and inexplicable death of a child. For the bereaved this type of death results in both shock and trauma. The shock is due to the death occurring suddenly and unexpectedly; the event is permeated with drama and results in the feeling of a lack of control. The trauma can inflict strong sense impressions or delusions, involving the potential creation of long-term psychosocial problems.

Psychosocial difficulties

Grief subsequent to traumatic death in varying degrees results in complex and compound processes for the individual, and for the individual in interaction with other people, respectively (Dyregrov, Nordanger and Dyregrov, 2000a, 2003; Li *et al.*, 2003; Schaefer, Quesenberry and Wi, 1995; Tedeschi and Calhoun, 1995). In this book the term 'psychosocial difficulties' is used as a general term for the emotional and psychological pain, the existential challenges and the social strains that arise after traumatic death.

The foundation and perspective of the book

An important point of departure for the book is that although people need one another when life becomes an uphill battle, they will not always succeed in functioning well together in life situations characterized by adversity. Further, the book is based on the fundamental view that social support and care are communicated and that this communication takes place *between* human beings (a relational and communicative perspective). There is a particular focus on the insecurity all parties feel in the situation, an insecurity which to a certain extent is a deciding factor with regard to support failing to reach the intended bereaved party as effectively as it might have done.

General insecurity on the part of the network is often formulated as: 'How should I behave in relation to someone who has just lost a child, spouse, or life partner? What can I do to help? What type of help do they need? Shall I contact them or would that be intrusive? Certainly enough time has passed now that I should stop bringing up the subject.' The bereaved ask their own questions when personal disaster has become a reality: 'What can we expect from our surroundings? Who can be expected to be there for us? Maybe others have enough of their own problems? What should I say or not say? Perhaps we should be able to manage on our own now?'

Because such questions will always be closely connected to the individual situation and the individual bereaved and network involved, it is not always possible to give a standard response. Nonetheless, some things can be more appropriate than others and some advice can generally apply for the majority of cases, given certain conditions. The conditions that we have in mind will be intertwined with the factors *surrounding* and the processes *within* human beings (social structures and social processes). We would like to give the reader an understanding of how the bereaved and networks experience support processes and how support can contribute to mastery through good relationships. In order to achieve this, both user-knowledge based on experience and theoretical knowledge are required. This book therefore takes as a point of departure the experiences and wishes that we have disclosed on the part of the bereaved and within their networks, when we point out possibilities for strengthening social network support. This is also in correlation with public authorities' emphasis on the need for an enhanced 'user perspective' in welfare states.

Who will find the book useful?

This book is first and foremost addressed to professional assistance workers such as clergymen, police, medical personnel, psychologists, people working in the school system, funeral homes, and others who come into contact with the bereaved. Such assistance groups are extremely important with regard to the mobilization of comfort and support for those who are left behind following a traumatic death and can give the bereaved advice about the significance and use of social network support.

The book is also intended as an aid for family members, friends, colleagues and neighbours who create social networks around those who suddenly lose a child, a spouse, a partner, or another person with whom they share an intimate bond. The large number of deaths (suicide, murder, individual and large-scale accidents, infant death, etc.) that occur suddenly and unexpectedly implies that an extremely large number of people every year find themselves in a situation where they would like to provide support for a fellow human being in the midst of a serious life crisis. As an example, one might mention that for the some 4000 suicides that take place in Great Britain and Northern Ireland each year, there will be an estimated 24,000–32,000 bereaved people who will receive support from various social network 'circles'. In our research, social networks are characterized as possessing not only a large desire, but also a large amount of uncertainty, with regard to how they shall support the bereaved in the context of a sudden death (Dyregrov, 2003–2004).

Because the success of any encounter between social networks and bereaved individuals is dependent upon both parties, the book is also directed towards those who have lost loved ones. In research studies the bereaved have confirmed that social network support is extremely important, but that very many things can go wrong between the bereaved and the network, and that quite frequently, they do. They are at the same time humble, thinking 'we would certainly be just as helpless as they are if we did not know what we know now'. The bereaved will hopefully be able to obtain knowledge from this book, particularly where the book gives advice regarding how they can accept friends' endeavours to offer support. Beyond this, the book discusses the network's experience of encounters with the bereaved – a reality that the bereaved and others have known little about.

Students attending university colleges that educate some of these professional groups (nurses, teachers, social workers, social educators, policemen and women, etc.) are also included in the target group for the book and we hope it can serve as an inspiration for those who wish to write papers about topics such as grief and crisis assistance, care for the bereaved and social network support following sudden death.

We would specify that although many of the examples take as a point of departure parents' sudden loss of a child, most of the information will also be applicable to the loss of other types of relationships. And although the book is written about sudden death, much of the knowledge presented here will also be valid for other types of loss situations. Many of the bereaved experience the same difficulties following anticipated deaths, such as by cancer. The book will therefore also be helpful for friends and family who feel a need for support after such types of deaths.

The chapters in the book

In order to understand how sudden death affects the bereaved and as a basis for providing good support and assistance, common grief and trauma reactions are addressed first. Other common reactions, social and familial challenges in relation to school, the workplace and social network, and the personal growth that many experience in the aftermath of a crisis are also illuminated (Chapter 2) for the same reason. To make support possible on the terms of the bereaved, their own wishes for help are illuminated through extensive user research. Adults' wishes for help are discussed first (Chapter 3), before a particular focus is put on children and young people's situations and support needs (Chapter 4). Chapter 5 addresses the challenges, dilemmas, and valuable aspects of support that members of social networks can experience when they have provided support for crisis-stricken individuals. The next two chapters are more theoretical and incorporate theories about communication, grief and crisis, and social network support. Our intention with the middle section of the book is to connect the first section, based on experience, to some general advice about network support. In Chapter 6 we address why social network support is so important for crisis-stricken individuals and why such support can be so difficult. We then expand in depth upon our perspective of social network support as communication. The subsequent chapter discusses important conditions and criteria for good network support. Here we address how one can create a good relationship, choose a form of support that is helpful, and otherwise provide support in such a way that it is experienced as beneficial (Chapter 7). In Chapter 8 and 9 some general advice is given regarding the type of support that family, friends, schools and the workplace can give, based on theory and the experiences of the bereaved and networks. The following chapter discusses which signs can be an indication that support from family and friends is not sufficient and that professional help should be brought in (Chapter 10). In conclusion, we give some concrete advice on support for social networks, because one knows that it is demanding to stand by a crisis-stricken individual for a long period of time. Here in particular, collaboration with professionals and the bereaved will be highlighted (Chapter 11).

How to read this book

This book can be read in its entirety, from cover to cover, or in parts and piecemeal. If one chooses the first, one will see a development that starts with a terminological background and foundation, moves through our own and others' empirical studies and theory, and continues with advice and guidance with a more practical orientation. If one reads the book in its entirety, one will understand that it is not our desire to provide handy hints for social network support in the event of a sudden death. Our wish is to give readers a kind of knowledge that will enable them to make their own assessments. This book can also be read more selectively and we have therefore permitted some of the key themes to overlap. If one reads only the chapters that address advice and guidance, we would ask that the reader exercise caution in interpreting our advice categorically. Although we have sought to provide some general advice, this must always be adapted to the situation at hand. This is exactly the predominant focus of the remainder of the book.

In order for the book to reach different target groups and be easy to read, we have (with the exception of a couple of chapters) sought to avoid excessive use of scientific terminology. We have therefore also provided a brief outline of the main themes at the end of each chapter. For professionals or others with a special interest who would like to read more on the subject in depth, we have included a number of literature references at the end of the book.

The book's characteristics

- The book's primary objective is to improve network support following death.
- The book shall contribute to increased insight on the part of both support 'recipients' and 'givers' in sudden death situations.
- The book addresses theory about important factors in social network support.
- The book gives general advice based on the experience and knowledge of the bereaved, social networks and professionals.
- The book's target groups are professionals, social networks, the bereaved, and university students.
- The book is based on research and theory.
- The book has a relational and communicative perspective.
- The book contains advice for professionals but also for social networks and the bereaved.
- The book has been written in a down-to-earth manner but also contains a few more challenging theoretical chapters.
- A summary of the main themes is presented at the end of each chapter.

2

How does sudden death affect the close bereaved?

If someone had dropped an atom bomb in the city centre, it could not have affected us more. It would not have been any worse...

This quote from a father who lost his young son serves as an example of the grief and despair parents can experience upon losing a child suddenly and unexpectedly. In this chapter we describe the common reactions of bereaved adults and the challenges they experience in interaction with their surroundings subsequent to a sudden death. Knowledge about such reactions is a prerequisite to enabling other people in the social network to contact the bereaved in a helpful manner. We will first present and discuss some common myths about grief reactions and grief processes because these contribute to the formation of our expectations of the bereaved.

Myths about grief

There is an almost universally accepted perception that we must pass through certain phases in our processing of grief. This idea has its basis in the fact that well-known theorists many decades back wrote about grief that followed such phases; since then this has been repeated so many times and in so many contexts, in textbooks, magazine articles, newspapers and in the public domain, that everyone believes it to be a fact (Parkes, 1998). The reality is that studies do not confirm such phases. Grief reactions never follow the simple stages often described in textbooks.

Because such models of the different stages of grief are described in the textbooks of healthcare personnel, many of the bereaved have unfortunately met with phrases such as 'now you are in the denial phase'. The interpretation of a bereaved person's reactions can accordingly be based on a perception regarding whether or not the person in question 'should' be in this phase and the attitude towards the grief-stricken becomes theoretical rather than empathetic. This shows how easily we can allow our encounter with the bereaved to become coloured by our theories about grief, with the consequence that we then behave insensitively and offensively. Phase theories about grief are not confirmed by grief research, apart from the fact that we can, for the majority of the bereaved, break down the reactions into a shock phase, which follows directly after the death, a reaction phase that comes when we absorb what has happened, and a reorientation phase, at which point we gradually lift our gaze and once again commence with life's duties. But even this type of structure does not fit everyone. The prevailing theories today emphasize that the bereaved individual alternates between addressing the loss and avoidance of things that recall it and that this alternation is a way of coping with the loss (Stroebe and Schut, 2001). The bereaved must be able both to approach what has occurred, and 'report' for life again. Such theories are more in harmony with the reality one encounters. The first myth that can be disposed of is accordingly that grief follows fixed stages, where emotions succeed one another in a characteristic pattern. Let us establish with certainty the simple fact that there is not only one way to grieve – that there are just as many different ways as there are bereaved people. That also means that each individual must find his or her own manner and own pace of grieving.

Myth number two is that everyone must go through a grieving process. Among both professionals and laypeople in the Western world there is a fixed idea that grief work is necessary. The term grief work means going through an emotional process where one is confronted with the reality of the loss, reviews the events that took place before and during the loss, and where one focuses on memories of the person one has lost and gradually achieves detachment from the deceased. The confrontation is often connected with a discussion about what happened, although the processing can also take place without discussion with others. Many will go through such a grief process and grief processing, but research shows that a relatively large sub-group, up to 20 per cent, do not feel a great sense of grief – neither immediately following the death nor later, even where the person they lost was a child (Bonanno and Kaltman, 2001). For people who have grief reactions that are neither intense nor long-term, it is of course completely inappropriate to pressure them into following a pattern dictating how they shall react, or requiring them to process their grief. If both healthcare personnel and family and friends believe that the bereaved are *supposed* to react visibly, the pressure can become enormous and problems can be created because the bereaved can begin to believe that there must be something wrong with them, in that their reactions are not more pronounced. Here it is society's expectations and its understanding of grief, which we as professionals have contributed to forming, that creates problems. For the bereaved individuals who experience their loss in this manner, it is wholly legitimate to continue with life as before, become involved with their surroundings and live the most active life possible.

For the large number of the bereaved whose reactions are both strong and long-term there is another myth that creates problems, namely the myth that grief is a process with a fixed beginning and end point. Even though this to a certain extent is true for grief following the deaths of people of an advanced age, it is not true when the death occurs suddenly and unexpectedly or in a dramatic manner. Those in the surrounding environment often have a time perspective according to which they anticipate that the situation will improve once the bereaved individual has put the first months following the death behind them. They will then frequently want an uplifting response when they inquire about how things are going. The pressure to respond 'things are going well' or 'things are better now' is enormous. More recent grief research, including research we have carried out on parents into the second decade after a child's death (Dyregrov and Dyregrov, 1999) shows that grief has a long-term timeframe, where its overall character is not necessarily as persistently 'heated' and exhausting as at the start, but one of a continual return, particularly in connection with the annual seasons, public holidays and red-letter days (Murphy, Johnson and Lohan, 2002). It is of particular importance to note that grief research has shown how meaningful it is for many to be allowed to develop and maintain an internal memory or a so-called internal representation of the deceased. From being a person inhabiting our external surroundings, the deceased will become a 'person' inhabiting our internal space. The deceased person becomes an active part of our spiritual life and can serve as a constructive value for us, as an 'inner helper' or advisor. It is accordingly not necessary to undo the ties to the deceased as was believed formerly. We can carry the deceased inside of us in a meaningful way (Neimeyer, 2001). If this holding on becomes extremely intense and prevents us from being able to function on a daily basis, this is of course cause for concern and professional help should be sought.

Although we have now emphasized the large range of reactions and possible progressions that grief can follow, some reactions will nonetheless be more common than others. In order to make it possible for the social network and other helpers to identify these, we will discuss some features of the psychosocial difficulties, grief and personal growth.

Common reactions

While the immediate reactions often include shock, disbelief and numbness accompanied by strong emotions, the subsequent reactions are often varied and distributed across many different life spheres. Many grieving individuals experience periods of weeping, intense sadness and yearning for the deceased (Cleiren and Diekstra, 1995; Jordan, 2001; Reed, 1993, 1998). Grief reactions vary in intensity and duration, and grieving people experiencing extremely strong reactions sometimes wonder whether their reactions are 'normal', or if they are in the process of going 'mad with grief'. Many of these individuals have a large need for confirmation that what they are experiencing is 'normal'. Many are relieved when they hear that such problems in principle are viewed as being normal reactions to an extreme event. It is when such reactions remain unchanged over time and prevent the individual from carrying out a normal life that they must be viewed as being destructive and inexpedient.

Immediate reactions

When someone suddenly dies, most bereaved people will experience a sense of the unreal as the death occurs, when they learn of the death or during the period of waiting up to the point when what has happened is clarified. The experience can be that of being in a dream, as if it is all taking place in a film or as if it were not true. If the death occurs in the home, the bereaved will often respond suitably and quickly until somebody else takes over responsibility. They call for help, start resuscitation attempts if they think this can serve a purpose and often conduct themselves wisely, rapidly and constructively. Previous experience, such as from a first aid course, is retrieved from the brain's experiential storage vault while information from the surroundings is absorbed quickly, precisely and in detail. On the whole, this provides a good point of departure for managing the situation. The sense of unreality reflects the fact that the emotions have been put on hold so that all of one's energy can be expended on handling the situation that has arisen, where it serves as protection against the pain in connection with what has taken place. The experience of time can be dramatically altered, often with the sense of time standing still so that bereaved people can subsequently berate themselves for being slow to act. The waiting period until help arrives can seem interminable, allowing time for many thoughts. A number of bereaved people will afterwards blame themselves for the way they reacted. Many think that their responses were insufficient. If the death is permeated with drama, as sudden deaths often are, the sense impressions can become 'permanently engraved' with an extraordinary intensity. This is due to the mental mobilization mechanism, which enables the brain quickly to absorb information from the surroundings that can then provide a basis for knowing which actions to take. Even in situations where this mental mobilization is not required, it will be activated and it can therefore appear to be a hereditary mechanism enabling action in critical situations.

In principle the first shock reaction guarantees quick reaction and a form of mental protection. The altered sense of time provides 'extra' time to act, allowing the affected individual to absorb what has happened little by little, and serving to postpone strong reactions so that the individual is not immediately overwhelmed by intense feelings, which otherwise can easily lead to paralysis in the situation. The shock becomes so intense that the bereaved cannot absorb everything that has happened at once and hours can pass, or days, weeks and even more time, before they fully realize what has happened. They know it intellectually but not emotionally. It is extremely important that those around the bereaved individual have an understanding of this initial reaction so that they do not expect the bereaved necessarily to exhibit strong reactions or otherwise put pressure on them to react. It is this reaction that can explain why those who are closest to the deceased sometimes end up consoling others with a less intimate connection. It is also easy to begin saying things such as 'you are taking this so well' or 'you are so strong' to describe the reactions of the bereaved, and thereby put pressure on them in the manner of expectations regarding how they should continue to react.

Bodily reactions such as shaking, palpitations, nausea, chills or dizziness are not unusual. For some people these symptoms continue beyond the first day and are intensified by a lack of appetite, too much coffee on an empty stomach, etc. Many bereaved people speak of a 'calamity' of different thoughts racing around in their heads: 'What now?' 'How is this going to be sorted out?' There is so much to be addressed at the same time, and everything appears chaotic and muddled. Others scarcely remember anything from this period of time.

Many find that they do not cry until later, at the wake, devotional service, memorial service, or funeral. These are important rituals for us. From experience we know that it is beneficial to attempt to manage grief without the use of sedatives. The medication diminishes our reactions and can result in further complicating grief processing. It is expedient for grief-stricken people to allow themselves to react emotionally and not attempt to be 'strong' and hold back their reactions. Often, people in these situations zealously set out to acquire medication, perhaps predominantly because it is so painful to acknowledge one's own sense of helplessness. Presence and support usually have a better sedative effect than any medication. Nonetheless, one must not avoid medication at all costs, but evaluate the need by listening to the bereaved and to medical and psychological expertise.

Long-term reactions

It is important to emphasize that long-term reactions are common reactions that many experience and that from nature's side serve a purpose for us. The anxiety or fear that many bereaved experience is a reflection of the fact that we have enhanced alertness subsequent to something having threatened our existence, while memories of what took place compel us to confront and process the death. The long-term reactions accordingly do not reflect unhealthy processes, but are reactions that in different ways help us in the period after a death (and after other situations which threaten our existence). Among the most common long-term reactions following sudden death are:

- feelings of loss, yearning and pain
- self-reproach and guilt
- reliving the events surrounding the death
- sleep disturbances
- anxiety and vulnerability
- concentration and memory problems
- irritation and anger
- physical ailments.

Feelings of loss, yearning and pain

The strong sense of loss, feelings of yearning and pain assert themselves as a rule with the greatest intensity after the funeral, in the encounter with daily life. The loss of the deceased is omnipresent. It is a matter of both the physical absence (holding a child, hugging a loved one, the person in bed beside one) and in particular the absence of all the activities that connect one with the deceased, which the bereaved encounter in everything they do. For many the time period of the first three to twelve months is the most difficult period. At all times one is surrounded by memories of the deceased and all holidays and annual celebrations (birthdays, the anniversary of the death) are experienced for the first time without the deceased. The daily sense of loss and the intense yearning are frequently intolerable, while at the same time one feels lonely because few can truly understand how one feels. Most bereaved people state that the most difficult period is when people in their surroundings no longer give them as much attention, when the expectation of others is that 'now he or she really needs to begin looking ahead'. The bereaved can personally have expectations such as 'now it must soon start to get easier', while simultaneously they experience that things are progressing in the opposite direction.

Self-reproach and guilt

Not infrequently, the bereaved individual will experience self-reproach and guilt although there is no actual basis for this. 'What could I have done to prevent what happened?' and 'If only...' or 'Why us...?' are common thoughts, particularly after a sudden death. After a suicide, such thoughts are particularly intense, and the bereaved individual may need professional help if they do not succeed in sorting out their thoughts (see Chapter 10). If it is a situation involving the deaths of young children the self-reproach can be particularly acute. Because young children are completely dependent upon their parents, it is easier to assume more responsibility in the event of such deaths than when the deceased is older. Many bereaved people regret things they have said or done in relation to the deceased, or they think of things that they would have liked to have said to the deceased. Many brood over or search for a meaning in what has happened, and sometimes the bereaved become preoccupied with the idea of it being a punishment for something they have done.

In line with our above statements regarding the constructive nature of the long-term reactions, it is appropriate here to say a few words about some of the positive effects of guilt. Self-reproach and guilt are perhaps the most important human reactions following critical or traumatic events. When we review in detail everything we could have done or should not have done, thought or said the brain is working at retrieving information from our experiences that can be utilized later in life. If we did not have this mechanism, we would not be able to learn from our mistakes, change our behaviour and develop as a species. In principle this is an important mechanism, enabling us to learn from experience, and it is only when we perpetuate the thoughts of self-reproach after all the experiences have been 'retrieved' that the mechanism becomes self-destructive. It is therefore important to respect that such a period of self-reproach will often follow on the heels of a death, that it must run its course and that only later will we be in a position to recognize whether the mechanism has become a fixation and the bereaved person needs help in departing from this state of self-condemnation.

Reliving the events surrounding the death

Some aspects in connection with the death can have become imprinted on the mind's eye, or – if we were not present – engraved as imaginary scenes or perceptions of the chain of events and of how one's loved one passed away. The bereaved can have seen or heard dreadful things, experienced unusual odours, or absorbed unpleasant things in connection with the death and this can come back to haunt them as recurring images. One frequently hears that the bereaved have so-called 'flashbacks', in other words, intrusive visual impressions on the retina from which they are unable to free themselves. Other things that can become acutely imprinted in one's consciousness can be the telephone call relating the sad news, the priest or policeman who came to the door to report the death, the time of waiting for news or the last thing one said to or did together with the deceased. Reliving such memories or images can be troublesome and they can reappear in such a way that the bereaved feels that they have no control over them.

Sleep disturbances

Often thoughts about what happened are activated when the bereaved goes to bed and many acquire varying degrees of sleep disturbances. Many struggle to fall asleep because their thoughts make them physically restless. Some sleep reasonably well, but awaken early in the morning without any chance of falling asleep again. Sometimes the traumatic event returns in the form of nightmares. If one must get up early to go to work or is responsible for getting children off to school, the night can therefore be very brief. Networks wishing to demonstrate involvement and support should therefore wait to make contact until late morning, so that the bereaved have the opportunity to sleep. Bereaved individuals with serious sleep disturbances will naturally not be able to perform to their best ability, neither in a school nor a work context. One otherwise sees that, when the quality of sleep declines over a long period of time, this can easily lead to exacerbating other long-term reactions.

Anxiety and vulnerability

Increased anxiety and fear is another extremely common reaction to sudden death. The anxiety can be connected with everything that recalls what one has experienced, but anxiety and fear that something else will happen to one's own family or self is even more common. '*One* death has taken place; what is to prevent the occurrence of another?' The world goes from being a safe place; to an unsafe place. The sense of security and invulnerability which many experience in daily life, which enables us to keep the misery of others at a distance and to think that 'such things happen to others, but not to me or my loved ones', is replaced by a new sense of vulnerability where anything can happen. If a child had passed away and one has other children, the fear that something shall happen to them as well is sometimes intolerable. Not infrequently this can result in overprotection of the other children. Because children's fear of losing their parents also increases after a death in the family, this creates the basis for a vicious cycle.

This type of anxiety has a number of dimensions. One of them is an increased sensitivity to change that many experience. The body is set in a state of emergency preparedness and all changes in the surroundings, from loud noises to sudden movements, are read as dangers triggering a reaction. Many bereaved people have their sense of insecurity enhanced by reading the newspaper, particularly the obituaries, watching the news, etc. with new and vigilant eyes, observing that, 'so much more happens now than before'. Many of those in the surroundings do not help matters when they tell the bereaved of their own or others' losses, often because they think it will help. Instead it can reinforce the bereaved person's experience that 'so much happens'.

Concentration and memory problems

For the bereaved who are to return to work (and school) concentration and memory problems are a source of concern. Many believe that they are in the process of becoming senile, or that their mental capacities have become permanently impaired. They speak of how they organize their lives by writing messages to themselves on Post-it notes in order to remember simple daily tasks. It is not certain what causes these mental difficulties but they can be connected with the state of heightened preparedness, geared to detecting danger that occupies a large portion of the brain's capacity for the processing of information, while at the same time intrusive memories and concerns continually interrupt the thoughts. A decreased mental agility resulting from sadness and efforts to keep unpleasant memories at a distance can also be a contributing factor. Regardless of the cause, there are many who speak of short-term memory impairment and problems in collecting the thoughts for tasks requiring complicated mental activity. Because such problems can last for a long period of time, they can create difficulties in a work situation. Colleagues and supervisors can become irritated over tasks that are forgotten, about more time being needed to carry these out or about reduced work quality. For those who experience many of precisely these types of reactions, it is crucial that the work situation can be adapted to the temporarily reduced capacity, so that the bereaved person does not burn out attempting to manage tasks in the same manner as before. The period of restitution can be long-term and if the bereaved puts pressure on him- or herself too soon or is pressured by others during this period, it can lead to long-term sick leave.

Irritation and anger

Irritability, impatience and anger are also common reactions. Many believe that this is due to some of the factors mentioned above: that the reactions also arise as a result of being drained of energy, sleeping badly, etc. But it is also the case that the sensitivity one has for one's surroundings, and the change in values that many experience, result in the bereaved imposing different requirements on their social environment and therefore becoming more easily irritated or angry. Frequently this is anger towards the individual held responsible for the death, whether this was due to a traffic accident, an error made in hospital, a murder or a person who has committed suicide. In our work we also experience that many have a justified anger towards a public health service that they feel did not do their job well enough or subjected them to considerable additional strain. Many sudden deaths result in an encounter with the media and this frequently results in anger about how the death, or how the bereaved themselves, have been portrayed there.

Physical ailments

Studies have shown that grief can lead to an increased incidence of physical illness due to the large psychological strain grief can entail (Li *et al.*, 2003; Schaefer *et al.*, 1995). This implies that one can become more receptive to different types of illnesses because the immune system is not functioning optimally. Increased agitation and anxiety can lead to physical ailments such as tension, headaches and digestive complaints. Being in a state of constant worry and on full alert for things that can potentially happen requires an enormous amount of energy. It leads to fatigue but not the kind of fatigue that enables you to sleep well. If the appetite has disappeared, there can be a deficiency of nutrients that the body needs. The combination of reduced sleep quality, the proliferation of somewhat confusing thoughts, and reduced appetite can lead to many bereaved people becoming physically tired in the aftermath of a sudden death. Some can feel constantly tired and run-down for a long period of time:

> It is almost as if a valve has been opened below, so that all of one's physical energy drains out. You have no motivation to do anything. You sit in the kitchen staring into space from 5:30 a.m., wide-awake, but with no initiative in the body to go to work. It is empty. No energy…

The bereaved personally often point out the connection between the death and family members' subsequent increase in physical ailments:

> All the colds that I had! I think your immune system… I believe you can carry a number of latent illnesses. When something like this happens, then you have no reserves. Then I think it happens very quickly. When I look at my father and everything that has happened afterwards… And it is obvious that when you are experiencing that type of grief, then you become even more frightened if you develop some illness, right? You don't need it, in the middle of all of this.

Because of the physical and mental strain brought on by the situation, a number of people are put on sick leave. Although this can be necessary, one should also be aware of the fact that this entails an increased probability of social isolation (Sèguin, Lesage and Kiely, 1995).

Complicated grief reactions

It is normal to feel sadness and grief when a person close to you dies. There are, however, several types of complicated grief reactions. One common type is characterized by strong separation distress. If, for many months (more than six months), one experiences an intense and persistent longing for the deceased, problems in moving on with one's life, and an experience that life and the future are meaningless and without purpose, this can be a sign of 'complicated grief'. This is also called 'traumatic grief' or 'chronic grief' of the separation distress variety. The separation from the deceased is at the core of the condition, and finds expression through persistent weeping, yearning and preoccupation with thoughts about the deceased, and in part this involves a denial and lack of acceptance of the death. In order to distinguish normal from complicated grief, it is important to specify that one is talking about complicated grief when the experiences are extremely intense, inhibit the functions of daily life and continue for a minimum of six months.

It is important to specify that complicated grief reactions of the separation distress type are to be distinguished from depression and anxiety-related conditions. The bereaved are neither, as some fear, in the process of 'going mad'. One can say that people who are experiencing complicated grief have a condition of extended or chronic grief (Prigerson and Jacobs, 2001). More recent research has shown that people experiencing complicated grief have an increased risk of long-term health impairment. This is particularly the case for the bereaved subsequent to 'violent deaths' such as suicide, murder, accidents or unexpected child deaths (Dyregrov, 2003; Prigerson et al., 1997; Stewart,

1999). In different studies of parents who lose a child, it has been documented that 20–70 per cent can experience complicated grief (Dijkstra, 2000; Dyregrov *et al.*, 2003; Jacobs, 1999; Prigerson and Jacobs, 2001).

The following is an example from clinical daily life, which we present in order to make complicated grief even more concrete and clear:

> Sandra lost one of her twin babies, and became overly fixated on the deceased twin and had problems with the contact with the other. She continued to use the baby carriage for the twins, where she had a picture of the dead child in the one end of the carriage and the living twin lying in the other. She longed intensely for the dead twin, heard him crying and even brought a shovel along to his grave to dig him up again. She continued to buy toys, which she put on his grave. For her, he was not dead; he was just waiting for her to come and get him. In addition, she replayed for her inner eye how she had found him dead. She also became almost fanatically obsessed with having another child and believed that her son would be reborn in a new child (but only if it was a boy).

This woman meets all the requirements of a complicated grief reaction, except the problems existed and were detected long before six months had passed. There is of course no point in waiting six months before helping someone who is obviously in distress.

Another complicated grief reaction is due to the trauma itself more than the loss. The way in which the death took place results in a pattern of posttraumatic reactions with three characteristics: 1) re-experiencing the death wherein traumatic memories invade the thoughts, 2) attempts to avoid thinking about, speaking about or approaching anything that recalls the death, and 3) an over-active nervous system.

A third, but less common, complicated grief reaction comprises a postponement of all reactions, but where people in the bereaved person's surroundings will notice that they are different from how they were before the death (for a more detailed presentation of this see Chapter 10).

When we miss somebody with intensity after a sudden death, the brain can 'build bridges' in this loss, hereby alleviating the loss by giving the bereaved a strong sense of proximity to the deceased (Prigerson *et al.*, 2000). This need not be a complex form of grief but can be if it proves to have consequences for functioning on a daily basis. The bereaved individual sees the deceased before them, wholly vital and lifelike, and only when they reach out to touch him/her do they understand that the person is not there. Sometimes they hear the voice of the deceased or feel as if the person is in the room. Many seek proximity by smelling the clothes of the deceased, retrieving items that they associate with them or they wear something that connects them to the deceased. It is important that the bereaved be allowed to clear away the clothing and other personal items of the deceased at their own pace, in consultation with others in the family. Many find the task of such clearing up or clearing away to be an extreme burden, but it must be done. If everything remains untouched for months after the death, this can be a sign that the internal grief processing has come to a halt.

For bereaved people who struggle with complicated grief reactions, good social network support is extremely important but not always sufficient (see Chapter 10). There are good therapeutic treatment methods that help those who are struggling to process their loss, and to identify and change difficult thought patterns and interpretations of the death. The social network will here, as with long-term reactions, potentially play a key role in helping the bereaved, in collaboration with professionals who have such expertise.

Challenges in the family

After a traumatic death the bereaved may over time acquire a strained relationship to their spouse, immediate family, other family members, friends or colleagues. Many bereaved people claim that others, to a very limited extent, understand how they feel and some experience that others pull away and do not want to be bothered. The reality is perhaps rather that others do not know how they should help, or are personally so affected that they cannot stand the thought of making contact or addressing the painful subject. In that the main purpose of this book is how one can best avoid having problems arise in the interaction between the bereaved and their social surroundings, we will discuss some common challenges in couples and in the immediate family, before in the next section discussing interactions with the social network.

Couples

> It is much easier for me to talk about it with others. If I need to shed a tear, I do it, but he does not. He puts on a front pretending that everything is fine. When I am depressed and cry, I get angry with him. Because I feel that he ought to cry too. But then he says, 'I am also grieving. I also feel loss, and am in just as much pain as you are but I don't cry.'

The above quote illustrates a typical example of how women and men can grieve differently. There can be considerable gender differences in grief, a point that is particularly noticeable after the death of a child. Mothers will usually react with greater intensity and for a longer period of time than will fathers, although for about one-fifth of all couples the opposite is true. Studies have shown that while fathers actively address and take action in relation to the outside world in making funeral arrangements, dealing with the police and funeral home, mothers have a greater tendency to set their sights inward, to feel and express strong emotions (Riches and Dawson, 1996a). Generally, women also seek out others to speak to about what has happened, to a larger extent than men, while men to a larger extent attempt to focus their thoughts on other things, including work. It is important to note that this does not necessarily mean that women are regarded as grieving more than men, but that they are far more capable of expressing grief. The differences in the reactions to and expressions of grief can frequently lead to mutual accusations between the parties involved and communication and mutual support can become difficult:

> Why are we so shut-off from one another when we are so open towards those outside of the family? We are incredibly sensitive, both my husband and I, and we are the worst when it comes to straightening out our relationship. We are both of us so fragile that we don't manage to help each other. My husband reacts by going out and working. That is his way of coping with this. The accusations come from everyday things and are not connected with that which is perhaps at the root of them. But why can't one do anything about it if one is aware of it? We don't manage it.

With the loss of a child, one can interpret the different types of reactions as mothers and fathers implementing different grief-mastering strategies, which to a certain extent are connected with a traditional distribution of labour. But if work has given men the greatest distraction from grief and served to reinforce the man's identity as something other than a father, the same is the case for those women today with a stronger work-identity. The home, however, represents a catalogue of losses: of the child, of the normal domestic routines, marital life and a predictable family life. For many women more of their identity is still connected with the home than is the case for men, who associate a larger portion of their identity with work outside of the domestic sphere. This, along with different personal grief reactions connected with gender differences, also leads to men and women often participating in different bereavement communities.

Very many couples also state that they 'grieve out of step', in that she is 'up' while he is 'down', or the opposite. It can appear as if many couples adapt this as a suitable interaction among themselves, in that the one spouse allows their grief to emerge while the other provides support. Some bereaved people point out the positive aspects of both spouses not being down simultaneously, and how they can then take turns helping one another up out of despair:

> In the beginning when Jane was up, then I was down, and vice versa. We supported one another. When things were really at their worst and I was at rock bottom, she would be able to say: now let's go for a walk, now let's do this or now let's do that. That lasted for two years.

Communication problems do not only apply to parents who lose a child. Many of the same problems can also be experienced by other close family members and with other forms of loss.

Climate of impaired communication

Communication is the easiest when one communicates about everyday, familiar things. Communicating about feelings is, for many, more difficult than speaking about events and facts. When a sudden death strikes, the bereaved experience an extreme situation and many families develop greater problems in speaking together about their feelings and thoughts. Any unresolved conflicts will easily surface, resulting in accusations and in the attribution of blame, particularly if the feelings have a connection with the deceased. As a result of the fact that individuals are struggling, the family is therefore affected as a unit when a family loses someone close. The family members' ordinary behaviour patterns, which function when everything follows customary, familiar routines, will be affected by individuals' grief and trauma reactions. For families that were already struggling with interaction problems, the death can create problems that are difficult to resolve along with individuals' personal crises. In most families the members manage to grow closer after a death but a significant number of families also struggle.

Some children and adults do not sufficiently communicate the grief and despair they are carrying, in order to protect one another within the family unit. They avoid speaking about the death when they are struggling personally, if they believe that other family members are momentarily untroubled. This takes place between adults and between children and adults. An important cause of a climate of impaired communication is that many parents want to protect their children from seeing that their mother and father are suffering from terrible pain. In the same fashion, there are many children and young people who do not communicate sufficiently the grief and despair they are carrying, in order to protect the parents. Mutual support in the family can also be made difficult if family members develop disaster anxiety out of the fear that something will happen to the surviving members. One often sees that traumatic loss can lead to an enhanced preparedness and fear of death or fear that another disaster will occur, 'because if this has happened, anything can happen'. This kind of anxiety can continue for several decades (Dyregrov and Dyregrov, 1999; Dyregrov, 2003; Yule, 1999). Disaster anxiety can result in exaggerated alertness or overprotectiveness. Young people can, however, also experience the same fear that something will happen to their parents.

In the initial period following the death, communication problems often have a connection with inadequate factual information within the family, where information is not communicated to all family members. If the facts about the death are kept hidden from parts of the family unit, this can affect the family's unity, internal dynamics and family members' grief processing over time. Sometimes one partner can keep things hidden from the other or parents can keep important information hidden from the children in the belief that it is best for them. Previously this happened (more) frequently after a suicide, where one hid the cause of death or other circumstances surrounding the death. This still takes place, but an increased focus on and knowledge about the significance of being open has had the effect of this becoming less common. 'Secret' information as a rule comes out into the open at some time or another, which can result in reducing trust or a persistent suspicion that other things are also being concealed. It is therefore of great importance that all family members are continually updated regarding important information about the death, but of course in relation to the age and maturity level of the individual.

Intimacy and sexuality
There are few studies done about how intimacy and sexuality are affected by a death in the family. In a study of 321 parents who had lost children (Dyregrov, 2007), about two-thirds of the parents reported that they had resumed sexual contact in the course of the first three months after the child's death and one-tenth said that this had happened almost immediately. On average, six years had passed since the time of death at the time of the study. Most parents then reported that the level of their sexual activity was as it had been before the death. Nonetheless about one-third had reported reduced activity. There were significantly fewer mothers, compared to fathers, who experienced sexual pleasure. Close to 30 per cent of the mothers experienced that their capacity for pleasure had been reduced after the death. The sexual activity had also declined for around one-third of the parents and only a few of the parents had experienced an increase. The reasons the parents gave for changes in sexual activity and related pleasure were extremely varied, but for both genders it was

first and foremost a matter of causes connected with the grief in itself and the physical exhaustion which grief entails.

The reported changes were given further nuance through written comments on the questionnaires. The women reported that their loss had had a much greater effect on their sexual life. The men most frequently wrote in their comments that the loss had not had any effect on their sexual life. Different aspects of grief were pinpointed as the cause of problems, whether it was a matter of mood swings, feelings of sadness, a lack of energy and fatigue, but also anxiety: anxiety regarding another pregnancy and another child who would perhaps not grow up. Mixed feelings, combined with a guilty conscience about feeling joy or satisfaction, and intrusive images of the child intervening in the course of sexual intercourse, explain why many, and women in particular, are not able to experience pleasure as before or to resume former activity.

Clear gender differences were disclosed in the study. Women more easily develop a guilty conscience in connection with sex; they experience sex as being inappropriate, that men do not understand that it is difficult to think about sex when one's child has died and it is difficult to open oneself up to good feelings when everything in life is currently terrible. Sex is also experienced as being more painful for women than for men. Crying during sex is not uncommon. More than one-half of the mothers in our study had experienced this and most of them just a few times, but close to one-fifth had done so for a long period of time. Fewer men had experienced the need to cry. Men for their part found that their partner was distanced and uninterested in sex after the death of a child. All in all, this can explain why many struggle with intimacy and sexuality after the death of a child. Men experience sexual desire more often than their partner, while women have a greater need for physical intimacy and also find intimacy to be difficult because it is so easily misread as a desire for sex. While men's desire returns more quickly after the death of a child, they also find sex to be more 'consoling' than do women. Nonetheless, both women and men find that sex can alleviate tension after the death of a child. The findings indicate that because of the different needs of men and women, the distance from pressure and conflict is not great. Men seem to have a physical need, which more easily comes into conflict with the fact that women have a greater tendency to bring their grief with them into sex. A large majority of both the women and men agreed that the differences in their mutual desires could create stress for both parties in married life/cohabitation. More women expressed that they did not feel 'whole', that something had happened to their identity and capacity as a woman. One woman, who had experienced a stillbirth, expressed herself as follows: 'I was almost convinced that I could not relate to it (my body). I couldn't stand my body, which had taken the life of my child.'

Parents who managed to handle or improve the situation in the area of intimacy and sexuality usually attributed this to a good interaction within the relationship, which included openness, understanding and discussion. Time in itself was also mentioned as an important factor, often in combination with having another child. An improved psychological state, as the grief began to loosen its grip, also contributed to normalizing the situation in these areas.

Unfortunately, sexuality subsequent to a death entails a double taboo (both death and sex are taboo areas), which is very seldom brought up in contact with professionals, family or friends. Only around 10 per cent of those who took part in our study reported that the theme was brought up in follow-up counselling sessions. Even fewer had friends or family members who brought this up, a point which is perhaps more understandable (Dyregrov, 2007).

High divorce rate – a myth?

When we meet parents who have lost children, they have all heard that there is a greater possibility that the loss will lead to a divorce. In the general population this is a kind of 'folklore' that lives its own life and as a worst-case scenario can become a self-fulfilling prophecy. Some even say that healthcare personnel have told them this (Dyregrov, 2007).

Different coping styles can make communication within the family difficult, resulting in mutual accusations. Nonetheless, it is a myth that many marriages fall apart as a consequence of the death of a child. Most couples grow closer over time, particularly if they manage to show respect for the differences in reaction patterns (see Cruse Bereavement Care, 2008 and SANDS, 2008). Schwab (1998) and Oliver (1999) have in summary articles reviewed research done on this subject, and have concluded that there is no clear documentation supporting the belief that the divorce rate is higher among bereaved parents than in the ordinary population. The main findings in well-controlled studies indicate that parents stay together, in spite of considerable strain. There is clear documentation supporting the fact that a child's death can have an extremely negative effect on the functioning of the family and on the parents' marital relation (Murphy *et al.*, 2003). The areas of the relationship that are often difficult are: a) a father's worry and frustration over a mother's grief, b) a mother's anger about a father not sharing his grief, c) a temporary breakdown in communication, d) a loss of sexual intimacy and e) a general irritability between partners (Schwab, 1998).

Here, as in other areas, there is now a greater emphasis on the fact that relationships can also be positively affected over time. In studies that we carried out in the 1980s (Dyregrov and Matthiesen, 1987), the 1990s (Dyregrov *et al.*, 2000a) and the 2000s (Dyregrov, 2007), we found that the majority of the couples grew closer, while a relatively large group grew apart. Few reported that the relationship remained the same. The ability to communicate within the relationship appears to be an extremely important component of that which contributes to the growth of a couple's relationship (Dyregrov, 2007; Riches and Dawson, 1996a). One also sees that couples who value open communication experience a higher level of grief during the initial period after the loss, than those who attribute less importance to such communication, but that those with open communication manage better over time (Kamm and Vandenberg, 2001).

What happens when a child dies is that the parents must construct or develop a new 'story' (narrative) about themselves and their relationship. The parents' ability to absorb and understand one another's new narratives can be crucial for their subsequent relationship. How can they, individually and together, find new meaning in their existence? How can they help one another to reconstruct their existence in a world where the physical and mental landscape has been dramatically altered? The differences in men and women's grief do not make this easier. The loss must be integrated over time; new roles in the family shall be allocated, and openness and intimacy shall be established or carried on in a new context. It becomes therefore a challenge to mobilize resources in the social network that can support the parents in this process, resources that to a large degree are available on the parents' own terms.

Reduced caring capacity

Bereaved people with responsibility for taking care of young children or elderly parents can have difficulties coping in the initial period after the death. Children and young people can change their behaviour patterns as a result of both the death and the caregiver's grief, and therefore can require increased attention (see Chapter 4). For bereaved adults, this can be an additional strain, carrying along with it guilt and a bad conscience if they find that they cannot be the caregiving people they used to be, because they are physically and psychologically exhausted. Here efforts on the part of the social network are of invaluable importance, for children, young people and adults (see Chapters 3, 4, 7 and 8).

Existential challenges

> I will never be the same person that I was before the death – that was the beginning of a new era. My priorities have changed completely. That which previously had great value and which you appreciated now means nothing. It is therefore so absurd sometimes when I watch talk shows on the telly. They use words like terrible tragedy and then it's like it's nothing. At work I hear colleagues sitting and talking about personal problems and then, it's like it's nothing. I prefer then to withdraw from the situation or leave. It's my priorities that have been turned upside down.

As this quote illustrates, very many bereaved people find it difficult to relate to the 'normal' world because they have seen the abyss. Chaos lurks in the background, a chaos that is not only about a lack of order in one's existence, but connected with the loss of other people (Giddens, 1991). Because when a sudden, unexpected death, possibly the death of a child, damages a human being's fundamental sense of security, it often leads to an existential crisis (Janoff-Bulman, 1992). The bereaved feel that 'the world has been turned upside down' and 'everything that was safe becomes uncertain', that existence is experienced as being extremely unfair and that they do not have control. This can affect them for a long time after the loss. Much of that which we all take for granted in daily life no longer applies and the brutal upheaval imposes difficult requirements with regard to adjusting to that which has happened, at both the mental and the emotional level (Janoff-Bulman, 1992). These difficult requirements lead to most of the crisis-stricken people reviewing both the event and the possibilities that they may have had to influence the outcome (self-reproach) over and over again. In the process of 'leaving not a stone unturned', they have thoughts and reflections that mark them permanently, in the manner of personal and social changes but also in the opportunity for personal growth through the creation of meaning. While the bereaved at an early stage after a death want an explanation for why the death occurred, many are later concerned with searching for or reconstructing meaning in their existence and in further integrating the experience of the death in their life. Those who are able to do so, manage best over time.

The reconstruction of meaning, change and personal growth

In sociology, psychology and related sciences there is a growing recognition of the fact that we create our own reality. To a certain extent we personally control how we experience our surroundings, how we organize our thoughts and the nature of the reality with which we surround ourselves. On the basis of this, the potential arises to imagine that the creation of new meaning is possible, regardless of what we have experienced. The form this takes can vary, and we will make distinctions between different ways of creating meaning and how this affects personal growth.

Many bereaved people find it helpful to find a way to invest their efforts so that the death, once it has become a reality, can serve to benefit others. They become active in different ways so that something meaningful emerges from the meaninglessness. Many parents, for example, volunteer to be available for other parents who find themselves in the same situation. They take part in bereavement support groups, associations for people who have lost children, meet other couples personally, take part in research projects about grief, etc. This offers the possibility for a belief that their child did not die in vain, that somebody else could be helped through the death of their child. This manner of creating meaning and mastery has an extroverted, social form and has helped many.

There is another and more private manner of creating meaning, which is more connected to the family unit. Here the bereaved allow meaning to find expression by emphasizing how the death has enabled them to appreciate in a more heartfelt manner those closest to them. The bereaved can later claim that they feel richer than before the death and that this relational wealth is more important than any type of material wealth. Loved ones are not taken for granted, because one knows the brevity of the distance between life and death. Here the creation of meaning leads to giving greater priority to close, personal relationships. The intensity of close relationships can also include other family and friendship ties, sometimes also with negative ramifications: people who were close friends before the death can be discarded because the relationship becomes empty and the conversations too shallow. But, as we will discuss in the next section, there are also many bereaved people who have found that this has brought them closer to other family members, or that ties to friends and fellow human beings have been strengthened. Many of the bereaved demand something more, something deeper, from their relations with others. Some characterize this manner of creating meaning as a change in priorities pertaining to values: one bereaved person says: 'I don't care about trivialities any longer. Now I know what is important and what is not.'

A third type of meaning creation takes place with those who emphasize the personal evolution and growth which they have experienced. This can also have a social dimension, in cases where the bereaved state that they have grown as human beings and understand better the needs of others in crisis and that they will now be far braver and more straightforward in relation to others experiencing bereavement. Simultaneously, these bereaved people emphasize that they would have preferred to be without this growth process, and to have the deceased with them, alive. Some feel more self-confident and state that they are now more assertive in relation to others; they speak up if they are treated unfairly at work, etc. Others emphasize that they have learned to put their thoughts and reactions into words – here it is perhaps men who experience the most development. The creation of meaning also takes the form of a greater sense of gratitude for life, over the fact that life is seen from another perspective, that life can be more greatly enjoyed, that one has a greater appreciation for the small, everyday things and that life is lived to the fullest every day. Some bereaved people state that being human has become a more intense experience, that the death has contributed to their living life more fully, while simultaneously that which they have lost is granted space in their thoughts, particularly on special occasions and important holidays.

Our own research and the research of others show that most who live through a serious crisis in the long run also experience personal growth. This is the case for both adults and young people. The concept of growth implies that the creation of meaning after a significant loss often can provide an experience of positive change; international research shows that 75–90 per cent of all people experience such positive personal changes after trauma and loss ('posttraumatic growth') (Davies, 1995; Dyregrov, Nordanger and Dyregrov, 2000b; Tedeschi, Park and Calhoun, 1998).

It is not our intention to portray life after having suddenly lost a loved one as a walk in the park. Because it is not. To the contrary, the creation of meaning occurs, if it does occur at all, against a backdrop of pain, longing and loss. Few of the bereaved speak of personal growth, at least not until long after the death. For many bereaved people, the experience of such processes is that of having to pull oneself up by one's bootstraps. They gradually reach an understanding that the way life will be for them, for the rest of their life, also depends on how they manage to create meaning in that which is meaninglessness. The creation of meaning which the individual is able to carry out, will affect the quality of life and growth that they experience personally and together with their family and social network.

Challenges in relation to the social network
Changes in the social network
As a consequence of the dramatic upheaval in the lives of the bereaved, changes and rearrangements in their social network often occur. In the Support and

Care study, 88 per cent reported that the family had grown closer, while few stated that the family had grown apart (Dyregrov *et al.* 2000a, 2000b). Similarly, three-fourths of the bereaved had grown closer to others in their network. This can be a matter of people who have experienced corresponding losses or who provide particularly good support following the death. One also often sees how the death has an unnerving effect on the family members of the bereaved. Being able to find an outlet for feelings and take part in intimate conversations with other people is often an extremely important type of social support in bereavement. This is particularly the case for women. For the bereaved in mourning and crisis, the experience of intimacy – or lack thereof – will potentially and fundamentally alter their sense of who is meaningful for them in life. One therefore often sees that some relationships fall by the wayside or become superficial, either in that friends and family members pull away or that the bereaved personally no longer find it meaningful to spend time together as they had done previously with certain individuals. It is experienced as being empty and meaningless to take part in conversations about trivialities, while they personally find that they are now interested in far more serious subjects. It is just as common for the bereaved to accept new people into their network, people who for various reasons were there for them and who acquire a great importance in the period following the death.

On the whole, the death will often result in large-scale upheavals in the social network of the bereaved. Some bereaved people can unfortunately be left quite alone.

Social isolation

A good number of bereaved people can feel isolated, particularly during the initial period after a traumatic death. This can be in connection with others' as well as their own withdrawal. In the Support and Care study almost 50 per cent of the bereaved stated that they had pulled away from others, and an even greater number experienced that others had pulled away from them (Dyregrov, 2003–2004; Dyregrov *et al.*, 2000b). This type of withdrawal can occur because the bereaved goes on sick leave, stops going out to the shops, drops out of club activities or fails to go to the cinema, the theatre, etc. Some do so because they cannot bear to meet others or because it feels meaningless to do that which previously was pleasurable. Others quite simply do not have the energy to do more than try to stay on their feet. They keep to themselves or stay with close family members or friends to a greater extent than before the death (Wertheimer, 1999).

Interaction with others is characterized by a number of questions. Who can we speak with? How should we behave? Can we say what we really feel? Shall we explain what happened? Do we have the energy to explain? What do I reply when they ask how it's going? What will they think of us? What if I meet someone who does not know what has happened? When is it appropriate to start going out again, to laugh and live a normal life?, etc. Often the bereaved will not mention the death because they experience a lack of acceptance for speaking about the deceased in 'normal' conversation. Our research has shown that those bereaved people who to a large degree struggled with trauma reactions and complicated grief reactions were also those who had an increased tendency to isolate themselves (Dyregrov *et al.*, 2003). The bereaved who reported good support from their network also experienced acceptance for speaking about their loss and altered life values. Those who reported good support were also willing to communicate feelings stemming from the loss and to listen when other bereaved individuals spoke about people they had lost.

The bereaved experience the network as insecure and helpless

When friends, family members, neighbours or colleagues pull away from the bereaved, the bereaved believe that the main reason for this is that both parties are extremely uncertain about how they are supposed to handle the situation. On this subject a father says the following about losing his daughter:

> We are taught to handle most situations in life, but when sudden and traumatic deaths occur, we are completely helpless, both in terms of handling it personally and giving others support.

Very many bereaved people express enormous frustration over other people's helplessness with regard to giving support and demonstrating compassion, empathy and caring. Simultaneously, they experience this as being more about their fellow human beings' ineptitude, rather than a lack of desire to be supportive. Such ineptitude is seen to a greater extent on the part of more peripheral friends and acquaintances than with close friends and family members. For some bereaved people who feel a strong sense of guilt and shame about the death (e.g. in the case of suicide), the insecurity of others can contribute to their further isolating themselves from their community. This is because a lack of social support is interpreted as a sign that one should be ashamed and withdraw. This can be a vicious cycle, where the bereaved isolate themselves more and more, and the social network gradually pulls away from them (see Chapters 3 and 5). The bereaved describe how many in their social network seem afraid and insecure about meeting them and that this is a difficult experience. Some bereaved people succeed in taking the initiative to accommodate the network's uncertainty, while for others this entails their choosing to cut off contact with them, either temporarily or permanently. In this dynamic lie some of the greatest challenges, particularly for the social network – challenges that we hope this book will contribute to resolving.

Light at the end of the tunnel

As we have shown, trauma and grief reactions can affect the individual bereaved person and family in varying degrees. In addition, most bereaved individuals find that they experience a change in life perspective and large-scale adjustments in their social network. Very often those in the surrounding environment underestimate these upheavals and the amount of time that will have to pass before the bereaved sees the light at the end of the tunnel. Some aspects of grief will last a lifetime and most bereaved people say that they never want to forget the person they have lost. However, it is very seldom the case that a person will 'cultivate' his or her grief. As a rule, the expression 'to cultivate grief' is a description of the behaviour of someone struggling with a complicated grief reaction. Most find that grief changes in character during the course of the year following the death: it is intensified on red-letter days or public holidays or when something reawakens the loss.

Over time, however, most families are able to establish a new daily life and live with both happy and sad memories. After a while, almost indiscernibly, it becomes easier. First, in that one passes a few easier hours or a single easier day among all the dark ones and eventually one finds that the death has gradually receded a little more into the background. Friends and family who want to give support should note and have an understanding for the fact that the long and demanding process that most bereaved individuals go through in reconstructing meaning and integrating the pain of what has happened is a process that can go on for years. How this process takes place depends upon a number of factors – where support from the social network can be one of the most important elements with regard to long-term adjustment.

Main themes

- We need to dispose of myths about grief.

  - There is not just one way to grieve.

- ○ Theories about stages of grief are not confirmed by grief research.

- ○ Not everyone necessarily goes through grief processing.

- ○ Grief is not a process with a fixed beginning and end point.

- ○ The bereaved need not detach themselves from the deceased.

- The individual must find his or her own manner and pace of grieving.

- It is important to be able to develop and maintain an inner memory of the deceased.

- The common situation for close bereaved after a sudden death can entail the following:

  - ○ Immediate reactions can include: a sense of unreality, shaking, palpitations, nausea, chills or dizziness and an altered experience of time.

  - ○ Long-term reactions can include: feelings of loss, longing and pain, self-reproach and guilt, reliving the events that took place, sleep disturbances, anxiety and vulnerability, concentration and memory problems, irritation and anger and physical reactions.

  - ○ Complicated grief reactions.

  - ○ Challenges in the family with regard to: grief in a couple's relationship, communication, intimacy and sexuality and capacity for caregiving.

  - ○ Existential challenges that contribute to: reconstruction of meaning, long-term adjustment of priorities and personal growth.

  - ○ Challenges in relation to the social network can include: change and replacement of the network, isolation from the network and the network feels insecure to the bereaved.

  - ○ There is light at the end of the tunnel!

3

What types of support
do the bereaved encounter
and what do they want?

In this chapter we focus on the type of support that bereaved adults often encounter and the wishes they commonly have with regard to help. In this way we hope to contribute to enabling the social network to assist the bereaved directly, or to help them in contact with other bereaved people or professionals. Children and young people will be addressed separately (see Chapter 4).

> When you experience a disaster of this kind you are not capable of asking anyone for anything at all. You are completely lost and feel as if you are drowning and need someone to rescue you.

The above quote is from the mother of a young person who committed suicide and exemplifies the large need for help and support that very many bereaved people experience after a traumatic death. In the vast majority of the studies done on this subject, the bereaved say that they need help and that it is not a matter of *either* professional help and public assistance *or* informal support from social networks. The bereaved maintain that they need both social network support and support from other bereaved individuals, as well as professional help where the need for this may arise. The reason for the potential need for help from all of these sources is that each addresses different types of need (Clark, 2001; Dyregrov, 2002b; Dyregrov *et al.*, 2000a; Murphy, 2000; Provini, Everett and Pfeffer, 2000).

Our experience, which is confirmed by the bereaved, shows that the support and care that the bereaved receive when they suddenly and unexpectedly lose a loved one varies enormously. Help and support varies, with regard to type, quality and quantity. The type of support the bereaved receive can vary, as can the person from whom they receive help, the frequency of offers, whether the support is offered or must be asked for and its duration. Last, but not least, whether or not the support is valued and experienced as useful by the bereaved also varies.

Support from social networks

For the most part there will be a consensus among the bereaved by a sudden death, in terms of the veracity of the following statement regarding the significance of positive support from social networks: 'I believe that when people demonstrate that they care and are supportive, that makes all the difference!'

The good support

Our research shows that the bereaved to a certain extent receive massive support from families, friends, colleagues, neighbours and schoolmates, particularly in the course of the first weeks following a death (Dyregrov, 2003–2004; Dyregrov et al., 2000a, 2000b; Nordanger, Dyregrov and Dyregrov, 2000). Most of the bereaved speak of valuable and beneficial support from their social network. The support and care of family, friends, neighbours and colleagues is experienced as being irreplaceable and wholly essential to surviving the first period.

First and foremost, most will receive 'an avalanche of flowers' for both the home and the funeral. Flowers come from the family, from close and distant acquaintances, from the workplace and clubs or organizations where they are members, and from the families of friends of the deceased. Although the funeral is as a rule an enormous strain, the bereaved also state that the funeral in itself provides them with a fortitude that enables them to move on, in that many people attend. It does not only feel like support at that particular moment, but also warms the heart after the fact, when they think back on this day. The bereaved emphasize the importance of somebody really caring and possibly also crying with them or holding them and asking about how they are doing. Sometimes this is experienced as intrusive and unsuccessful, in the event the bereaved person feels that the time and place are inappropriate or that the person exhibiting compassion is not close enough to them that such demonstrative behaviour feels natural.

The bereaved relate that families, neighbours and friends contact them by coming to their homes or by calling or writing to them. Good friends and close family members step in to help around the clock. Some come with books or poetry to express their compassion or bring information materials in the manner of brochures and books. Others are physically present if only to hug and embrace the bereaved during the first days. They arrive early in the morning and remain by their side until they go to bed and help them essentially to continue living during the first surreal days. The bereaved also tell of close friends or family members who spend the nights immediately following the death with them and talk with them if they are unable to fall asleep. They have someone with whom they can cry and express their despair and who comforts them as best they can. The bereaved may ask the question 'Why did it happen?' over and over again. Friends and family often receive the difficult task of seeking answers together with the bereaved and frequently experience feelings of inadequacy, because there are no answers.

Particularly women, but also some men, refer to the importance of having a person with whom they can talk about 'everything'. And they appreciate that friends can listen to their stories, experiences and thoughts without asking anything in return. Neither do the bereaved necessarily expect any answers or advice. Because virtually all bereaved people wish to be reminded of the deceased, there are very many who want the person to be mentioned by name in conversations where this is natural. The bereaved experience this as a good thing because they are afraid that their loved ones will be forgotten. It is particularly positive when somebody over time remembers and mentions the death and the deceased.

After the initial, most surreal weeks have passed, when the bereaved are struggling to function in a purely physical sense, they also appreciate that friends, neighbours or colleagues attempt to bring them back or seek to motivate them to return to a more normal daily life. Most experience it as being positive if network members call and encourage them to take part in social activities or simply come to the door to take them out at a time when they are experiencing a complete absence of any initiative or joy. When network members accompany the bereaved to the burial grounds, invite them to their home for an evening or help them return to work, this provides beneficial support. They greatly appreciate colleagues who seek them out and attempt to motivate them to return to work, preferably to an adapted and flexible working situation. Many of the bereaved speak of a great willingness to implement flexible solutions at the workplace, either to work according to their day-to-day ability, to take advantage of the social community or to withdraw on a need-to-retreat basis. Such flexibility is experienced as providing an important assistance. Colleagues and supervisors whom, at the request of the bereaved person, assume responsibility for the task of informing others at work are also greatly appreciated.

A number of parents who have lost children speak of enormous support from their children's friends and acquaintances. They speak of young people who pay them a visit, sit in the girl or boy's bedroom and play the deceased's music or just talk about how they knew the deceased. In many cases this does not disturb adults, as one might think – many parents experience this as a beneficial type of support in the midst of all of their pain. Still, it can be experienced with mixed feelings, as being 'painfully good' – good to hear young people in the house again, but painful to be reminded that one young person is missing. It is comforting to acquire insight into new and perhaps unknown sides of one's deceased child and the adults and young people can give one another mutual support in their grief. Many young people also dare to be extremely direct and open in their bereavement, which bereaved parents often appreciate, such as this father:

> Johnny's friends sat here and cried. They managed so well to show their feelings. They just came here and put their arms around us. And that's all that we needed, you know? One came and delivered a bouquet of forget-me-nots that he had picked himself. That alone had an unbelievable impact.

When the network succeeds in communicating support so that it is experienced as helpful, social network support is greatly appreciated. But this does not always occur, and many of the bereaved relate negative experiences with this type of support.

The network's helplessness

In spite of all the positive experiences, research as well as experience from clinical practice shows that network support can also be insufficient or even destructive. Sometimes its effect can be the opposite of the intention (Dyregrov, 2003–2004).

A mother's experiences after her son's suicide illuminate very many aspects of what the bereaved experience as the network's helplessness and evasiveness:

> Friends were very much there for me, immediately, then. But then, gradually, there is nobody around who can be bothered to hear how it's going. But they certainly experience me as a person who is taking it well. I neither cry nor...not any longer. But now for the most part, I control it. So now, no...we need not speak any more about it. Or perhaps they are thinking that it is so painful to speak about it, that it is best to navigate

around it in case she reacts like this or that. And they don't want to remind me of it. But the thing is that it is always there, so there is nobody who can remind me of it more than I do myself! So that is why I am a little disappointed; people could just touch me and ask: 'How are you, Susan? Are you ok?' Then I can say: 'Sure, of course I am managing. Life goes on.' And then we can speak about something else afterwards. If only they would not, like, silence it to death. I would like to speak a little about Peter. I want to remember him all the time. He will never be completely gone for me. So I would like to talk about him a little. So if they could only say 'Peter'...work him into the conversation somewhere. Then I would be more than satisfied. But that doesn't happen, you know. It's exactly as if it is a taboo, just mentioning his name. That is how it feels to me. I understand that people should basically receive some kind of training. Me too, of course, for I have certainly behaved foolishly in many such situations before. One doesn't know what is involved before one is in such a situation. People should know more about how to behave when crisis strikes. Just the fact that they touch upon the subject, that they know that I have such a thing. I have this grief, although it is not always apparent to the outside world. If they could only just *mention* it, from time to time, then it would be...to the limited degree that this is done, it is good for me. I have said it to many people, that I would like to talk about it. But I receive no response. On a few occasions, perhaps. And I have said, 'Let me be allowed to speak about it.' But it is certainly just as difficult in spite of that. I believe it is much easier to steer around it.

Almost all of the bereaved that took part in the Support and Care project mentioned shortcomings with regard to the support they had received and almost half had experienced that the support from one or more in their social network had vanished (Dyregrov *et al.*, 2000a; Dyregrov, 2003–2004). The bereaved found that people from whom they expect to receive support avoid them by 'crossing the street', neglecting to contact them or ignoring them at times when they, under normal circumstances, would have spoken together. Others state that they become very hurt or angry when such people say 'I have been thinking about you so much' or 'I have so wanted to come and visit you' when they can no longer avoid the bereaved. As one bereaved person fittingly stated: 'It does not help the bereaved that others are thinking a great deal about them when one doesn't know about it.' Friends and family should instead pay a visit to the bereaved. The bereaved experience it as particularly hurtful when network members excuse themselves, by saying that they have been so busy lately or have had to work so much and therefore have not been able to come to visit.

Many workplaces now have organized emergency plans, and this includes showing compassion with regard to crisis-stricken staff members. Nonetheless, many of the bereaved experience that the support and attentiveness to their needs also fails to materialize in this context. In the Support and Care project, approximately one-third of the bereaved parents had not heard anything from their place of work in connection with the death. It is disappointing for the bereaved when colleagues, to whom they believed they were close, do not make contact after a death. For many, this is experienced as a hindrance to returning to normal life and resuming work. The more time that passes after such an event without returning to work, the more difficult it is for the bereaved. The bereaved also experience that people, both in the inner and outer network circles, pull away from them, either physically or in conversation. Avoidance and evasiveness take place more frequently when the bereaved meet others in a public setting, such as on the street, in the store or at the workplace, than when friends and acquaintances visit them in their homes. This type of behaviour involves their changing direction, crossing the street or looking away when they catch sight of the bereaved in order to avoid addressing the traumatic event. In the home it is far easier for the bereaved to take the lead in conversation, also because those who come home to them, through this act alone, are signalling a willingness to broach the subject of the death. A mother who abruptly lost her son gave an everyday example of such evasiveness:

> The first time I met a close colleague after having lost my son, he sat directly facing me in a meeting. He turned away from me and conversed intensely with the man beside him in order to avoid meeting my eyes. When he left the room, he did not say good-bye to me… That has never happened before.

Quite frequently some members of the network avoid broaching the subject of the death and the loss in the course of ordinary conversation. As soon as the topic is brought up or the name is mentioned in passing, the conversation comes to an abrupt halt. 'It is as if they have swallowed their tongue or had their lips suddenly sealed,' as one described it. It is experienced as both hurtful and insulting when it would have been natural to talk about what happened and the bereaved have a need for this. Instead they find that the people in their surrounding environment avoid them and from the perspective of the bereaved, speak instead about the most trivial things in the world. Such conversations become as a rule meaningless for relatives of the deceased, who want to inform the people in their surroundings of what has taken place and that it does not matter if the deceased is mentioned in conversation where this otherwise would have been a matter of course. If one has covered this subject, hereby lancing the boil, so to speak, the bereaved generally have less of a need to put the death at centre stage. 'Then everyone knows that everyone knows.' A father expressed it in this way:

> It is frustrating to spend time with people who know what happened and who know that we know that they know, without our being able to speak about it. By talking through it, at the very least once, we establish a common starting point and then it is easier to address everyday tasks.

Inconsiderate behaviour on the part of the network

In our research, the bereaved give many examples of types of support that are not experienced as being helpful, but to the contrary, detrimental. These examples include well-meaning advice, inconsiderate actions, and thoughtless and even cruel comments. Some of the advice that is given is not only bad but is also experienced as being without empathy or respect. This is particularly hurtful. The bereaved are told how they should grieve or that they should not have so many pictures or candles placed out in the open, should visit the graveyard less, go back to work or stay at home longer, etc. Such 'advice' hurts the bereaved; they ask that nobody give advice, believe themselves to be experts on how others should grieve, or instruct another on the right or wrong way to grieve. A mother, who abruptly and unexpectedly lost her son, expressed herself as follows: 'Nobody can ever enter my soul and know how horrendous my situation is for me. So nobody can therefore tell me what is the right or wrong thing for me to do.'

The bereaved often hear thoughtless comments such as 'the grief will disappear in time', 'everything happens for a reason', 'there were so many problems with him, it must be something of a relief' and 'luckily you have other children'. Such comments can become permanently engraved, although many know deep down how thoughtless such comments are and that they should not let these comments upset them. An example from a mother who lost her 19-year-old son by suicide shows how stigmatized suicide still is. The comment came from an older relation who failed to conceal her attitude in her misguided attempts to console the family: 'I believe nonetheless that Tony is with God because God does not distinguish between people.'

Some bereaved people also experience imprudent actions on the part of people in their surroundings. It can be a matter of rather peripheral individuals who pay them a visit in their home and who want to explain that they have had the same experience. While some may find support in this, there are others who will experience it as neediness and a strain, in that they are thus obliged to address the grief of another in addition to their own.

The bereaved make excuses for the network

A large number of the bereaved understand that it is difficult for the social network to address acute grief and despair. They understand that friends, family members, neighbours and colleagues pull away due to their own uncertainty and helplessness with regard to how they shall behave towards people who have been through such a tragedy. The majority therefore excuse their network. A common observation from a bereaved person regarding inconsiderate comments and advice is that: 'They were certainly trying to be supportive, but it was just all wrong,' and 'The fact that they do so badly is certainly just due to ignorance'. But in spite of the fact that the bereaved point out that the difficulties are certainly due to the network's ineptitude and that they understand their insecurity, the experiences add to the strain of their bereavement (Dyregrov, 2003–2004).

Nonetheless, very many of the bereaved say that they would probably have personally behaved in the same manner if they had not learned through their own loss. They see the paradox in that they previously had also been perfunctory and behaved in a superficial manner in relation to the grief of others, while they now expect other people to understand them. Although they have specific wishes concerning how they would like the network to greet them and have had a number of unfortunate experiences, they feel that they cannot really make any demands. As a mother says:

> You experience after the fact that you are expecting something specific from some particular individuals. But then you realize that they have their own life and you cannot expect that people are always going to keep returning to what happened. We must, in the end, carry the burden of our son's death.

Different types of support from inner and outer circles

When one speaks with a bereaved person about a support network, one frequently experiences that there are large qualitative differences. And the expression 'it is in grief that one learns who one's true friends are' is absolutely valid after a traumatic death. An extremely large number of the bereaved find that they have a small 'inner circle' of close friends and a larger 'outer circle' of more peripheral friends and acquaintances. The inner circle includes those who spend the night with them in the beginning, come to the door and offer their support, and who most intuitively know how they should approach them.

These are the friends who know them best, who make the fewest mistakes, and who are less likely to abandon them over time. These are people who support them through 'thick and thin', who demonstrate the greatest willingness to provide support and who are permitted to give support. It is however not a given who these might be – they are not always family members, as one might think. Just as often the bereaved say that the inner circle comprises best friends and close colleagues or neighbours. They are most often people whom they have known for a long time.

Frequently it happens nonetheless that new people will have entered the bereaved person's life after the death, because they have supported them or approached them in a unique and particularly helpful manner. They might be people who have experienced similar type deaths, or people from the outer circle who have proven to be particularly compassionate and supportive after the death. But a rearrangement frequently takes place in the opposite sense as well, in that some friends or family members whom the bereaved viewed as being close become more insignificant in their lives. These are moved from the inner to the outer circle, either temporarily or forever.

The outer support circle is as a rule larger and is made up of a larger number of people than the inner circle. In this outer circle one finds those who come to the funeral only, colleagues with whom one has purely a working relationship, those one meets in the store, neighbours whom one knows only to say 'hello' to, family members with whom one perhaps does not have a particularly close relationship and people with whom one associates to a greater or lesser degree in various social contexts. These often demonstrate the greatest insecurity and ineptitude in the encounter with the bereaved. They have a greater tendency to avoid the bereaved or do not speak about what has happened or they say and do hurtful things. As a rule the network in the outer circle has not had as close a relationship to the bereaved before the death, and subsequently knows neither the deceased nor the bereaved particularly well.

It is experienced as being particularly hurtful when people whom the bereaved had considered a part of the inner circle, such as family members, behave as if they were part of the outer circle. We meet accordingly many bereaved people who are disappointed over the fact that their biological family had not given them the support they had hoped for or expected. Bereaved people who have this experience will often make excuses for them by saying that they are certainly so deeply affected by the loss for their own part and that this is why they pull away – something which is often the case. Some, however, become extremely saddened and feel abandoned by their loved ones, those from whom they had expected to receive support. How then do the bereaved wish to be approached by their social network?

The network support wishes of the bereaved

The primary wish with regard to network support is that friends and family take the initiative for various support measures, while attempting as well to give support on the terms of the grieving individual. The bereaved experience network support as being 'alpha and omega' and want personally to contribute to reducing the social network's insecurity. In order to make it possible for the people in their surroundings to understand and respect the individual's manner of grieving and provide the best support, the bereaved see the need to inform their surroundings. They perceive the necessity of giving family and friends clear signals and information regarding how they are feeling and about the kind of support they want and need.

One of the most important things for which the bereaved need understanding is the fact that they can no longer spend time with friends and family in the same way as previously. They request that the people in their surroundings understand that they, for a period of time, will not have the same amount of energy for the give and take of an equal relationship with friends and family. Because they are exhausted and perhaps are sleeping and eating poorly, many need more than an offer to 'just say the word if there is anything that you need'. Some feel incapable of action. Therefore one needs friends who personally make contact and do not leave it to the bereaved to take the initiative, at least for a period of time. A mother who suddenly lost her child expresses this clearly:

> Very many came and dropped by here. They stood in the doorway and said: 'If there is anything that you need, just contact us. Pick up the phone and come by.' You don't *do* that. And I believe that friends and neighbours quickly lose any desire to come by if they feel that now I have been there twice, three times and she has not reciprocated. They expect one to initiate contact on an alternating basis, the way things are when everything is normal. They follow the ordinary routine while we are in another place altogether. We must be sought out.

Very many specify that more open communication about the death, about how they are feeling, and about the type of help and support that they need, will increase the network's possibilities for supporting the individual and the family on their own terms. They believe that this is difficult to bring about for different reasons but believe that it would help if the surroundings could understand more of their reactions, and the duration and intensity of the grieving process (Dyregrov, 2003–2004; Murphy, 2000; Wertheimer, 1999). Because many have experienced a lack of understanding for their own way of grieving, they ask that others show respect and patience for the particular manner in which they need to grieve. The bereaved want empathy and support that is direct and sincere, without there always being the need for so many words. The most important thing is that the people in their surroundings show that they care. On the other hand, they have a good understanding of the fact that the networks are uncertain, but believe that it would help if the networks dared express this directly or just showed compassion in other ways. When the bereaved describe the type of compassion they need, they make reference to those members of the network who listen with sincerity to their despair and grief. In addition, they would prefer if a few, select individuals could be there for them when they needed this, individuals whom they trust wholly and fully and to whom they can tell 'everything'. Practical help, such as helping out with the children or with cooking in the initial period, can be invaluable. Advice regarding how they can handle the situation, however, is not usually at the top of a bereaved person's list of the ways in which social networks can make a contribution.

Receiving acceptance for their need to remember the deceased, also together with the network, is given high priority by most bereaved people. It is therefore a significant wish on the part of the bereaved that the person they have lost be mentioned by name or spoken about where it would be natural in everyday conversation, particularly as time goes on. The bereaved are in a sense asking the network for 'permission' to bring along the deceased and to remember him or her as the person he or she was. It is experienced as extremely supportive that neither friends nor family have forgotten the child, spouse or boy/girlfriend that they also once knew. Because a large majority of the network appears to have 'forgotten' what has taken place, believe that they can protect the bereaved from thinking about the death, or have an inadequate understanding of the duration of grief, long-term support is a primary wish on the part of most bereaved.

A bereaved person's relation to the social network is accordingly not streamlined. While each greatly values the support of friends and family members, they also experience some frustration and strain, which they feel is due to the network's ineptitude and thoughtlessness.

Support from other bereaved people

The insecurity and negative experiences described above are virtually nonexistent when the bereaved by sudden death meet with 'peers' – or other bereaved. This type of support from others, whom as a rule are peripheral or complete strangers, comprises a special type of support.

Peer support: a special type of support

'Peer support' is that which occurs when the bereaved meet with other bereaved people through bereavement support groups, peer organizations, private initiatives and connections or when the public assistance scheme provides this type of contact. The bereaved find that others who have experienced approximately the same type of loss are in a unique position, because they 'have been in their shoes'. 'We need not say very much when we meet, because we know' is what one often hears regarding such encounters. Many, though not all, bereaved people wish to meet others who have experienced losing someone through a sudden and unexpected death.

First and foremost, the bereaved experience that they can be themselves when with other bereaved people. They need not pull themselves together or pretend. They can cry and receive acceptance and understanding and tell their story to someone who really listens and understands. But it is also easier for the bereaved to allow themselves to laugh and enjoy themselves with other bereaved people, without the risk of being misunderstood by their surroundings. Time spent together with peers is experienced as a 'time out', because they can be wholly and fully themselves and need not hide their sadness and continually pull themselves together. The bereaved experience being met with sincere and implicit understanding and recognition, and having painful and somewhat confusing feelings, thoughts and reactions confirmed by others. Through the community they receive confirmation that their reactions and thoughts are normal and natural. Along the same lines, they also receive opportunities to express thoughts and feelings on their own terms. They need not hide 'the very worst' – that which they often spare others in their social network – as other bereaved people 'can stand to hear it'.

It is not just conversation with other bereaved people that is emphasized as being a particularly important form of help. Many receive (and give) valuable information and good advice. Advice that comes from others in the same situation is experienced as extremely credible. This can be a matter of advice concerning coping strategies, assistance programmes that are available or that have worked, useful literature, etc. The fact that both parties give and take contributes to a good feeling of equal worth and increased self-respect at a time when many bereaved people otherwise experience crushing blows to their self-esteem. They will in particular be able to share and receive support within a long-term perspective when others will appear to have forgotten the deceased and what has happened. Because different periods of time may have passed since the time of death for the bereaved individuals who meet in such situations, this type of community gives hope for the future in that one meets others who have advanced further in the grief process than oneself. Over time many of the bereaved also experience it as being extremely meaningful to be able to provide support for other bereaved people. It informs the meaningless event that has occurred with a kind of meaning. Some of the bereaved undergo training to operate bereavement support groups through peer organizations, such as FSID – Foundation for the Study of Infant Death, Roadpeace – Supporting bereaved and injured road crash victims, SANDS – Stillbirth And Neonatal Death Support, and Cruse – Cruse Bereavement Care.

Bereavement support groups

Information about bereavement support groups is often passed on by other bereaved people in volunteer organizations, by the church or by healthcare professionals or can be found in adverts in the daily newspaper or on the Internet. The establishment of contact between bereavement support groups and the bereaved takes place more or less as with public assistance schemes. Some bereaved people make contact on their own initiative, while others receive help from people in their social network or from public assistance schemes, who contact those who have lost someone in a similar way. The point in time when a given individual is prepared to take part can vary greatly, from just after the death to up to several years later. For most it is the case that some time must pass before they are prepared to encounter the grief of others in a bereavement support group. Whether or not the bereaved receive such an offer varies from place to place both within and between countries. On the other hand, there are bereaved people who receive such an offer but choose not to participate in bereavement support groups. What we know about this is that some of those who decline do so because the offer is made prematurely in the course of their grieving process. They say, however, that they would have liked to have received the offer again at a later point in time – they would then have reconsidered. For others, grief is too private a matter to invite strangers into it. The bereaved who have positive experiences from participation in bereavement support groups emphasize the community aspect, of feeling that they 'are not alone', the normalizing effect with regard to the extreme situation in which they find themselves and that they, in time, are able to share feelings and express grief with someone who understands – in other words, the same benefits as with peer support in general.

The challenges of peer support

Although the advantages of peer support clearly outweigh the disadvantages, there are some challenges inherent to this type of support. The bereaved can, for example, find that 'the personal chemistry does not work', or be 'overwhelmed by the grief of others'. Although other bereaved people are perceived as being an extremely important source of support in the context of a sudden death, the bereaved also have clear requirements. The contact 'one on one' or in bereavement support groups must have a certain quality and content, and the personal chemistry must be right. An important challenge of peer support in general is that it can be too much to take in others' problems and grief on top of one's own. This is particularly the problem for the bereaved early in the grief process or when bereavement support groups are too large. And there will always be large differences between the contents and styles of individual bereavement support groups, depending upon the leader of the group. The most common reason given by the bereaved who have tried, but then withdrawn from bereavement support groups, is that the groups are undifferentiated, in other words, that there is too great a variation in the types of deaths that the participants have experienced. A mother who had lost her child reported that she found herself in a group with a woman who had lost her husband. She commented upon this in the following manner:

> We started attending a bereavement support group through our parish but stopped going. There one met people who had lost a spouse and an elderly woman, and it just wasn't really suitable… It didn't feel right and we said so after the first meeting. There was a large focus on us and 'poor you' and that's fine, we were feeling pretty 'poor'. But it was certainly just as bad for the elderly woman who had lost her husband of many years and I understand that very well. But the focus was wrong.

Some bereavement support groups for parents who have lost children start with two or three couples and then it is difficult to withdraw from the group if one does not feel that it is providing support or help. Parents feel guilty about letting the other parents down, although they would prefer, for their own part, to stop attending. This, and other examples that will follow below, illustrate how important it is that such groups are well planned and well led. Another important reason why the bereaved stop attending bereavement support groups is that they do not feel as if they are getting anywhere. Some have a need for a more therapeutic perspective in bereavement support groups. While some groups have a focus on venting emotions and mutual support, other groups to a larger degree have a therapeutic objective. A mother who had taken part in two different support groups maintained that more serious requirements should be imposed with regard to a therapeutic objective in order for participation to have meaning:

> When the first pastor led the group, he had a theme for each meeting – such as Christmas and 'What do you think about it?' Now the new pastor just sits and listens, but he does not say anything. He just sits there and listens to us. I miss it the way it was, that there was a progression in the process. Now there is nothing. I feel that there is no point in going there.

Despite the challenges of peer support the benefits are clearly greater. Common experiences and pain provide a sense of community and comfort. One sees that the bereaved find meaning in life by supporting other bereaved individuals, in that which is described as the principles of 'self-help' (Riches and Dawson, 1996b). That which is of great importance to the bereaved and which distinguishes this network from others, is that the bereaved need not explain so much about the circumstances because others have experienced the same type of loss and they can speak with greater ease and less difficulty about seeing the corpse, the funeral, the return to work and about their grief. Because bereaved people go through so many of the same rituals and experiences in connection with grief, solidarity is strengthened and it contributes to a common identity that differs from that found in other network relations. This is particularly the case for bereaved people who have lost their loved ones under similar circumstances and at approximately the same time. It leads to a community of 'insiders'. As one bereaved father expressed: 'This is a very exclusive club. I pray to God that you never have to join it!'

Help from professionals
What kinds of professional help do the bereaved receive?
The Support and Care study showed that 85 per cent of local governments in Norway offered some form or another of immediate contact with professionals – such as a pastor, physician, police or mental health nurse – after a sudden, unexpected death (Dyregrov, Dyregrov and Nordanger, 1999; Dyregrov *et al.*, 2000b; Nordanger, Dyregrov and Dyregrov, 1998). Nonetheless, more than half of the bereaved wanted more help than they had received. Very few of the local governments had follow-up schemes that lasted beyond the first year (13 per cent), while almost all of the bereaved sought this. To the question

regarding how as a rule the contact between the local government assistance schemes and the bereaved was established, 42 per cent of the local governments replied that this took place on the initiative of the public authorities. All of those in need of help from the public sector (88 per cent) held that the initiative for this should come from the side of the public authorities and not from themselves. The most common type of help that was provided was support in the form of counselling, provided by a pastor, physician or nurse. Relatively few local governments (38 per cent) focused on bereaved children. Although we do not know of any British studies, similar results have been found in Australian, Belgian and American studies (De Groot, De Keijser and Neeleman, 2006; McMenamy, Jordan and Mitchell, in press; Wilson and Clark, 2005).

After the study was completed in 1998 a large number of local governments and their crisis teams in Norway have taken the crisis-stricken and their situation far more seriously. There is therefore cause to believe that help from the public sector, according to the wishes of the bereaved, has improved today. Nonetheless, reports from bereaved people who come for follow-up and reports from the peer organizations would appear to indicate that some of the main tendencies continue.

What kind of professional help do the bereaved want?

The bereaved want more, or other types of professional help, than that which they receive (De Groot et al., 2006; McMenamy et al., in press; Wertheimer, 1999; Wilson and Clark, 2005). At the same time they specify that they are not asking to become lifetime clients in a treatment system but that they would like help towards self-help, in order to get on with their lives in the best and most expedient manner. They ask for routine and quick assistance so that they can avoid becoming long-term clients. They would like to receive help as early as possible in understanding what happens and they want, in varying degrees, to be 'taken care of' for a while, either by the social network or professionals. They seek systems that ensure automatic contact with public assistance teams. They want support with stability and continuity, qualified assistants, but at the same time, an assistance scheme that is flexible and adapted to the individual (Dyregrov, 2002b). A large group of the bereaved claim that professionals will be crucial in some phases of the grief process, but that social networks will have a central role for far greater portions of the process. The bereaved ask that local governments take responsibility for mobilizing social network support when this does not occur automatically. Last, but not least, some would like help in acquiring contact with others who have experienced similar type deaths, through peer organizations or through bereavement support groups.

Our research shows that a large majority of the bereaved by sudden death are not satisfied with the assistance provided by the public assistance scheme. Very many of the bereaved express frustration and bitterness over what they experience as discriminatory treatment in comparison to the assistance schemes for somatic illness or large-scale disasters. Many of the bereaved have said that they know that professionals and psychosocial first aid exists and that they have the right to help, while simultaneously they maintain that they do not have the energy to ask for help. The clear dissatisfaction with professionals is therefore to a large extent focused on the help being short-term or non-existent, rather than the help that was in fact received being of a poor professional standard. We will elaborate below on some of the most important aspects of the professional help requested (Dyregrov, 2003).

EARLY AND OUTREACH ASSISTANCE

The bereaved want early and outreach assistance, where they need not take the first initiative for contact. Many are not capable of asking for the help they really need, although assistance workers on the first day tell them that they have only to make contact if they feel a need for help. A mother, who had experienced two traumatic deaths in her immediate family, expressed her despair over the fact that the assistance scheme had not offered her psychosocial crisis assistance: 'I thought about how I could break both my legs so that I would be taken care of by someone in the assistance scheme.'

In correlation with findings from other studies (De Groot et al., 2006; McMenamy et al., in press; Provini et al., 2000; Wilson and Clark, 2005) the bereaved in the Support and Care project experienced help needs throughout the grieving process that varied enormously and emphasized that the offer of assistance should be repeated throughout the course of the first year after the death. As a father says:

> If the municipal healthcare service had contacted us and offered us some kind of regular assistance after the suicide, I could have used this contact as a lifeline, known that it was there and used it if necessary.

The bereaved have many different explanations for why they do not ask for the help for which they claim to have a great need. First of all, a loss of energy and exhaustion disables many bereaved people from contacting the assistance scheme. In this way, paradoxically, one of the most important reasons for the need for help becomes a hindrance to its acquisition. Feelings of shame or guilt, or prejudices from the surroundings, can also contribute to the bereaved hesitating to seek out the help they need. Beyond this, many of the bereaved are unable to put the type of help they need into words or do not know the types of assistance programmes available from different professional groups.

INFORMATION

After a traumatic death the bereaved have a large need for different types of information. They seek information about medical aspects of the death and the grief process and they want knowledge about how the death can affect family members and the family as a unit. In particular, adults ask for advice in helping bereaved children and young people, and with handling communication problems that arise between family members and live-in partners. They request both written and verbal information.

VARIED HELP

Most grieving families have a need for various types of help. Beyond psychopedagogical information, help is also wanted with regard to the existential, practical, economical and juridical questions, as well as therapeutic help and advice. In particular the need for more specific psychological assistance and advice on self-mastery is emphasized, to reduce stress reactions, nightmares and flashbacks (intrusive images stemming from the death). Many do not know who or what they need, but often express a need for 'psychological assistance'.

HELP FOR BEREAVED CHILDREN

Parents are often unsure as to whether or not they are 'doing the right thing', and whether their children might need help beyond that which they personally can manage to provide after a traumatic death in the family. In the Support and Care study two-thirds of the parents sought advice in this regard from professionals and almost half (45 per cent) maintained that they needed a psychologist's help for their children. Parents also sought family counselling to improve the family dynamic, to resolve conflicts in parent–child relationships and to receive support and discuss their own thoughts about the best possible way to provide care for their children. Young people bereaved by suicide specified the need for more professional support that directly addressed their needs as independent individuals and on their own terms. They communicated a particular request to the assistance scheme to help the parents so that young people could be spared having to do so or being burdened with caregiving tasks, such as responsibility for younger siblings (Dyregrov, 2001b).

LONG-TERM FOLLOW-UP

The duration of follow-up is a key topic in the context of sudden death and very many of the bereaved maintain that the ideal assistance programme must have a time perspective of a longer duration than is usually the case. The Support and Care study showed that 73 per cent would have liked to have been offered contact with the assistance scheme for the duration of at least one year. Such requests were specified as 'for at least two years' or 'for as long as necessary' or 'for the rest of my life' and provide a striking contrast with regard to the experiences of the bereaved, which often entail that they receive help during the first week(s) while they are still in shock or busy planning the funeral and then, subsequently, are left to their own devices. The greater majority of the bereaved specify that they struggle with difficulties for a much longer period of time than either the assistance scheme or social network appear to be aware of (Dyregrov, 2002b; Dyregrov et al., 2000a).

A clear parallel can be seen between bereaved people's wishes for an ideal follow-up programme and that which is recommended by professionals in the field (Murphy, 2000; Provini et al., 2000), as well as the requests of bereaved people in other countries (Clark, 2001; De Groot et al., 2006; McMenamy et al., in press; Wertheimer, 1999).

Why does not everyone receive psychosocial crisis assistance?

There are a number of different reasons why psychosocial assistance after crises still varies from place to place (municipality to municipality in Norway). An inadequate focus and organization or a lack of professional expertise are among the most important reasons. These inadequacies can be solved and a good number of Norwegian local governments have invested considerable resources here during recent years. Another hindrance to improving the assistance schemes for the bereaved is the professional and ideological resistance that has traditionally been present in professional communities. This resistance is predominantly based on the idea that such help should not be provided or made a priority, or on the idea that it is unnecessary. The bereaved, and those of us who work in the crisis assistance field, find that some professionals as well as politicians believe that the bereaved by traumatic death do not need help. Crisis-stricken people, however, point out that there appears to be a higher level of tolerance for suffering within the realm of psychosocial difficulty than for somatic illness, before the assistance institution perceives assistance measures as being a necessity (Dyregrov, 2004b). The reasons for this response stem from attitudes such as 'grief is a natural part of life', 'one must not make that which is normal into an illness', 'this will go over time' or 'the social networks are the only ones that help in such difficult situations'. Such attitudes not only totally overlook those of the bereaved who specifically ask for professional help in addition to other types of support, but also reveal a great amount of ignorance about the actual life situation of traumatically bereaved people (cf. Chapter 2).

As the bereaved point out, emergency help and routine follow-up is provided after a heart attack or for a broken bone but if one experiences an enormous life crisis resulting in psychological, physical and social difficulties, there is little help to be found. There are many bereaved people who ask the same question as this bereaved father: 'Why is it so much more important to trust natural healing processes for emotional suffering than for physical suffering?'

A main argument on the part of professionals who resist the concept of professional help following traumatic losses is that this deprives people of the possibility of taking responsibility for their own lives and health and that professional help makes them powerless and dependent upon others. On the basis of our own research, it is difficult to understand how traumatized people's independence would be in any way reduced by professional crisis assistance. There would appear to be a far greater risk involved in allowing the bereaved to be overwhelmed by trauma reactions, isolation and a lack of social support than by providing crisis assistance where the objective is to enable them to regain control of their own lives. Those who are critical of implementing professional resources according to need, should not ignore the fact that traumatized individuals who wish for help are perhaps the best experts with regard to assessing whether or not such help is in fact needed (Dyregrov, 2004b; Dyregrov, K., 2006a).

Main themes

Bereaved persons' wishes for support from social networks

- Give support on our terms through communication and knowledge.
- Be open, direct and sincere about:
  - one's own insecurity with regard to how to be supportive
  - the need for the bereaved to express how they wish to be approached.
- Take the initiative so that we do not have to.
- Be present and available.

- Listen sincerely and in earnest.
- Show empathy, respect and patience for our way of grieving.
- Remember the deceased.
- Give practical assistance.

Bereaved people's wishes for peer support

- Conversation, comfort, advice, information, community, 'time out.'
- 'They have been in our shoes.'
- 'We need not say so much when we meet because we know.'
- Bereavement support group adapted to individual wishes and needs.

Bereaved persons' wishes for help from professionals

- Help us to say good-bye in the best possible manner.
- Make contact – offer help, do not leave it to us to take the initiative.
- Be organized and create routines; the help should not be offered at random.
- Take turns, don't all come at the same time – and not only at the beginning.
- Be flexible, listen to what we need, but take over when necessary.
- Inform us of how the death happened, what will now take place, where and from whom we can receive help, grief and crisis reactions, how men, women and children react differently.
- Help us to come into contact with a psychologist and other relevant professional groups.
- Help our children and/or help us to help them.
- Do not forget others outside of the immediate family who have been hard hit.
- Help us to make contact with others who have experienced the same thing.
- Be there as well when everyday life returns.

4

Children and young people

Their situation and help needs

The situation of children and young people

Bereaved children and young people struggle to a certain extent with some of the same psychosocial difficulties as do adults. Nonetheless, children and young people's level of maturity and development implies that they will experience certain aspects of a sudden death differently to adults. In addition, children and young people have a number of different reactions and experiences due to their different relationship to the deceased which can result in other psychosocial difficulties and challenges than those experienced by adults.

Reactions and relational difficulties

For children and young people, the reactions of their surroundings and adults' attentiveness can often be decisive to how they cope with the situation. Research has shown that the degree of severity with regard to children's problems subsequent to a traumatic death bears a connection to the degree of caregivers' psychological and social difficulties. In some cases one sees that children and young people's normal development can be retarded due to a lack of emotional availability on the part of bereaved and distraught parents (Calhoun, Abernathy and Selby, 1986; Pfeffer *et al.*, 1997). In addition, children's age and gender, along with the type of death, and the amount of time that has passed since the death, will all heavily influence how the death is experienced. Further, young people's level of development and resources, including their ideas about death, will be of significance with regard to how they will cope (Davies, 1995). It is nonetheless young people's daily surroundings that are particularly crucial to the grieving process. Children have the best conditions for coping if they are living with resourceful parents in a stable life situation, if the climate of communication is good and mutual support exists within the family. For older children and young people, support from friends, the school, and other social networks plays an increasingly important role. We have summarized key information about children and grief in the form of a pamphlet, and in that context came to the conclusion that most children manage well at home, in school and in day care (Dyregrov, 2008). This feasibly has a connection with adults' increased knowledge on this subject. A relatively large sub-group of children and young people, who experience a sudden death, can nonetheless have difficulties coping and we will describe some of their most common problems.

On the part of children and young people who experience the traumatic death of someone close to them, one observes a lack of energy, sleep disturbances, appetite and weight problems, increased emotional and physical restlessness, guilt, social withdrawal, concentration problems and varying degrees of difficulties at school (Dyregrov, K., 2005a, 2006b, 2006d; Dyregrov, 2008). Some children and young people can be angry, frustrated, experience suicidal thoughts, depression or anxiety reactions. Others speak of a reduced self-image and identity crisis, particularly in the case of a family member's death by suicide. Similar to adults, many young people struggle with reactions following bereavement in the form of intrusive memories and images, physical restlessness connected with memories of the incident, or they use a disproportionate amount of energy on avoiding thinking about or addressing anything that can remind them of the death. One also sees that young people can at times experience a reduction or lack of energy with an increased incidence of physical illness. The lack of energy can also result in their feeling that they cannot be bothered to spend time with friends as they have done previously.

Children and young people who lose parents or siblings describe the sense of loss and sadness in different ways. The sense of loss is often the heaviest to bear, and for some it is so critical that they do not succeed in functioning on a daily basis or in attending school immediately subsequent to the death. In daily life young people are continually reminded of their loss and yearning for their mother, father or sibling, in that other children as a matter of course speak about their parents or siblings. A 17-year-old describes her sense of loss and vulnerability in connection with the loss of her mother:

> For me, the fact that I cannot cry out mummy is the worst. Because it was like, that was what I did the most. No matter whether I was afraid or what, like…everything. Yes, having a mummy, just that. There are very many

such comments in my class: 'I have to call my mother,' 'my mother is coming to pick me up,' etc. You remember it right away.

Frustration, anger and instability are widespread reactions among young people. Both girls and boys speak of how they 'have become more angry' or 'are more angry and stressed out'. Small things can appear very unfair after the death and trivialities can trigger feelings of anger and frustration that have never before been experienced. This can also be taken out on younger siblings or others among those closest to them. One young person, who lost her mother, says:

> I go around with so much inside of me that if one tiny thing pops up, that can irritate me in a way more than the daily…then it's like I just lose it. It's no good. I feel pretty unstable sometimes.

The difficult situation can also make young people more vulnerable in relation to their network of friends. Particularly young people in the more peripheral network of friends can make comments that are potentially hurtful without their being aware of this in any sense whatsoever. The everyday vernacular of young people, including statements such as 'why don't you just go out and hang yourself and get it over with', 'so shoot me' or 'take a long walk on a short pier' can have an extremely hurtful effect on young people who have experienced that a loved one has just performed precisely such actions. Children can also be so thoughtless and mean to one another that they in the heat of an argument throw out comments such as 'it was a good thing your mother died'. Such comments can easily trigger a violent rage or turn a good day into a terrible day.

Troubles at school
Very many bereaved children and young people experience to a greater or lesser extent difficulties concentrating in connection with school. In our studies of young bereaved people (the Support and Care study, the Young Suicide Bereavement Study and the Children and Cancer study; see Appendix) we found that young people struggle most with difficulties at school. All the young people had, or had had, difficulties learning new things and concentrating at school after the sudden death of a close loved one (Dyregrov, 2005a, 2006d; Dyregrov and Dyregrov, 2005b; Nordanger et al., 2000). Almost half of the young people stated that they 'almost always' had difficulties concentrating and all said that it was difficult 'once in a while' or 'always'. Concentration problems at school for many young people entail their needing more time and explanations than previously to learn new and difficult things. These are the

words of a 14-year-old who lost his brother by suicide: 'It's just like you can't even do the multiplication tables, right? It takes me a lot more time to understand that an arithmetic problem is right. I need a much better explanation.'

That concentration difficulties at school can also be connected with sleep deprivation, is something this 12-year-old who lost his mother mentions:

> You try to sleep but you just can't. And it's like even though I have to get up and go to school the next day, I still can't fall asleep before 2 or 3 o'clock and then I have to get up very early, so then I only get to sleep for a few hours.

Although children and young people can experience a lack of concentration throughout the entire day, it is in the context of school that this is the most evident and the most troublesome. A clear pattern is that thoughts of what has happened arise when there is little to distract them. It is easier to concentrate on tasks that are pleasurable and require more activity in dialogue with teachers or fellow students than on quiet work done alone and difficult or boring assignments. Young people can fail exams or their marks can suffer as a result of such extensive concentration problems. Painful thoughts create a distraction from what the teacher is presenting and reduce learning capacity or concentration on assignments they have been instructed to carry out. Such thoughts, along with brooding about the death in particular, will become prevalent when it is quiet in the classroom or while doing homework, causing young people to be distracted and disturbing their concentration on school subjects. New and difficult assignments suffer especially, because new material is not 'stored'. One young person, who lost a brother, put it like this: 'I am very good at simply listening, but I don't retain anything. It goes in one ear and out the other.'

Our research also showed that, in addition to the fact that many young people struggled at school, their experience in this context was that they were not believed. They were therefore subjected to an external pressure with regard to performance and coping ability, in addition to the intense internal pressure they were suffering. These young people gradually came to feel like losers because they did not manage to deliver at the same performance level as previously or in accordance with teachers' expectations. Many felt that they were distrusted, put under great pressure and lacking the support that they found themselves needing. A clear pattern was that the young people managed to keep the intrusive thoughts and memories at a distance when they did pleasurable things or were active, such as during recess. Teachers who observe such a pattern and do not have knowledge about traumatic reminders, particularly as these function for young people, can suspect a pupil of taking advantage of the situation to get out of doing their schoolwork. The young people who did as well as they could, in spite of concentration problems and headaches, often had depressive thoughts because they felt as if they were under constant pressure, not least with regard to marks (Dyregrov, 2004; Dyregrov, K., 2006b). Although the most common reaction is that of concentration difficulties, one should also be aware of the fact that some children and young people 'overextend themselves' during the first period after a death. This manifests itself by such young people actually improving their marks during the first chaotic months, as they use school and homework as a means of escaping from the painful situation and creating order in all the chaos. For the external world it appears as if these young people are managing the situation well until they 'deflate' and their marks nose-dive.

The wide range of difficulties at school must be seen as being a result of the great psychosocial strains and turbulence in the affected children's surroundings. In spite of the frequency of difficulties at school, children are nonetheless often alone with their problems. Enhanced efforts on the part of the school to safeguard these young bereaved people are therefore extremely important and even though schools today do many things well in this regard, additional and improved assistance is needed.

The family is affected

Although young bereaved people often paint a more favourable picture of the situation than do adults, they also speak of a range of family problems after a sudden death. They experience a reversal of roles and a difficult communication climate within the family. When parents lose children or one of the parents dies suddenly and unexpectedly, one frequently sees that this affects the child–parent roles. Sometimes parents can be so worn out that for a short period of time they cannot even take care of themselves, so that the children become their caregivers unless somebody else steps in. Older siblings can assume responsibility for younger siblings or they can temporarily assume responsibility for cooking or other aspects of the caregiver role that the deceased mother, for example, formerly carried out. It also happens that young people living outside of the home move back in to take care of parents and younger siblings. Young people often think that the parents are much worse off then they are themselves and do not dare express everything they are feeling. This is illuminated by a 16-year-old who suddenly and unexpectedly lost his father:

> I couldn't accept support from mummy or the family at the time – it would
> not have worked. You see that she is in great pain and you have no wish – I
> had to feed mummy the first 24 hours, it didn't work.

Many young people do not tell parents that 'they are terrified that something
else will happen' because they believe that the parents 'have more than enough
on their plates'. Some young people avoid their parents so as not to become
personally dejected. Many parents also overprotect their children after such an
incident, because their fear increases that something shall happen to them. In
addition, they want to protect their children from exposure to the horrendous
amount of pain their mother or father is suffering. Some children and young
people can have difficulties in relation to overprotection while others
understand that it 'just means that they care about me very much'. Other young
people want to protect their parents from seeing how much pain they are in
personally. They pull themselves together or take off in order not to add to the
strain that they can see the parents are already struggling with. This represents a
form of pressure on young people and presumably some of the descriptions of
anger and lack of self-control in other situations can be connected to this. A
17-year-old who lost his mother, says: 'I can't manage to scream in front of my
father – I will manage on my own. But this works up to a point where I can't
take any more and then I fall apart completely.'

Bereaved children and young people who are living with parents who have
lost a child or a partner often have stronger reactions than those with their own
partner and family or who live outside of the parental home. One explanation
for this can be that the burden for the youngest is heavier in that they are living
close to their distraught parent/parents and in close contact with memories of
the deceased, than for young people who are surrounded by their own, separate, immediate families. Then it is no longer mother or father who is the most
important and closest relative but the new family (Brent *et al.*, 1993; Dyregrov,
2001b).

> We are sort of like *only* siblings. I believe you feel that, because your parents
> are in very much pain, right? And you understand that, because they have
> lost their child. But I have lost my brother…

This painful statement, made by a 20-year-old who lost her brother, illustrates
that many understand that parents suffer and are therefore not able to give their
children the support that they need. Nonetheless, this does not remove the need
for support and help. Children and young people experience in many ways
having to be alone in their grief, because the parents for a period have more

than enough in coping with their own bereavement. Months can pass before they feel that they can begin to lean on their parents once more.

The difficulties of family communication

If a parent/parents and children have a different amount of information about the death and the circumstances surrounding it, this can create difficulties in the relationship between children and parents. After a brother or sister's suicide, young people may have knowledge of circumstances that they have promised not to tell their parents, or they may have heard or seen things that siblings rather than parents more commonly will find out about other young people. While very many parents with their background knowledge about the deceased do not understand why the suicide happened, siblings can have had access to other kinds of information, which enables them to know or guess why. This can of course be reversed, for there will certainly just as often be situations where adults will have more knowledge regarding a death than young people. If over time the death becomes the most important subject, adults and children, due to extremely different perceptions or different amounts of information, can be prevented from sharing their thoughts with one another. This can lead to a debilitated communication climate within the family, which also makes mutual support difficult.

Because grief is influenced by how one thinks about the causes of the death, black holes can arise within the bereavement, which hinder adults and children from sharing all of their feelings and thoughts. In studies carried out long after a suicide has taken place, adults who were in their childhood at the time of the death expressed great frustration in connection with what they experienced as a keeping of secrets, silence and blocked family communication following the tragedy (Demi and Howell, 1991). Family secrets frequently arise in connection with death, where some know and others not. Such secrets can, in the worst case, potentially affect the family for several generations, and at best, become information that is to be shared before too much time has passed. Healthcare personnel, pastors and other helpers can contribute to openness and be models of direct communication about difficult topics.

Although there are difficulties associated with the child–parent relationship and the basis for communication in crisis is found in previous family communication patterns, there are also families who manage to solve such difficulties. By putting into words the fact that communication is difficult, and subsequently, what the difficulties are based on, some of the hindrances to communication between parents and siblings can be reduced. But as one sibling after a suicide pointed out: 'If children have not been able to speak with their parents about difficult things previously in life, this is not the point in time to learn how to do so.'

The relationship to friends

As is the case for adults, children and young people's social networks also play an important role after a sudden death. While younger children often confide in and speak with their parents in grief, there are fewer teenagers who do so. They open up much more frequently to close friends in their own age group. Young people therefore stress the importance of their friends and girlfriend/boyfriend being there for them. In the Support and Care study, siblings spoke of the need to pull away from the parental home for hours at a time, particularly during the initial period. They need to get away from their parents' grief and despair, all the hubbub of people coming and going and all the telephone calls and flower deliveries. The most important friend is the one with whom a young person can share 'everything' and in the Young Suicide Bereavement project 72 per cent of the young people reported having had such a friend (Dyregrov, 2006d). Two-thirds of these took advantage of this opportunity. Here as well there are clear gender differences; girls have a greater tendency to seek out girlfriends to talk to, while boys do so to a lesser degree. When a young person suddenly loses a sibling, many will later seek out the sister or brother's friends, regardless of whether or not they had formerly been part of their social circle. These friends knew the deceased, and are often of great importance because siblings and friends can share their memories, grief and sense of loss and serve as a support for one another since they are 'in the same boat'.

Alongside of the community of friends

For various reasons, not all children and young people receive the support they so sorely need from a community of friends. For some this can be due to the fact that they personally pull away from parts of their previous social network, because they find that they have grown away from it. They can experience that they have suddenly become many years older and those of the same age group now seem childish, immature and concerned with wholly insignificant things. Due to what they have experienced, they do not manage to have fun and be carefree like the others or they can feel that they are thinking adult thoughts for which they receive no understanding. In the Young Suicide Bereavement study, young people pointed out that they felt that they had missed out on a part of their youth because they had not been, mentally speaking, present (Dyregrov, K., 2006b). The young people felt that they had lost important months or even years of their lives. Some could not bear to take part in graduation festivities or refrained from attending parties as they had done before and when they again managed to take part, it was as if 'they had missed the boat'. Similar to adults, young people also experience that many people in their surroundings do not understand that grief takes time. They receive signals from friends implying that they are tired of hearing about the death, perhaps because it becomes too much of a burden to absorb the grief of others in the long run:

> I feel as if my friends say it, even though they don't, that now so much time has passed that it's enough. The old friends, those who have known me the longest, are actually those who back out. It becomes too much for them and they cannot handle it themselves.

Gaining maturity and growth

Due to the growth processes initiated by crisis, many young people can experience an 'abrupt maturity', which entails their growing away from former friends. In our studies of young bereaved people by suicide, 84 per cent of the young people had experienced personal growth in the aftermath of the death (Dyregrov, K., 2001b, 2006b). Our findings indicated similar figures for children and young people whose parents had been afflicted by cancer and for young people who had lost a sibling by sudden infant death or an accident (Dyregrov, 2005a; Nordanger et al., 2000). In many cases, this results in increased self-awareness and personal maturity. At the same time, it calls for great resources on the part of young people because the changes affect their relationship to their surroundings. A young person in the Support and Care study spoke of how his brother's death had thrown him into maturity:

> You feel as if he sort of has entered into you, so you are now twice as old. Now I no longer spend time with people my age, because they are so immature, but instead spend time with people much older than me.

Gradually and perhaps only after many years, young bereaved people will speak of how the death has changed them radically as human beings. Over time many experience that they come out of the difficult situation with greater strength. They speak of a new time era, a new scale of values, a new perception of life or even a new identity in the aftermath of a traumatic death. Because it is almost always difficult to speak about something positive after a traumatic death in the immediate family, few bereaved people will do so, and at the very least not until a long period of time has passed. The concept of growth in this context entails the development after a significant loss potentially resulting, over time, in an experience of positive change. The growth is accordingly experienced as an unintended positive consequence of something extremely negative (the death). This is wholly in accordance with many adults' experiences and can be connected with that which we know about personal growth and development in the aftermath of crises, known as 'posttraumatic growth' (Tedeschi *et al.*, 1998).

For young people this growth entails a change in priorities with regard to lifestyle, increased contact with their own feelings, that they more greatly appreciate life and small things and have a greater focus on that which represents important values. Like the adults, young people say that they are concerned with safeguarding each moment and living in the present, that they have greater self-reliance and feel stronger, more mature and independent. Some also experience an understanding that life to a larger degree is up to the individual, and what he or she makes of it, that they have become more understanding, more accepting and more compassionate towards their fellow human beings. The latter implies that young bereaved people experience being a good support resource for other young bereaved people. Other young people experience increased spiritual and religious development and a reinforced bond between friends and family members.

What kind of support and help do young people want?

Both directly and indirectly young people relate that they have enormous resources and a fighting spirit that enables them to move on in life after a close loved one has died suddenly and unexpectedly. Nonetheless, in the difficult struggle through extremely demanding and unknown territory most young people experience a need for help and support. Because various groups fulfil various types of support needs, they want support from family members, friends, the school and healthcare personnel – and for a much longer period of time than most are aware of.

Support from adult networks

Outsiders often provide more support for children and young people when the latter have lost one of their parents than when they have lost a brother or sister, in spite of the fact that parents can actually be more affected and incapable of taking care of surviving children when they lose a child than when they lose a spouse (Worden, Davies and McCown, 1999). In our research siblings stated that they had only been cared for in part by the family's network because the attention was focused primarily on the parents who had lost their child. The Support and Care project showed that siblings who lived with the parents at the time of death, often experienced 'disappearing' in the subsequent chaos that arose. Parents also confirmed that surviving siblings 'were forgotten' in the initial hours or days. During the initial period it was more frequently (elder) siblings who supported parents, than the reverse (Dyregrov, 2001b; Dyregrov *et al.*, 2000a). Older siblings still living at home point out that it is therefore particularly important that someone outside of the immediate family take care of the surviving siblings.

Although bereaved children and young people often experience that the effects of the death are greater for the parents than for themselves, they do find it painful to come in second. This is reinforced by the fact that the assistance scheme as a rule addresses the adults in the family and seldom the children directly. In the midst of this, their life's nightmare and crisis, young people nonetheless often experience expectations that they shall perform, learn new things, function as before and be responsible for caregiving duties at home. Over time, children's problems can increase in correlation with the surrounding world's gradually forgetting what they have experienced. An increase in level of maturity implies that many have a need to understand and speak about what has happened – long after everyone believes that they have 'forgotten'.

If they do not receive support from someone outside of the immediate family, they can come to feel quite alone in their grief. There is therefore a need for someone outside of the immediate family to take care of children and young people who have lost a caregiver or a sibling, so that they have the opportunity to speak about their difficulties with someone who can tolerate hearing about how much pain they are in, who can simply be there for them over time and not request anything in return. Young people are therefore wholly dependent upon other family members, the social network or the public assistance scheme stepping in when there is a sudden death in the family.

In that young people often understand the parents' difficult situation just after they have lost a child or spouse, they do not reproach them for the fact that they, for a period of time, cannot carry out their role as a parent as they had previously done. But they speak of the importance of professionals being aware of these factors. One young person says:

> It is not just a child sitting there and feeling horrible. It is the rest of the family and there are limits to what the adults in the family manage to give. If, for example, one has lost one's child or husband or wife, yes, there are in fact limits to how much he or she can help. You see how the person is personally dying from grief. Perhaps instead clearly inform the professionals who are nearby that: 'I can't manage to take care of my child right now, can you speak with him or her, can someone provide some support?'

Support from friends

Young bereaved people want the support of friends on their own terms! This involves the support being adapted to their state of mind from day to day, so that the young people can speak together when they like, receive comfort when they need it and have fun when they want a 'time out'. Often young people have a need to spend time with friends who knew the deceased, to be able to speak about painful things, cry with them or just have some time off and listen to music. Both young people and young adults appreciate being met with empathy and care from their network, also months after the funeral. After the first period, a select few best friends become the most important supporting players, helping the bereaved to get out and do pleasant things. The best friends are those who know about and can relate to what the young bereaved person is struggling with and those with whom he or she can also have fun. As one bereaved person says:

> I would prefer to have both for if one day we are doing something and I break down, then they know what it is. And then we can talk about it and then we can start having fun again.

Teenagers speak about a select number of close friends being the most important discussion partners and often pull away from parents when they want to open up and speak about the most painful issues. First and foremost, they want friends who can be there and listen when they have a need to talk about what has happened or how they are feeling. They stress the importance of having someone whom they can call or visit at any time and who then is there for them and does not back away:

> They told me very clearly to 'come whenever you want, call when you want, come and cry, come and be happy, do what you want but just know that we are here…' And they dared to say it.

One often sees that young people want to have a few friends who take care of the need for intimacy and with whom they can share their painful thoughts, while they have contact with others in the circle of friends when they need 'a time out from grief' and to have fun. Those who are just 'party friends' have frequently become so because they have not demonstrated much understanding of the situation or have never been among the closest group of friends:

> I feel that I have different friends for different needs. I still like that silly girl gang that I go out with and have such a good time with. But I also need the others whom I can talk to.

To the extent that younger children speak about their situation, adults are the most important discussion partners and it is with adults that they release their sadness, tears and despair. For these children, friends mean to a greater extent playmates, with whom they can share a 'time out'. Younger children, who experience that friends are interested in their situation and want to show empathy, often have a limit for how often they want to receive questions about it. A nine-year-old says: 'If they ask every single day how it's going, then I get all confused. I get tired of their asking.'

Some children, regardless of their age, do not want to burden their friends with everything they are struggling with. It does not feel natural; they can become embarrassed or they cannot handle seeing their friends become saddened as they listen to them:

> It just becomes totally strange for me to begin to speak to friends. They know how I am feeling; they help me and support me. No, I feel almost embarrassed; I don't want them to think about problems that they don't need to think about.

However, like the parents, most young people experience that it is not possible to receive too much support and attention from their own social networks (Dyregrov *et al.*, 2000a). The young people ask for respect and understanding and direct communication in this situation. Therefore most find it beneficial if good friends take the initiative in relation to them, ask how they are feeling and are able to speak naturally about the deceased. In particular they need the distractions and 'time outs' from grief provided by doing fun things together with friends.

Support from other young people in the same situation

Not all young bereaved people meet others who have experienced the same or similar types of losses. And it is neither the case that all will want or benefit from this. Nonetheless, several of our studies have disclosed that young people who have met other young people 'in the same situation' greatly appreciate this (Dyregrov, K., 2005a, 2006b). They say that the encounter removes the sensation of being the only one with such experiences, thoughts and reactions, and enables a sense of 'being normal'. One young person, who had been to a gathering for young people bereaved by suicide, put it like this:

> You walk around by yourself on the streets and believe that you are the only person in the whole world. Then you come here, and you see that there are some others as well. It doesn't occur to you when you are walking

down the street that some of those walking by have experienced the same thing.

In spending time together with other similarly bereaved people young people receive confirmation for the issues they are struggling with; they can speak about thoughts and feelings and find themselves being taken seriously when others listen. They do not have to say very much, are truly understood and 'the others can stand hearing about it'. By speaking with other young people for whom a long period of time has passed since their loss, they are given hope and belief in the fact that the issues they are struggling with will not last forever. The young people's experiences of encounters with other bereaved people are, in other words, more or less identical to those reported by bereaved adults. And like the adults, young people want to meet others with a background as similar as possible to their own. This would imply that young people want to meet people of their own age group and, ideally, who have also experienced the same type of death, because they have some unique experiences and needs. They want to air thoughts and emotions, which they otherwise seldom express with others of their age group, something which spending time with other young bereaved people provides the possibility for. They find that the need for the outer protective shell, in which they so often hide themselves, is gone, and they can dare to be themselves. The grief community enables them to become acquainted and feel secure much more quickly than they ordinarily would when they otherwise meet new young people. A 14-year-old says: 'When we meet other bereaved youths, we start with the inside, not the outside as we usually do.'

Young people exchange and give advice and information about what has helped them in the difficult situation in which they find themselves. This can be in the form of advice on what they can do personally or information about where they can apply for professional help and the kind of help available. Advice from other young bereaved people often gains a far greater significance than if the same comes from adults or young people without the same experiential background. But above all, the opportunity to have fun and 'do amusing things' and 'to be allowed to be young' in the company of others is extremely important for young bereaved people. Taking a time out while at the same time remaining in contact with what has taken place is of inestimable value. As is the case for adults, it is meaningful for young people to be able to support other young people after a traumatic death. Last, but not least, young people report that other young bereaved people understand the meaning of giving and receiving support and understanding over time – when everyone else has forgotten. The young bereaved people who have experience from contact with other bereaved youths therefore specify the importance of all young people receiving such an offer of support. This can be done through professionals with knowledge of the existing and relevant peer organizations and who provide, and motivate, such contact. Then it is up to the individual young person to accept the offer or not.

Professional help

In Norwegian as well as international studies, the majority of the young people involved indicate that they needed support and help from outside of the family after a sudden death:

> There are very few who can get through such things without receiving help. I think most people need to receive help. I believe regardless that it is important to speak with someone outside of the family.

For various reasons young people discover that the support of parents, close family members, friends or other bereaved people is not sufficient. This can be because they are struggling with special issues, lack information that only professionals can provide for them, or do not wish to burden their network with specific problems. Young people therefore request that the public assistance scheme assume responsibility for ensuring that those in need of professional help receive an offer of this. In the Young Suicide Bereavement study, 88 per cent of the young people stated that to varying degrees they experienced a need for professional help (Dyregrov 2006c, 2006d). Young girls and those who lack the support of the family or isolate themselves reported the most acute need for professional help. Another group of young people in greater need of help than others includes those who experience the most intrusive memories and the most intense grief reactions.

When young people ask for help from professionals, they simultaneously make many recommendations regarding how such help should be organized. Like the adults, the young people communicated the need for a programme providing routine care subsequent to a sudden death: 'There are routines for the deceased but not for those who survive them.' The young people point out nonetheless that although they would like routine professional help, this must be carried out in consultation with the young people. The young people want first and foremost for somebody to see them as separate individuals and to evaluate each individual situation. Many young people feel a large amount of uncertainty in relation to their own reactions because these are so intense and they are unsure of where it will all end. They therefore express a need for the security provided by 'somebody' standing by, ready to help out if the need should arise. This certainty that help will be provided if they should have a need for it is like a lifebuoy and the knowledge that they will not 'go under' gives them a greater sense of security.

The helpers must not wait to be sought out – they must make an offer, because one often is not able to ask for help personally. At the beginning one is completely in shock and 'does not know up from down in the situation' or what one needs or what kind of help is available. The young people suggest that if a young person refuses help because it is offered prematurely or because one does not understand the point of it, one should receive a business card. In this way the young person can make contact at a later point in time, should he or she feel a need and can manage to do so. But the best solution is if the potential helpers make contact once again at a later point in time, according to the young people. They could say 'we will call you again after the funeral' – and then do it. One young person who lost his father had the following to say about this:

> It's not always when you are sitting there, a few hours after having found out, and someone comes and asks if you need to speak with someone or 'are you all right now', it's not always so easy to answer. Because at the moment you can't tell up from down, with regard to yourself or the situation. One needs to talk; one needs a chance to sort things out and perhaps in a very gentle fashion. But to ask for help personally, that is at any rate extremely difficult.

Based on negative experiences, many young people stipulate that it is important to be informed and included in a direct and sensitive manner. They want information about what has happened, the contents of a suicide note, of police investigations, autopsy reports, about what will happen next, etc. At a later point in time, information is often wanted regarding the normal reactions of young people (and adults/parents) in a crisis situation. Further, young bereaved people want help from qualified professionals. In particular, counselling is sought, with psychologists, nurses and social teachers.

Simultaneously, young people ask that all key assistance authorities in connection with sudden deaths (pastor, police, physicians, teachers, funeral homes, etc.) focus on the young bereaved person's special situation. With a point of departure in unfortunate encounters, young people specify that a condition must be that involved professionals have the required knowledge and qualifications for meeting young bereaved people in crisis. By speaking with a professional about the most painful, difficult subjects, they are spared having to burden other bereaved people who can be more than overwhelmed for their own part, or friends who perhaps will not tolerate hearing about it or understand. The fact that professionals are bound by rules of professional confidentiality is also important, as this gives young people the courage to express everything that they are struggling with. Further, it is crucial for the chemistry to be right, for young people to experience that they are receiving good help. Many communicate well with nurses or school welfare officers, who frequently function as an outreach programme because they are stationed at schools:

> It is so good that you can just go there and talk (with the school nurse) if you need to; it is very good to know this if something should come up. It doesn't take very much and then it's easy to feel completely alone, but then it doesn't take very much either for you not to feel this way.

Young people also want advice and information about any peer organizations from nurses or others in the assistance scheme and maintain that the collaboration between the assistance scheme and such organizations should be reinforced.

Push us a bit more – find the 'traction point'!

Many young people state that they personally have contributed to not receiving the help that they would have liked to have received at a later point in time. They are not always adept at expressing themselves and informing helpers that they are not doing well. Appearances can be deceiving; many try to cover up how they are really feeling. Because young people for different reasons try to hide this, they realize that it is not always easy for those around them to give them the help they need. Some refuse the help that is offered and they therefore say 'push us a bit more' and 'repeat the offer of help'. They ask that helpers dare to be a bit more on the offensive and not just accept the first refusal at face value. Other young people, who have never received help, can imagine it being difficult to accept such an offer, but believe that they would have done so if outsiders had motivated them. But some young people are also sceptical about being pressured to open up too quickly and too much, such as with a psychologist. In such a case it is a matter, as this young person put it, of 'finding the traction point':

> The psychologist that I had was all about trying to get me to say absolutely everything. I actually did not want to say very much, but he got me in fact to say a lot. So that is certainly what ruined it for me, that I did not get the kind of help that I needed. Maybe not pressure, but in a way, a little pressure...sort of find the traction point. But we want to play a part in deciding.

Young bereaved people understand that it is not easy for professionals or family members to find the 'traction point', or to know how much they should 'push' the individual young person in order to give them the help that they need or can manage to accept. Many young people indicate that they had to push their reactions aside in the beginning, simply in order to keep functioning. Right after a death, many must take in the reality little by little and then one does not have the emotional space to relate to well-meaning helpers or family members, however deeply they may want to help. Therefore, proximity and repeated, careful offers of help and support are the best solutions.

Some young people are very disappointed about the absence of help from society, particularly when the family has been unable to do its part. They can later experience strong reactions. Particularly vulnerable are young people who have lost their best friend or boy/girlfriend and feel that they are not taken into consideration. Other young people report that close friends of a deceased brother or sister are struggling but that they do not receive the help they need. They experience that the focus of assistance measures for young people, at best, is only on the immediate, biological family while young friends who perhaps have been the closest of all in the final years before the death are not included in any follow-up measures.

Support from the school

The young people state that they receive some help through the school and they are often more satisfied with the schools and teachers than with the public assistance scheme. Their accounts reflect that very many schools have taken charge and have plans for or thoughts about taking care of pupils after a sudden death in the immediate family. This finds expression in a good number of encounters between young people and the school. Many young people want to return to school as quickly as possible if they can be there a bit on their own terms at first. They want 'psychological time outs' from the sad atmosphere at home, while they feel that the school, teachers and fellow pupils can also give them important support. A girl who lost her father when she was 15 years old says about this:

> I managed to hang on by clinging to the fact that I was going back to school. That alone was what was in my head, hang on for two days, I will soon be back in school. I believed that I would receive an extraordinary support there and so I did.

One type of help that is stressed as being beneficial is that of teachers who offer to inform the class about the death or do so in collaboration with the pupil and family. Further, it is experienced as extremely positive when teachers show them a little extra consideration, bring the matter up with them and implement concrete measures if necessary. They especially appreciate teachers who follow up over time on a regular basis and (discreetly) ask how they are doing, although certainly not too often. In particular (head) teachers, school welfare officers and school nurses are central, significant helpers. A young boy says:

> The teachers I have had, they have been like nurses, the entire gang. They are full of compassion and you gain a very good kind of contact with them. Then you can dare to say everything as well. But you don't have such good chemistry with everyone you meet.

Although the young people give the school and teachers relatively good references, there are many important factors that can be improved. In the Young Suicide Bereavement study better care measures on the part of the school were extremely important to the young bereaved people and approximately one-third would have liked to have received more support from the school (Dyregrov, K., 2006b, 2006d). A large problem for many was the experience of pressure in the way of performance expectations, that they should attend school and continue to function exactly as before, despite having been through such a difficult time. In addition, some of the young people found that different teachers at the same school had different procedures for taking care of the same student subsequent to a suicide. Very many young people express the wish that their teachers to a larger extent could understand the nature of their struggles after the death of a close loved one. They want someone to observe and make the connection between increased absenteeism, a lack of concentration, reduced learning capacity and lower marks, and the difficulties they are going through. Unfortunately some can fall through the cracks at school if they are not seen and helped out. A 14-year-old who lost his brother when he was ten years old says:

> It should have been like if I needed to calm down that I would be allowed to sit alone and maybe talk with a teacher – because you can't just get up and walk out of class suddenly. I skipped school because I could not stand to be there and only after a year and a half was able to concentrate and began to work with school again. It would have maybe gone a bit more quickly if I had received more help with my concentration. It is going tolerably well now but right after it had happened, it didn't go well at all.

An extremely sensitive subject for young people is empathy from teachers and the manner in which this is expressed. It is important for young people that teachers proceed with caution, and indicate that they understand their situation but without 'jumping all over them' in front of everyone. Due to both the extreme nature of what has happened and their age, young people can be extremely vulnerable and particularly sensitive to their surroundings. While they want sincere empathy from teachers, the way in which the empathy is expressed must be such that they can accept it. The type of compassion young people can accept will depend upon their day-to-day state of mind, the type of relationship the young person previously had with the teacher, and – in particular – whether the setting allows for intimacy. Taking all of these factors into consideration is extremely demanding for teachers, who are for their own part often very unsure about how to approach young people in crisis. The challenges are not lessened when one takes into consideration that the young people as individuals have different support and intimacy needs: 'Everyone is different, some need lots of hugs and some don't want them at all.'

Lack of time perspective on the part of professionals and networks

Wholly in correspondence with what the adult bereaved reported, the young people stated that everyone, with the exception of the closest affected individuals, forgets about what has happened long before they themselves stop thinking about it. This is experienced as a great hardship and problem, and contributes to increasing difficulties in coping with the situation and in asking for help as time passes. This is the case both with regard to the healthcare system, the school, some friends and family. One 14-year-old, who had lost his brother three years earlier, put it like this:

> This has its claws in you for a long time and it is not even finished after a whole year has passed. It takes time to get over it and those who have not experienced it do not understand this. They do not understand that it takes time to get on your feet again and that you need support all along the way, not just from your parents.

For the majority of the young people, the shock, grief and pain diminish over the years and they see that it is possible to integrate the memory of the deceased into their lives. This process can take time and is very burdensome. Through help and support, networks, other bereaved people and professionals can alleviate and abbreviate the duration of these arduous years for young people in the aftermath of a sudden death.

Main themes
Young people's support requests from adult network individuals

- Give information that is accurate and sincere. Do not refrain from giving us information that we want to receive or will hear from others.

- Do not pressure us to grieve like parents/adults.

- Do not pressure us to speak, but signal that it is ok and be there when we are ready and want to talk or share our feelings.

- Do not impose too much of the adults' despair upon us or allow us to assume adult roles.

- Do not despair unnecessarily over insufficient reactions or talk on our part (most of us talk to our friends).

- Pay attention to whether or not we function well on a daily basis after the first few months (sleeping well vs. nightmares and sleep disturbances, eating normally vs. changed eating patterns, meeting friends vs. isolating ourselves, school performances as before vs. enhanced performance/drop in marks).

- Try to give/accept that we need 'time outs' to do amusing things and to relax with friends, even at an early point in time when adults cannot conceive of such a thing.

- Talk to the school about how we are doing, check whether the necessary support measures have been implemented (in collaboration with us).

- Ensure that a close relative/acquaintance is available to serve as a 'support figure' at the start (someone with whom we already have good contact).

- Make it clear that it is acceptable to speak about the deceased and the event over time.

Young people's support wishes from friends

- Express that you have no words for the situation or do not know what to say.

- Do not think/say that you understand how we feel.

- Do not try to say the 'right' things or give advice.

- Speak with or ask us how you can provide support in our bereavement.
- Respect our wishes regarding how you shall behave and ask whether what you are doing is ok.
- Remember that you do not reopen a wound when you speak about the deceased in a natural manner. We think about the deceased frequently.
- Create time outs from grief; have fun – when and if we can manage it.
- Avoid hurtful comments such as 'go out and hang yourself and get it over with', and do not allow others to get away with this.
- Take the initiative and give support in the long-term.

The support derived from meeting others in the same situation

- We meet others and see that they are in the same situation.
- We receive confirmation for the issues we are personally struggling with and acquire confidence in the fact that we are completely normal.
- We have the chance to speak about our thoughts and feelings, are listened to in earnest and feel truly understood by other young people and adults.
- We have the opportunity to express thoughts/feelings that we seldom air with others in our age group.
- We do not have to say so much; we are really understood and the others can stand hearing what we have to say.
- We receive advice and information.
- We acquire hope and faith in the fact that it is possible to move on.
- We can take 'time outs', do fun things, 'are allowed to be young' with the others, while we do not escape from the serious issues.
- We have the opportunity to support others – and that is meaningful.
- We can give and receive support over time.

Young people's wishes for help from professionals

- Automatic offer of help.
- Flexibility as a main rule.

- Early and extended offer of help that is repeated.
- Information.
- Stand-by help if/when one needs it.
- Counselling with qualified professionals.
- Chemistry with the helpers.
- Personal focus – speak freely.
- Information about and contact with support organizations.

Young people's wishes for help from the school

- Schools/teachers should acquire knowledge about the situation of young bereaved people following traumatic death by making this a part of teachers' basic and continuing education.
- Plans should be made for a follow-up strategy for young bereaved people following a sudden death.
- The school/teachers should be responsible for contacting the pupil/home to inquire about the necessary adaptations and plans for care. The pupils should be involved in the collaboration with the school and parents.
- The school should take the initiative/help the pupil to inform the class about what has happened. It is important that the teacher takes the initiative and makes it clear that this can be done.
- The school/teachers must anticipate that the pupil may need to return gradually after the funeral and be on the lookout for concentration difficulties.
- Young people want more sympathy/empathy from some teachers – but expressions of sympathy must be adapted to the individual and situation so that teachers do not 'fall all over' the pupil.
- More flexible school attendance rules are needed – so the young person need not attend school if they do not feel up to this on a given day (of particular relevance for more advanced pupils).
- Young people want the option to take a 'time out', particularly in the beginning – e.g. to be allowed to retreat to a separate group room or to be allowed a distraction such as working at a PC.
- Young people propose exemption from (some) tests and exams according to need – particularly immediately following the death.

- There can be a need for an adapted solution for tests – such as a separate room, a longer allotted time period, possibly an oral examination if this alleviates concentration problems.

- The school can ease up on the pressure to achieve good marks and try to see new tests in connection with the pupil's former performance and with what he/she has been through when marks are given.

- The pupil can be permitted to be more passive in class for a period without this having any repercussions for marks.

- Where necessary, practical outplacement/apprenticeships or leave from school for short time periods can be considered.

- Teachers at the same school must coordinate strategies in relation to the same pupil.

- The school must have a realistic time perspective with regard to bereavement and the need for care, and not expect the grief to pass after a few months.

- Young people want routine contact with school welfare officer/ nurse/psychologist, which in addition to serving as an outreach programme provides fixed appointments for contact throughout the term.

- Offers of adaptation and help should be repeated if pupils who are clearly not coping refuse these. The school/teachers must show that they care and understand the difficult situation following the death.

5

How does sudden death affect
social networks?

In this chapter we will look at how social networks experience supporting family members, friends, colleagues and schoolmates after a sudden death. The majority of the network knowledge in this book is based on research carried out within the parameters of the Network project (Dyregrov, K., 2003–2004, 2005b, 2006c). As we have seen earlier in this book, the bereaved find that it is difficult for family members, friends and colleagues to approach them after they have been struck by tragedy. They also believe that networks wish to provide more support than they are managing, and share some thoughts here about what is needed to improve the situation. In this chapter we will see that the bereaved are correct in their conjectures, and the network members will explain the difficulties that they personally experience while also indicating solutions. By having both parties (bereaved people and network members) indicate challenges, dilemmas and solutions, we lay the foundation for the mindsets and measures necessary to derive the greatest benefits from the type of network support that we will later propose.

Painful, difficult, but incredibly rewarding!

It is important to make her understand that I am always here for her – regardless of when and where or whatever it might be.

The above quote comes from a female friend who represents the close social networks, the members of which as a rule express deeply felt compassion and want to do 'everything' to support the bereaved. We can see the same kind of reaction with other kinds of loss, such as of a spouse or other close individual. The networks want so much to help out but nonetheless feel a large degree of uncertainty in their encounter with crisis-stricken individuals. The reasons for this are many and complex. In summary, one can say that social networks describe the support they provide for bereaved people as: 'Painful, difficult, but incredibly rewarding!' When we discuss support from the network it is important to make a distinction between support from close social network people and those who are a bit more peripheral. In general, we can say that the more peripheral the network members are and the poorer the quality of contact between bereaved people and the network, the greater the uncertainty. When speaking about network support we also want to distinguish between its quantitative and qualitative aspects, as reported by the network itself.

Quantitative aspects of support

Friends and family members in the Network project were thrown into shock and disbelief when they received word of the death, and had difficulties functioning during the first few days. Nonetheless, they did their part from the moment they learned of the death and for many of them this meant from the first day. Almost all of the 101 network members (90 per cent) personally took the initiative and contacted the bereaved if the bereaved had not phoned them personally. This is wholly in accordance with the wishes and needs of bereaved people but not with their experiences on the whole, a reflection of the fact that the participants of our study to a large degree represent the inner circle of friends and family (see section about inner and outer networks below).

On average, the network members had been in contact with the bereaved more than once a day during the first week following the death, more than five times a week during the month following the death, and four and three times a week during the six and twelve months following the death, respectively. On the average, network members provided support for some two years, an impressive length of time, taking into account the fact that not all of the members had known the bereaved for such a long period of time previous to the death. In addition to the need for support over time, the network had experienced the significance of contacting the bereaved at an early point in time and of offering support – without the bereaved being obliged to contact them personally. The network members found that the most important things that they had been able to do had been to speak about what had happened (99 per cent), be physically present (98 per cent), offer consolation (97 per cent), or provide social stimulus (95 per cent). While three-quarters contributed with help of a practical nature, half provided support for the surviving children. Few had perceived it as necessary to provide financial assistance (10 per cent). Most friends, family members and colleagues expended an enormous amount of energy on assisting the bereaved during the initial days, the period during which they felt that their need for support had been most critical. As a result of this, the homes of the bereaved could be quite chaotic and full of people during the first week and a certain amount of unnecessary overlapping of well-wishing helpers occurred. As we shall see below, some of the network members observed this and implemented corrective measures.

Qualitative aspects of the support

Friends, neighbours and family members in the Network project stated that they virtually moved in and lived with the bereaved families during the initial days. Some friends and family members had been extremely aware of the fact that the bereaved should not be left on their own after the death. During this period they experienced that the most important contribution that they could make was simply 'to be there', to listen and hold the grieving adults and children. In addition, they helped out with the preparations for the funeral and arrangements for the viewing, with practical things such as housework and cooking, paying bills or accompanying children to school. Some of the members of the inner circle of the friend-network had discovered that it was wholly necessary that they assumed an active role. They had seen that very little happened unless they called and visited the bereaved or basically took over some of the tasks in the home for a short period of time. In most cases it did not help to offer one's help and then wait for a phone call, at least not during the first week following the death.

After the first week the network support entailed listening to accounts of the traumatic event over and over again, crying with and sharing feelings with the bereaved. The network discovered the importance of allowing the bereaved to determine the pace of the grieving process, without pressuring them or asking too many questions. In addition, the network attempted to be receptive, to listen and respect the intense emotions and sadness as expressed by each individual bereaved person. Over time they had experienced the importance of adapting the degree of intimacy to the individual needs of each bereaved person for closeness, consolation and other forms of support. They had also learned the significance of speaking about and sharing memories of the deceased, speaking his or her name, visiting the grave and remembering important days in connection with both the deceased and the death.

Gradually the network also attempted to provide stimulus for the bereaved by encouraging them to resume social activities. They invited them for a meal or asked them to come along and take part in something enjoyable, preferably activities that they had enjoyed before the death. This type of crucial encouragement to 'continue living' also included efforts to help the bereaved return to work. Nonetheless, most of the members of the close social networks had learned that they must not pressure them too much or give too much 'good advice'. They had learned this by making some mistakes, particularly during the first year. They had become extremely aware of their limited capacity to fully understand the unique situation of the bereaved. Gradually they had learned to provide support that was a reflection of the reactions of the bereaved, so that to the greatest possible extent they attempted to provide support that corresponded with individual wishes and circumstances.

Some of the networks had organized their resources and planned out who in the circle of friends was to be on duty on specific days, to do what, in relation to whom in the family. In this way the mother and father could receive support from their best friends while a neighbour took care of the children and a colleague informed the workplace. This type of organization was in many ways an efficient means of managing the available resources, in that one person could step in when it was their turn and then withdraw to regain their strength, with the knowledge that others were now assuming responsibility. The organization of resources also contributed to making it possible for network groups to provide support in the long-term. When compared with the wishes of the bereaved with regard to network support, the support from those who took part in the Network project was virtually ideal. Nonetheless, these close social network members also experienced a large amount of uncertainty with regard to what was the best thing to say and do, and how they should behave.

Learning through ineptitude and uncertainty
Friends and family members who support those bereaved by sudden deaths experience an enormous strain but also have many positive experiences over time. This was confirmed to a very large extent by the Network project. A total of 81 per cent of the participants of the project maintained that it had been 'a little' or 'extremely difficult' to provide support for the bereaved after a sudden and unexpected death, while three-quarters had experienced it as 'strenuous'. At the same time, 99 per cent of the network members said that it had been a positive experience to be allowed the opportunity to provide support and almost just as many had experienced personal growth due to the experience.

The experience of strain was first and foremost related to a person's own uncertainty and ineptitude in terms of dealing with the situation. Almost one-third thought that they had probably hurt the bereaved through their behaviour, such as through ill-considered advice or comments or by talking too much. More than one-half thought that they had examples indicating that they had provided support in an inappropriate or incorrect manner, which they later understood as they learned to interpret better the needs of the bereaved. There was in particular a large degree of uncertainty with regard to if and when the bereaved wished to speak about what had happened or if they wanted to shift the focus to other things. While some felt that they could step beyond the boundaries of the private sphere, others were afraid of 'destroying a good day' by beginning to speak about what had happened, if the bereaved themselves had not taken the initiative to do so. Others admitted that over time they grew weary of the subject constantly returning, so that they once in a while avoided the subject. To the extent that they were aware that this took place, it also was the source of a guilty conscience. A close female friend of a woman who lost a child through sudden infant death said the following on this subject:

> I know that I should have brought up the subject of John's death and life more often, but sometimes I get tired of it and wish that we could meet and speak about other things. I know that my evasiveness hurts them sometimes but it is such a burden to have to speak about it over and over again. On the other hand, perhaps the parents could start speaking about their son if they missed doing so.

For some friends and family members this becomes so difficult that they either avoid the bereaved for periods of time or wait until they personally take the initiative to speak about the event. Later as many as 70 per cent in the Network project thought that they had probably been too passive and had waited for the bereaved to give an indication or tell them how they wished to be supported. Gradually, the close friends and family members had understood that it was they themselves, and not those who had suffered the loss, who had to make contact and the initiative most frequently in the relationship. They acquired such knowledge over time, first and foremost through the passivity and weariness of the bereaved. The impression that this was about a learning process between the parties was reinforced by the fact that those who had supported bereaved people from between one and two years (83 per cent) gradually experienced less uncertainty over time.

Most of those in the network had experienced the futility of their efforts when they had attempted to give advice or had tried to 'push' in the grief process. They had eventually recognized that only the bereaved were in a position to know what was right for them and that they therefore were obliged instead to attempt to be the best possible 'sparring mates' in relation to the thoughts and feelings of the bereaved. Further, the network members learned that parents appreciated their speaking the name of the deceased/child in conversation in a natural way, sitting together and reminiscing about the child, accompanying them on a visit to the grave or commemorating birthdays or other important occasions. In particular, friends and family had learned the importance of staying in touch and indicating a willingness to provide support over time, even when they received little response from the bereaved. A colleague and female friend says:

> Close social network members should not stop making contact even if the bereaved person cannot bear to talk. Sooner or later they will want to talk and the fact that you have demonstrated that you have been thinking of them all along is very supportive.

The friends or family members who had personally experienced loss or previously stood by bereaved people in the same situation had far greater self-assurance in the encounter with the bereaved. These individuals had not been afraid to contact the family immediately and were not uncertain about what they should say or do in the first encounter. They just came, were present and met with the family at an emotional level. These friends emphasized the importance of assistance on the terms of the bereaved; in other words, of doing what the bereaved needed one to do, virtually regardless of what that was. Because such an attitude could lead to very intense involvement, this became difficult for some, particularly during the first period after the death and also, for some, over time.

Stress factors in the inner circle and the risk of burnout

If the majority of those who assist the bereaved immediately following the death withdraw after the first few months, the overall strain in the long-term is often too great for the inner circle of friends. As explained above, this inner part of the network has very frequent contact with the bereaved immediately after the death and frequent, almost daily contact throughout the first year. Even one year after the death, when the majority of the people around them seem to have forgotten the incident, the inner circle continues to assist its grieving friends. Because this circle is constantly shrinking, the stress and strain on the remaining friends increases. In the Network project, more than two-thirds found that assisting the bereaved over time was 'stressful'. Beyond the fact that it was time- and energy-consuming, it was first and foremost difficult to provide support due to constantly having a guilty conscience because they felt they were not managing to do enough.

Despite a decrease in uncertainty through increased experience, very many therefore experienced that it was difficult to provide support on a long-term basis. This was essentially associated with strain and fatigue combined with a guilty conscience and feelings of ineptitude. The desire to support friends in the throes of boundless grief, combined with the stress of witnessing the amount of pain they are in and the sense of being able to do so very little, is a strain. The best friend of a mother who lost her child through sudden infant death explained it as follows:

> I had such a feeling of helplessness and ineptitude in the situation – you cannot do anything whatsoever about the extreme, horrendous despair. You want to give them the entire world, but are not capable of alleviating the pain of the situation. It is really difficult to experience that there is so little that you can do.

Some common stress factors that network members otherwise struggle with are trauma reactions after having heard repeated accounts of horrible details in connection with the death. The deceased is as a rule also a loved one for the inner circle of friends. Over and over again they listen to the grief of close relations, to their pain and agonizing: over the person who had lived, the death and the day of the death, the first painful period, the reactions of the surviving children, spouse and effects on the home life, and also about the future – in the event the bereaved person is in any sense able to envision one. Some network members struggle with their own sense impressions stemming from the first period before the funeral when they provided assistance. They may have seen things in connection with a child's death or taken part in actions that left permanent traces. Although they would not have wanted to have been without the experience of clipping off a lock of hair or taking part in helping to dress the deceased – indeed to the contrary, they are grateful for having been trusted with such an important support function – these are nonetheless experiences that leave lasting marks on close friends and family members (cf. Chapter 11).

In order to prevent burnout for their own part, it happens that some network members who are struggling with a guilty conscience are obliged to take a break from their contact with the bereaved. In order to avoid misunderstandings, they have realized that it is important for the bereaved and for the network itself, not to mention the friendship, that the strain is communicated in a manner that the bereaved can understand. The worst thing would be for the network just to pull away without giving the bereaved any type of explanation. A woman in the Network project who had given support following three sudden deaths in the course of a short period of time had experienced that there are limits to how much a single person can step in at a time. If one becomes too exhausted, it is not possible to be a good support person.

Growth, development and learning for life

Although the task of supporting good friends experiencing serious bereavement is described as being strenuous and demanding, it is also as a rule a positive experience for close friends and family. This was heavily emphasized in the Network project. Almost all participants (95 per cent) experienced personal growth and learning from having been there for a bereaved person in a difficult life situation. The experience of being permitted to come so close to the bereaved gave the network a great deal in return. They pointed out the positive aspect of the fact that they had acquired a new perspective on life, an increased understanding of grief and of the bereaved, increased self-knowledge, a greater ability to provide support and care and a new depth in the friendship. We will now look more closely at what each of these points entails.

NEW LIFE PERSPECTIVE

Similar to the reports of the bereaved, friends and family members experience being challenged in terms of existential life-questions. The close contact with sudden and incomprehensible death compelled them to stop, reflect upon their own lives and put things into perspective: a female friend says: 'I have now understood that I do not have a single real problem in life and I understand how fragile and arbitrary life actually is.'

Through proximity to the bereaved person's crisis, the network members also came to appreciate life and non-material values more. They had eye-opening experiences with regard to what was most important in life when one gets right down to it, and appreciated life, their own health and happiness more. Like the bereaved, they did not take things for granted as they had done previously. They realized that life is short and limited, that one must live in the moment and take care of what one has. An additional effect was that they understood the significance of taking better care of and appreciating their own family. Some said that they now refrained from arguing about trivialities. The participants in the Network project maintained that these new realizations would affect them for the rest of their lives.

INCREASED SELF-KNOWLEDGE

As part of the personal growth that the networks experienced through close contact with the bereaved, they also derived increased self-knowledge and increased awareness of their own emotional reactions in connection with the suffering of fellow human beings. The experiences had given them a new understanding of themselves as human beings and they had matured. They now dared to cry in front of friends and showed their feelings with greater ease than previously. They had learned the importance of being more in contact with their own feelings, of being open and sincere about difficult issues. This was a lesson that many reported that they had transferred to their own family situation, including their own children. They had gradually improved their ability to listen and speak to their family and the bar had been lowered regarding that which constituted 'a serious problem' worth discussing.

INCREASED UNDERSTANDING OF GRIEF AND THE BEREAVED

Friends and family members also experienced an increased understanding of grief and trauma reactions, and greater humility with regard to sudden loss and death in general. They had witnessed how the sudden loss of a child sapped all the energy of the close bereaved, how siblings involuntarily ended up on the sidelines and how frightening the reactions could be, for both the bereaved and the network. Beyond knowledge about the large variations found in grief processes, they acquired intimate contact with the vulnerability as well as the strengths of those bereaved by sudden death. Friends and family were impressed by the willingness and resources that the bereaved mobilized in the midst of all the pain. One man who provided support for his best friend said: 'I have learned so much about trauma, grief, pain and vitality.'

INCREASED CAPACITY TO PROVIDE SUPPORT AND CARE

The network's insight, maturity and knowledge evolved little by little in interaction with the bereaved. Immediately following the death many had been frightened by the powerful reactions of the bereaved and were extremely uncertain with regard to how they should behave. But they gradually acquired greater confidence in their abilities and became more secure about their own significance in terms of providing support for the bereaved. They gradually improved their abilities to listen to and speak with the bereaved and many were surprised about the support that they had managed to give. Through a process where openness and honesty were of central importance, friends and family members learned some fundamental 'rules of conduct' regarding how they should behave in relation to the different bereaved people in order to provide support for them. Through the support process the network acquired increased knowledge and self-confidence, which helped them to maintain the friendship as well as carry out a role of support in the unique situation. They became extremely aware that support in the event of a sudden death was never about the right or wrong way to proceed but that to a large extent it was a matter of providing support on the terms of the individual bereaved person. Nonetheless, they had learned that how this took place also bore a connection to the relationship that already existed between themselves and the bereaved. Friends and family reported that they had become secure about their ability to support human beings in crisis, and that this represented a learning experience that they would not be afraid to put to use in the event other close acquaintances might need them. The importance of having a solid and intimate social network became very clear for the network and many had thought about how they themselves would have liked to have been approached in a crisis situation.

NEW DEPTH TO FRIENDSHIPS

After long-term support many of the network members experienced having acquired wholly different and more profound friendships with the bereaved. This was due to the unique situation, the new insight and knowledge, and intimacy with the bereaved, which emerged over a period of time: 'Being a friend in a situation of deep bereavement is difficult but it has bound us together in a stronger manner. It has added new dimensions to our friendship.'

Because the parties had shared so much pain and personal thoughts and feelings, a new depth was added to the friendship – a friendship that they maintained would last for the rest of their lives. A new trust and intimacy developed between the two parties, which resulted in a deeper understanding between them. The network found that the mutuality and trust which had developed through discussions about such losses could be transferred to other meaningful subjects between the involved parties. The network members expressed great humility about the trust and confidence that providing support for their friends through grief and life crises after traumatic losses entailed. Such friendships were seen as being extremely valuable and were greatly appreciated. The networks studied therefore maintained that such life experience, in spite of the fact that it is extremely demanding, would have a positive effect on them for the rest of their lives: 'It has, I hope, made me a better person!'

Different types of support from inner and outer networks

Most of that which is described from the network's experiences comes from what can be referred to as the inner network circles. These are networks that already knew the bereaved well or that grew very close subsequent to the death. These friends or family members often also provide the best and most important kind of support. Such people make fewer mistakes in relation to the bereaved, essentially because they have a better basis for understanding them than people in the outer network.

The outer networks comprise more peripheral friends and acquaintances of the close bereaved people and are people whom they will meet on a daily basis in various social contexts. It can be a matter of acquaintances with whom one has informal meetings or people one knows only very superficially from the neighbourhood, a training studio, at the store or workplace, from church, etc. Because the number of people in the outer circle is greater than in the inner, the outer circle usually also acquires great importance for the bereaved. Very often many people in the outer circle will know of a dramatic or unusual death so that the bereaved will be obliged to relate to them in various ways in their bereavement. The large degree of uncertainty and helplessness that bereaved people experience on the part of networks frequently stems from the outer network. And although bereaved people understand their difficulties to a large extent, thoughtless comments, evasiveness and inexpedient advice have hurtful consequences.

The outer networks find themselves in the midst of a difficult dilemma. On the one hand, they do not know the bereaved well enough to know what the individual would appreciate in the way of support, so that they can give support on their own terms. On the other hand, it is interpreted as evasiveness if peripheral friends and acquaintances fail to say something or otherwise fail to address the death once they have learned of it. Due to a lack of knowledge about the situation of the bereaved, about their needs and wishes for support, many of those in the peripheral networks fall back on a myth that states that one can 'reopen the wounds' by asking how things are going. It is better then to act as if nothing were out of the ordinary, so that the bereaved are not obliged to think so much about sad things. To avoid the risk of being intrusive, some pull away and behave as if they do not know what has happened. But such an unnatural, evasive attitude gives them away to the bereaved – due to the latter's extreme sensitivity to others' body language and behaviour following a traumatic death. The outer networks will therefore perhaps have as much to learn from this book with regard to both listening to the bereaved and the close social networks that have learned how to be good support people.

When support networks are also bereaved people

Some close friends, grandparents or other biological family members will find themselves playing double roles in relation to the bereaved. They often have, because they are relatives of or know the bereaved very well, also known the deceased well. They want to provide support while at the same time they struggle with their own reactions to that which has happened. In this way some close social networks will also be bereaved people who are experiencing stress and strain at many different levels. While they suffer in witnessing the family of their relative or friend in such pain, they can be struggling with their own reactions and grief for the deceased. In addition, such supporters must often take care of their own family and children, who can also be taking the death very hard.

Grandparents are in a unique position as a support network because they have so much to give and because they are vulnerable. In the UK, SANDS has focused on this group in particular and published leaflets according to the special needs of grandparents (SANDS, 2008). When parents lose a child, the grandparents are often concerned about how they can support their children. For many the grief involved in seeing one's own child in terrible pain is just as painful as the grief over the loss of a beloved grandchild. One therefore sees how some grandparents wear themselves out in efforts to support their children, because they forget about themselves, their own needs and their own grief in the midst of it all. Some grandparents can become so run-down that they develop serious physical and psychological reactions and are eventually obliged to seek professional help. Other family members, good friends and neighbours can of course also experience the same difficulties and challenges that are described here for grandparents. Awareness of this fact is the first step in the process of preventing the development of serious consequences and preventing these important support individuals from burning out (cf. Chapter 11).

The significance of inviting the network in

Network support can only occur if both parties want it. Bereaved people must permit the support of others, while the network must have a desire to provide support. When bereaved people sometimes wish to have the funeral 'passed over in silence', they are not always aware of the consequences of such a wish. For networks, inner as well as outer, it can mean their being cut off from participating in the grieving process, in the short-term and possibly also the long-term. Close friends who find that they are not welcome at the funeral can take this very hard. Not everyone manages fully to understand and respect such a wish on the part of the bereaved, although it can basically be due to the fact that they do not feel up to meeting others on this day. One must of course respect such a choice, but it is important at the same time for the bereaved to think about the signals they are sending to their surroundings. In the long-term such an 'exclusion' from the funeral can lead to the network withdrawing, in part or completely, from providing support to the close bereaved. Many can misinterpret the wish for a private funeral as a wish on the part of the bereaved to be left alone, also after the fact. Friends and family members, whose involvement as providers of support is wanted later on, can feasibly experience a vacuum, and neither are they able to share the experiences of the bereaved from the important day of the funeral. Bereaved people who are encouraged to include their social network in the funeral are often very grateful for this later. Although they at the outset may not have wanted to meet with others on this day, they experience it as being extremely important to allow others to participate in order to enable them to provide continued support.

How can network support be improved?

When friends and family members in the Network project summarize what they could have done better in relation to the bereaved, they point out the significance of an interaction, wherein both parties contribute to making the very most of the support. While friends and family recognize that they can be more active and take initiative, more signals are wanted from the bereaved.

In particular the network points out that they could have made contact and taken the initiative more often in relation to the bereaved. Many see later that they should have allowed themselves to have been even more open and communicated their uncertainty about the situation more directly. Would the bereaved have liked anything done differently? Are our contributions good or bad? Do we come too often or not often enough? Is our help experienced as intrusive in any way? Are there other types of help that would be more appropriate? Do we ever hurt the bereaved? How can we work together to find the support that works best, for both parties? A very close friend of a mother who lost a newborn tells of how she solved the problem of her uncertainty regarding how often she should contact her friend over the phone during the initial weeks. She lived out of town and therefore could not visit the mother in person. She revealed her uncertainty to the mother and they agreed that she would call every day, but it would be up to the mother to read the caller display and determine for herself the occasions when she needed to speak with her or had the energy to answer the phone.

In order for the network's openness to function, good signals are needed in return from the bereaved. The network members who have experiences with bereaved people who gave clear signals about how they were feeling, and the type of support that they needed, found that they were most successful in providing support. They emphasize the importance of both parties being open, listening to one another, speaking about and creating a kind of agreement regarding how they need and wish the contact to be. And not least, both bereaved people and networks must give one another clear signals regarding how they experience the (support) relationship. The network therefore also encourages bereaved people to think about the fact that they can improve their situation themselves by being aware of the fact that the people in their surroundings need feedback from them. A woman who provided support for a neighbouring family after a suicide had the following to say on this subject:

> One must not simply say that one is there for the bereaved and leave it to them to make contact but rather make contact personally. It is important that the bereaved person personally explains the type of contact that he/she wants and speaks up if one does or says something wrong.

Friends and family who have stood by the bereaved over a period of time have also learned that it is important for the bereaved not to isolate themselves, because then the people around them can far too easily pull away. The network maintains that they perhaps could have taken the initiative even more frequently to spend time together, do enjoyable things and be social on an everyday basis. In particular, friends and family emphasize the significance of being even better at providing consistent support in the long-term and at remembering the deceased:

> I believe it is important for later that the contact is maintained and that we remember to speak about the deceased. I know that I must continue to maintain contact and provide support as best I can.

Some participants in the Network project experienced the entire situation as extremely difficult. They would have preferred there to have been compulsory professional help for the bereaved, with guidance also provided for those close to the family. They would also have liked recommendations on relevant reading material for themselves and the bereaved, which could contribute to their acquiring greater insight into grief and support processes.

'Straightforward bereaved people make for a good support network'

A primary finding from the study of networks that have provided support for bereaved people following sudden deaths is that bereaved people who are straightforward result in a good support network. Such straightforwardness implies that the bereaved must give clear indications regarding how they would like the people in their surroundings to relate to them. By addressing such indications, the networks can develop into good supporters in relation to the bereaved. Indications signalling how the bereaved are feeling and the type of support they wish to receive can be given through direct speech, through actions or through explicit verbal cues and body language. The better the social network knows the bereaved, the greater the amount of non-verbal signals that can be interpreted – such as through body language, overtly expressed or understood by the network's 'intuition'. A best friend says: 'I just know how she thinks and feels.'

The expertise that close social networks possess with regard to the bereaved is connected to two areas in particular. One of these types of expertise is connected to knowledge about the bereaved, their situation after the death and how this develops from day to day. There are few others besides those who have been by their side, at close hand, over a period of time who have the knowledge of the bereaved person's personality type, ordinary behaviour patterns and how they usually handle difficult situations (inner and outer resources). The second type of expertise entails the resources that everyone in the network directly or indirectly has access to and that can be mobilized in a problem-solving process. Here we are thinking of an open form of communication and dialogue, the will and courage to provide assistance, stamina and sensitivity, and the ability to interpret and identify with the lives of fellow human beings. Close social networks, and perhaps in particular those who participated in our research, have had or have acquired this expertise. There are many indications that the network members who took part in the study have had a much lower quota of errors than that which is common for more peripheral social networks. Their experience with regard to what leads to good support has that much more value (cf. the next section on main themes).

Main themes
It is painful and difficult but incredibly rewarding to provide support after a sudden death!

- Close social networks make a large and important contribution – which is often quite intense at the start.
- Groups of friends who organize their efforts to allocate responsibility manage to relax once in a while and endure over time.
- Support networks learn and become gradually more secure over time.
- It is strenuous, challenging and difficult to remain close at hand and provide support over time.
- There are also extremely positive consequences derived from supporting bereaved people over time: one acquires valuable learning and life knowledge, one develops as a human being and the friendship with the bereaved acquires greater depth.

Experiences from the support network: about support for bereaved people

- Be open, direct and honest about one's own uncertainty regarding support and ask the bereaved to explain how they wish to be approached.
- Take the initiative.
- Be present and available.
- Listen with sincerity and in earnest.
- Show empathy.
- Show respect and patience for the bereaved individual's manner of grieving.
- Commemorate the deceased.
- Give practical help when everyday life returns.
- Provide support over time.

6

Social network support: challenges and solutions

As illustrated in the foregoing pages, bereaved people greatly appreciate social network support, despite the fact that they indicate some disappointments and weaknesses with regard to such support. Further, we have seen that the large majority of those in a bereaved person's network both wish and attempt to provide support although they experience that their efforts are insufficient and that they may make a number of mistakes. The experience of uncertainty is mutual for both parties. But both parties have thoughts and proposals for how the challenges can be met. The proposals show that the solution for better social network support is actually about better communication. In this chapter these factors are clarified. The chapter addresses the significance of social network support and the challenges of and solutions for network support are subsequently connected to a more comprehensive communication model. In this manner we will ground the experiences of both the bereaved and the network in theory.

The significance of social network support

> I believe the fact that people show compassion and support, that that is everything. We received many hundreds of pounds' worth of flowers for the entire year after Jonathon died. I put them on his grave and by his photograph. Some people did not manage to meet with us, but were able to write a few words or show compassion through physical contact.

The quote is from a mother who suddenly lost her son and shows the significance of social support while it also points out the challenges for the network, with regard to encountering people in shock and in the depths of grief.

The experiences of the bereaved

Social network support is important first and foremost because bereaved people experience it as being meaningful (cf. Chapters 2–4). The extensive support that many receive from family, friends, colleagues and neighbours is greatly appreciated. The most important thing, according to the bereaved, is that the network 'cares': that they make contact and are available on the terms of the bereaved, listen, show empathy and are willing to speak with the bereaved about the deceased. Support can also be in the form of flowers, visits, telephone calls and letters, or that someone steps in to help out with children and practical matters in everyday life. The network can gradually help bereaved people to return to a more normal daily life through work and social activities. Loved ones and friends become an important part of daily life at a time when the world has fallen apart and everything is turned upside down. One therefore often hears bereaved people say that 'without family and friends I would have never managed', or that the support is 'alpha and omega'. What is the explanation for the importance of this type of support?

Theoretical explanations

Social support is one of the most studied social phenomena of recent decades and many researchers stress its significance for physiological and psychological health. This significance has been connected to a greater life-expectancy, reduced incidence of various forms of illness, more rapid recovery from illness, improved coping skills with chronic illness and better psychological health (for a review of relevant literature see Albrecht and Goldsmith, 2003; Berkman *et al.*, 2000; Sarason, Sarason and Gurung, 1997; Schwarzer and Leppin, 1989). In terms of the grief-stricken it is pointed out that good network support both assuages and alleviates grief and stress reactions, and reduces psychosocial problems (Dunne, McIntosh and Dunne-Maxim, 1987; Johnson, 1991; Reed, 1998; Sherkat and Reed, 1992; Thuen, 1997a and 1997b). In this way, social support can contribute to improved psychological adaptation and coping skills, in that the crisis-stricken better manages the traumatic event and acquires a reinforced self-image and optimism about the future (Burleson, 2003).

The two main prevailing theories offering explanations for this effect of social network support are 'the buffer theory' and 'the recovery theory' (Cohen, 1988; Cohen and Wills, 1985; Sarason, Sarason and Pierce, 1990; Thoits, 1995). The buffer theory explains the effects of the support as being due to its mollifying the negative influences of the crisis event through the concrete support the crisis-stricken receive from their surroundings. An example of this can be when friends step in after a death to provide comfort, practical assistance or simply to be present. In the recovery theory, social support has a broader and more independent impact that is not necessarily connected to the support surrounding the event in question. The support can be in the form of a more or less constant climate of daily care, daily encouragement, good feelings and togetherness with others. The idea behind this is that the crisis-stricken more quickly recover because the positive ballast they have diminishes the great strains that serious life events represent for psychological and physical health. According to the theories, grief- and crisis-stricken people with a good support network are not as critically affected as others and they will 'recover' more quickly. With traumatic loss one can envision both explanatory models as being at work, either simultaneously or individually.

However, how network support works in a concrete situation will always bear a connection to the crisis-stricken person's personal and social resources. By personal resources we mean particular personal characteristics, gender, age, coping skills, knowledge, values, life situation, experience of self-worth and of oneself as worthy of support, and the ability to accept support, as well as previous experiences with accepting support. Such factors function in conjunction with the social resources, which among other things entail a degree of social connectedness, the features of a person's social network, social participation, the concrete support and any conflicts or other social stress factors. The research also indicates that the effect of network support is connected with the severity of the event, the type of support provided and the nature of the relationship to the person providing the support (Goldsmith, 2004). Although there are many common features pertaining to what is 'suitable' in various local communities, every family, circle of friends and other 'mini communities' has its own unwritten rules regarding what is appropriate in the situation, which in turn affects how bereaved people and the network interact. How one behaves in relation to the bereaved will otherwise be quite different in a large city versus a country town, between young versus old and between groups with different ethnic origins. In order to be able to anticipate how support will affect health and coping ability, one must also include the parties' norms regarding what comprises good coping abilities and theoretical reflections about that which characterizes adaptation to stress.

As we see, social network support is influenced by complex factors and conditions. In order to improve network support it is therefore important to attempt to understand how various factors influence the different participants in each situation and context. But in spite of the enormous amount of research that has been done, there is a large gap in the knowledge regarding the effective mechanisms behind good network support subsequent to a sudden death. Such knowledge pertains to how, when and particularly *why* social support is helpful or unhelpful. There is much to be learned here from both a bereaved person's and their network's experiences of challenges and solutions for better network support.

The challenges of social support

In the same fashion that the effects of successful support are outlined, the effects of negative support are also discussed in relevant literature. Inexpedient or poor support can result in the individual in need of support feeling worse, handling problems badly, destroying the relationship to the 'helper' or can lead to triggering stress-related illness (Greene and Burleson, 2003). Some people are more successful than others in expressing themselves so that the support has positive ramifications. Others do not manage this, although they have the best intentions. Communicating social support that is adapted to the individual and situation is accordingly associated with many challenges.

The uncertainty of bereaved people and networks: an analysis

The challenges of social support are described by both bereaved people and their social networks (cf. Chapters 2, 3 and 5). In correlation with findings from the limited amount of research literature found on the subject (Brabant, Forsyth and McFarlain, 1995; Dakof and Taylor, 1990; Thoits, 1995; Wertheimer, 1999) almost all of the bereaved taking part in the Support and Care project verbalized either something that they were missing in the existing support, the absence of anticipated support or negative encounters with members of the social network. We refer to this as 'social ineptitude'. Social ineptitude means that the network surrounding the bereaved is not always helpful because it fails to provide what is needed in the unique situation. This can entail anticipated support that fails to materialize, friends and family who pull away, advice and support given that is not helpful and support that is terminated far too soon in relation to the needs of the bereaved. The uncertainty in the encounter between the network and bereaved person can be characterized through a number of questions. Bereaved people ask themselves: 'To whom can we speak?' 'How shall we behave?' 'Can we say what we truly feel?' 'Shall we explain what happened?' 'Can we be bothered to explain?' 'What will they think of us?' 'What if I meet someone who does not know what has happened?' And 'When is it suitable to start going out again, to laugh and begin living a normal life?' The network asks: 'Are we close enough to mention the death?' 'Can we or should we speak about what has happened?' 'Do we dare mention the name of the deceased?' 'Shall we bring it up again the first time we see them?' 'Should we ourselves or they begin to speak about what has happened?' 'Should we show them how sad we think this is or will we then only drag them further down?' 'When will they want to attempt to live normally again and focus less on the loss?'

Although most of the bereaved experience a lot of support and consideration, particularly following a traumatic death, many bereaved people quickly find that a deeper understanding of their reactions is wanting, with respect to the type, intensity and duration of these. They describe how sometimes, even as soon as after a few weeks they experience a pressure to return to normality as quickly as possible because others want to hear that things are going better and that everything is the way it used to be. Many, particularly in the peripheral network, would prefer to avoid having to confront and absorb the situation fully and want things to return to the way they were before the death as quickly as possible. The majority of the bereaved express the desire for a better understanding of the actual duration and intensity of the grief process.

The descriptions of a bereaved person's and their network's questions and challenges with regard to network support illustrate that the parties experience two sides of the same phenomenon. They point out the positive aspects of network support, while at the same time the experience of a less than ideal situation is central for both. Both parties also realize that this is predominantly based on uncertainty. Friends and family obviously want to support the bereaved following a sudden death but find it to be difficult and demanding. They are afraid of being importunate, and struggle to find a suitable level of intensity for their efforts and appropriate forms of expression for their support. They are uncertain about whether they may have said or done unsuitable things. In addition, those who provide support over time find that it is a strain and they are afraid that they perhaps have been too passive at times. This is wholly in accordance with the bereaved person's experience of the network support (Dyregrov, 2003–2004, 2006c); the bereaved find that they need support but are uncertain about from whom they can expect to receive it. In addition to this, there are many who lack the energy to take the initiative personally in relation to the network. They must cope with disappointments over expected support that fails to materialize, inappropriate advice and that many disappear just when they need them the most. They can find that both friends and family abandon them and although it is difficult when friends fail them, it is even worse to experience this from the family.

What role do I actually have?

In addition to the uncertainty in the encounter with the bereaved it is not unusual for even the inner network to be quite unsure and ignorant about the importance they may have for the bereaved. Although they have provided support and been in contact with them after the death, many think that 'there are many others who are certainly closer'. In the Network project, a number of friends and family members were surprised that they had been mentioned as the closest friends. They had perceived others as being more important and emotionally closer to the bereaved. Many were saddened and distraught when they understood that they could have played an even more important role and been even more active in relation to the bereaved had they understood that their support was so greatly valued. Others felt guilty for having pulled away after a period because they believed that there had not been a need for them or that they were imposing at a time when close friends were wanted. It is therefore of great significance, in order to ensure the ideal type of support, that the members of the network understand how significant they are. One friend, feeling true sadness, relates:

> I was told how important my support had been when my friend contacted me for this research project. But I wish that I had known that immediately following her son's death. I did not understand how important I was and that she needed *me* the way she did.

Reproach and criticism

'Bad blood' can also arise between bereaved people and their social networks. Bereaved people can fault family members or friends for insufficient understanding, for not making contact, for forgetting them or not helping enough. Members of social networks for their part can experience bereaved people as being demanding or overly sensitive and irritable, or even reproach them for cultivating their grief for the deceased. Sometimes such accusations can break down and destroy close relationships. The network can signal that they want the bereavement to pass quickly; they can be overly protective or express things that deeply violate or disappoint the bereaved (Harris, 1992; Sarason, Sarason and Shearin, 1986; Thompson and Range, 1992). Dakof and Taylor (1990) found that networks of friends often avoided the grief-stricken as a means of resolving what they experienced as a difficult situation. Several researchers came to the conclusion that 'abandonment' on the part of the network affected different bereaved people differently, depending upon the degree of intimacy that they attributed to the relationship between themselves and the potential support individual. The sense of betrayal is experienced as being the most profound when individuals whom the bereaved define as close friends or family members fail to provide support (Dakof and Taylor, 1990; Lehman, Ellard and Wortman, 1986; Sarason *et al.*, 1990).

Why do some friends pull away?
The explanations regarding why it is so difficult to provide good social network support following a sudden death are many and with all likelihood are interrelated. Still, there is a fundamental difference between someone who disappoints the bereaved by completely failing to appear and the uncertainty one witnesses with support that is less than expedient. One explanation for why networks withdraw partially or completely can be out of a sense of self-preservation. By pulling away one avoids being reminded of one's own vulnerability and the fact that such terrible things can happen to all of us. Others who pull away perhaps already have a stressful and difficult life situation and cannot manage further responsibilities on top of what they are already carrying. Still others do not experience that they are in a position where it is 'natural', or believe that it is expected of them, to provide support. Those who do not pull away but attempt and wish to provide support, in collaboration with the bereaved, make many attempts to resolve the challenges implicit to network support.

How do the parties attempt to resolve the challenges?
Our research indicates that although bereaved people and the network experience many, relatively large challenges between them, there is a genuine desire and will on the part of both to find solutions, so as to improve the network support. Bereaved people understand the network's uncertainty and difficulties and wish to do their part to alleviate these, while the network for its own part sees its own inadequacies and wants help from the bereaved. Both parties have constructive and important suggestions for how to make the most of the important network support.

'Openness is the best coping strategy'
In spite of the fact that the bereaved experience pain and can be hurt by thoughtless comments, or inadequate or nonexistent support, most are able to understand the situation from the perspective of the network. They understand that it cannot be easy to relate to people who have experienced traumatic death, particularly if it is the first time one has had such an experience. Many bereaved people spontaneously comment that they can identify with much of the

uncertainty experienced by family and friends. They understand only too well that it must be difficult to contact them and to know what to say. Most understand, either immediately or at a later point in time, that when the network lets them down, it is more about a lack of ability than lack of will. A number of bereaved people therefore realize at some point that they must personally take control by participating in the creation of the kind of support they desire and need. Other researchers have also found that bereaved people who experience being abandoned by their social network attempt to reduce the pain, anger and social isolation by trying to 'educate' family and friends with an eye towards their providing better social support (Brabant *et al.*, 1995).

In the Support and Care project, 81 per cent of the bereaved suggested that 'openness' represented their most important strategy for coping with the difficult situation after the death. This word for them implied sincerity, honesty and direct speech, so that to a large extent it was a matter of giving clear signals to their surroundings. They had experienced that such signals were an important means of informing others of what had happened, how they were feeling, the type of support needs they had and how others could best support them (Dyregrov *et al.*, 2000a; Dyregrov, 2002b, 2003–2004, 2004a). When the bereaved inform others of what has happened, they give the network an understanding of the situation. In this way they also have an opportunity to speak about their reactions to the death, something that they experience as having a 'therapeutic value'. In that the bereaved address the situation with family and friends, they also signal to the network that they subsequently are permitted to speak about the situation with them. The network's response is usually relief over not having to feign ignorance about what has happened, because as a rule they hear about it from others anyway. Another way in which the bereaved can educate their network is through the power of example. One young person who lost his brother said: 'In that I was able to mention his name and speak about him, my friends understood that I would not be embarrassed if they did the same.'

In addition, the bereaved find that an open information strategy at schools, workplaces or with other large groups helped them to avoid the spreading of rumours. Some people bereaved by suicide, who find that guilt and shame complicate their relationship to the network, write 'he took his own life' in the obituary precisely for that reason. One final significant factor with regard to openness is that bereaved people clarify their needs for help and support in relation to the network of friends, schools or workplaces.

Bereaved people describe many active strategies for making contact with networks, initiating conversations about the loss, ways of seeking out support and the importance of inviting people home. Bereaved people who give family, friends, colleagues and neighbours honest and direct feedback on their endeavours to provide support find that such networks more easily manage to meet their support needs. In this way openness can help the network get over its helplessness. Some bereaved people even seek out those network members who have avoided them and confront them directly. They tell them that they would like to speak about the death and the deceased and about how they would appreciate being approached by others. Such an attitude is however not always easy to assume, as it requires an enormous amount of resource and of course, can also be risky, according to this mother:

> It is not easy to take the initiative because you then, of course, risk rejection and experiencing yet another disappointment. But once I realized that a person avoided me because she was afraid of meeting me, I then understood that she had a larger problem than I did in handling the situation. I therefore went out of my way to run into her and we ended up standing there and talking for half an hour.

Despite the apparently positive aspects of a strategy of openness and active initiative on the part of bereaved people, one should also be aware that it also has clear limitations. Not all bereaved people have the energy to take on an active role in relation to their network. The Support and Care study showed that those who were struggling the most did not have the energy to 'educate' the network but instead isolated themselves (Dyregrov, 2002b; Dyregrov et al., 2003). Other bereaved people are confronted with the fact that not everyone in the network manages to address the pain in the situation, despite the efforts of the bereaved to be open in relation to them. One also finds that the bereaved people who were closest to the deceased can disagree about which facts should be made public, either because they have different perceptions of privacy or disagree about the facts in themselves.

The network wants more signals

> The bereaved could perhaps have asked more for help and I should have been better about offering it.

The prevailing impression from the Network project can be summarized by the above quote. When the close social network that had provided support for the bereaved over time was asked about what could be done to make the support even better, the members of the network mentioned factors pertaining to themselves, the bereaved and the interaction between them (Dyregrov, K.,

2005b, 2006c). The prevailing message was that they wanted to support the bereaved but that they were dependent upon having the bereaved act as guides in order to be able to provide support on their terms. They had otherwise experienced that understanding and learning this kind of interaction was a time-consuming process. They found that they learned through experience and that the bereaved person's responses to their attempts to provide support were crucial to the learning process.

Friends and family members maintain that improved support requires their taking the initiative more frequently in relation to the bereaved. The initiative for socializing, providing support, comfort and practical assistance must predominantly come from the network. A network that observes how grief and trauma drain bereaved people of all of their energy recognizes that it is not realistic to expect the usual 50–50 type of relationship, where one alternates with respect to making contact and taking the initiative. Friends and family members realize that they must dare to take the initiative at the risk of being rejected. They point out the importance of being available for the bereaved, particularly during the initial, surreal days and of resisting the temptation to escape from the situation. Many members of a close social network understand the significance of support provided over time, of being patient and attentive and of trying to allocate time for the bereaved, also after some time has passed. They therefore emphasize the importance of each individual network member taking the time to consider whether support provided over time is actually something they can live up to, before getting involved with the bereaved following a sudden death. It creates false expectations and is a source of great disappointment for the bereaved if one steps in during the first couple of weeks only to subsequently pull away. The good networks see the value of remembering the deceased over time, such as by naturally speaking about them in conversation or by simply mentioning their name. This requires a dialogue where the network members themselves must dare to be more open and direct in relation to the bereaved. Friends and family members, who support the bereaved over time, have a need for guidance and advice from professionals to acquire security in the situation and maintain that this will contribute to improved support for the bereaved. Such guidance will also potentially contribute to preventing burnout and excessive strain within the network (cf. Chapter 11).

With regard to understanding the needs of the bereaved, almost half of the network members in the Network project stressed the importance of listening to the bereaved. Providing support on the terms of the bereaved was viewed as being the most important demonstration of respect and they warned against giving too much advice along the way. Another way of showing respect was to keep to oneself the things one learned throughout the course of the support process. The networks gave advice regarding how members of future networks should share their feelings and, to a certain extent, speak of their own vulnerability, so as to be able to provide emphatic support and confront the pain of the bereaved. Friends and family should be prepared to tolerate rejection by bereaved people from time to time without feeling hurt.

The majority of those who took part in the Network project emphasized the importance of being honest through advice such as 'be yourself', 'be honest' or 'don't beat around the bush'. An honest relationship will make it possible for the network members to ask the bereaved about how and when to provide support and about what type of support they want. In order to achieve this, friends, colleagues and family members must endeavour to be active listeners and dare to speak to the bereaved about how they experienced the situation. They must be honest about the fact that they would like to help and provide support and express any difficulties and challenges that they may be feeling in the situation. As a male friend stated: 'Have faith that you can help. If it is difficult to know what you should say – then that is exactly what you should say to the bereaved.'

The networks taking part in the Network project also indicated that in the event network members experience such excessive strain that they need a break for a period of time, they should have both the right and the obligation to communicate this to the bereaved. This will in any case be better for them than if network members suddenly and inexplicably pull away after first having been involved.

While the network is self-aware, they believe that the situation also requires the bereaved meeting them halfway. Experiences from other studies have shown that when the bereaved are straightforward and direct this brings about a better and more individually adapted form of network support (Dakof and Taylor, 1990). The bereaved must attempt to make contact more frequently, refrain from isolating themselves and be more active in relation to the person(s) from whom they want support. They must personally be open and provide more signals regarding the type of support they want, from whom they want to receive this support, and preferably also feedback regarding what they think about actions and statements intended as support. Although the network knows that such requirements with regard to bereaved people are in contradiction to what they observe in the manner of the latter's exhaustion and fatigue, they ask for understanding from the bereaved for the fact that without such feedback they become quite helpless. They ask that the bereaved, instead of withdrawing, clearly speak their minds when someone upsets them, has said or done the wrong thing or fails to turn up, so network members can learn from this and subsequently modify their behaviour. They can try to explain how they feel the person providing support should behave and give signals regarding the type of contact they need.

The network also clearly stipulates measures towards improving the relation and communication between them as a means of improving the network support. Like the bereaved, they use the term 'openness' as a catch phrase representing an important instrument to this end. But it is not sufficient for either the bereaved or they themselves to be open. Both parties must be open, listen to one another, and speak about the support and about the nature of the contact wanted. Both parties must also be able to set limits for what can be given and received and both parties can have a need for time to themselves:

> Setting limits, both as a support provider and bereaved person, is important. We must be allowed to say that enough is enough. If one has an open dialogue about this, it is not difficult to say that now I need a little time to myself.

Networks also point out that if bereaved people keep their emotional state to themselves, this will also influence what they are personally capable of expressing. In order to share their grief, friends and family need verbal, non-verbal and emotional signals from the bereaved.

Some network members point out that the openness must include conversations about the situation itself, as a support provider and bereaved person following a sudden death. When it is important to listen must be made clear, as well as when the support provider shall set limits. Beyond this, it is important to speak about and accept that friends and family members are not always at their best or do not always manage to tolerate the pain of the bereaved. Other times it can be important to speak of, for example, having a bad conscience because one's own baby was permitted to live, while the baby of a friend died. As an aid to managing the advanced forms of communication, network members point out the importance of meeting often for pleasant social activities on an everyday basis. The network, in other words, also imposes stringent requirements on itself in an extremely difficult situation. Are we now beginning to approach a solution that can optimize network support following a sudden death?

Is there a key?

As we can see from both the bereaved and the network's descriptions of the challenges between them, both express a great need to understand one another better. While the bereaved refer to openness, which involves *giving* clear signals, the network is concerned with the significance of *receiving* clear signals. Viewed in correlation, the Support and Care study and the Network study illustrate that bereaved people and their networks want to arrive at a mutual understanding of how they shall behave in relation to one another. The bereaved experience that network support can be improved by their personally being open and informative and managing to see the situation from the perspective of the network. The network, for its own part, emphasizes the significance of receiving feedback and instructions from the bereaved, so as to enable it to enter into support relations. This is supported by the fact that helpful support relations arose when the clearest signals were given by the bereaved. Signals are given through direct, honest and open communication in the support process. One sees that the parties experience the necessity of communication about, and through, the support process. The involved parties thereby indicate the key to better network support – namely to give and receive better signals to and from one another. They speak of reciprocity and they speak of communication. Such communication has a far more difficult dynamic than in most other types of interactions and conversations we might experience. As we have seen, communication is seriously put to the test when a situation as unique as a sudden and unexpected death arises. Can we connect the experiences of bereaved people and networks to theories about communication, which can further assist us in solving the challenges inherent to social network support?

Social network support is communication

'You cannot not communicate'

Communication is about trying to create a community around something that previously was not held in common. The word communication comes from the Latin *communicare*, meaning to do something in fellowship. In that a relatively common interpretation of the world around us is made possible through language and signals, people's ability to interpret and attribute meaning to their world is fundamental to communication. We can of course exchange information and signals but there is no understanding if we do not understand one another's experiential background and cognitive models.

One of the earliest theorists who viewed communication as a reciprocal relationship between different parties was Paul Watzlawick (Watzlawick, Beavin Bavelas and Jackson, 1967). He claimed that if one accepts that all behaviour/actions mean something for somebody, in other words, *are* communication, it follows that regardless of how much you try you cannot *not* communicate. Other sociologists, anthropologists and psychologists who followed up within the sociocultural tradition, emphasized that everything that is communicated has a relational and a content-related message (Bateson, 1972; Briggs, 1986; Watzlawick *et al.*, 1967; Wertsch, 1988). While the content-related message refers to what is said or done, the relational is about the relation between the parties that meet. Watzlawick (Watzlawick *et al.*, 1967) pointed out that in 'healthy relations' the relationship between the parties to a lesser extent influences the content of what is communicated, while in 'unhealthy relations' communication is characterized by constant 'negotiations' about the type of relationship one actually has and here the content-related message recedes into the background. In our case this implies that all encounters between social networks and the bereaved must be understood as communication and whether the encounter is experienced as supportive, non-supportive, indifferent, successful or a failure depends upon the parties' interpretations of the encounter. Which paradigms can we apply to understand the parties' respective experiences of one another?

Social praxis and social processes

Daena Goldsmith is one of the few researchers who have addressed social support in the context of illness, death or serious crises in a communication perspective (Goldsmith, 2004). She points out that it is not sufficient to view such support as concrete actions that can be quantified or as subjective experiences on the part of the person receiving the support. The support must be seen as meaningful social actions that take place in social contexts and for special purposes. The success of such actions can be evaluated by bereaved people and the networks and by externally positioned researchers on the basis of central key points. Social praxis and social processes are two types of social resources that we will focus on in order to understand the dynamics of social network support.

Social praxis means actions that are repeated on a regular basis within groups in society and which are thereby recognized and meaningful for the group. An example in our case is when networks send flowers after a death and other rituals in connection with funerals where networks are invited to participate. *Social processes* on the other hand are different forms of adaptation to a situation with regard to what one says or does – such as in conversations about grief and death. This implies that the parties' experiences, interpretations and evaluations of social support must be connected to the context in which it takes place (Goldsmith, 2004). With helpful support such an interaction is 'characterized by a mixture of successful application of routine knowledge and situational exploration and negotiation' (Luckmann, 1995: 179). When networks support bereaved people following a sudden death, there is often little routine knowledge in connection with the situation, so that the support process predominantly takes place as learning through 'negotiations'. In order to understand the micro-dynamics of such negotiations, we will connect these to a communication model.

A communication model for understanding social network support

According to Goldsmith (2004) previous models that have attempted to describe social support communication have underestimated the complexity when the support takes place in stressful situations. She claims that the models are inadequate in terms of being able to explore how the parties (network and bereaved) carry the burden together (or fail to do so) so as to adapt the support to the situation (Goldsmith, 2004). Previous research, which has been dominated by a view of social support as something taking place between a giver and a receiver, proves to have serious limitations when the model is applied to the interaction between friends and acquaintances. Close partners who seek to resolve a difficult situation do not solely implement giver and receiver roles but also other interactive roles and conversational frames. Various theorists have therefore over the years stipulated the need for understanding communication and interaction between individuals in connection with their unique social and cultural contexts (Bateson, 1972; Briggs, 1986; Watzlawick et al., 1967; Wertsch, 1988).

The challenges which bereaved people and networks experience are therefore connected to a communication and interaction model that focuses on processes at a micro-level (Briggs, 1986). By analysing processes between the parties when they meet, we will be able to find answers to some of the questions we have asked in this book: Why do network members feel so much uncertainty? Why do they pull away? Why do they say hurtful things? How can grief-stricken individuals and social networks communicate about this difficult communication? How can practical matters be organized so that the bereaved experience better support and the people in the surroundings can better provide the support they wish to give? The communication model is an important tool for illuminating both parties' experiences of the encounter, where social support is viewed as an action between two parties that is dependent upon their respective interpretations of a series of basic communication elements (see Figure 6.1).

Network members' social ineptitude and the uncertainty of the bereaved in the encounter with the network are illuminated by connecting the difficulties they experience to basic elements in the communication model: type of social interaction, goal of the interaction, social roles, social situation, the form of the message, communication channel and code, and linguistic message (Figure 6.1). The terms will be further explained in the context of the discussion about them below.

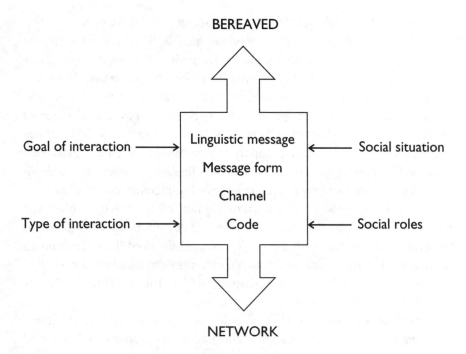

Figure 6.1 A micro-sociological model for social support communication[1] (based on Jacobsen and Hymes in Briggs, 1986).

Note 1: Goal of interaction: the motivation for engaging in the encounter. Social situation: the framework for the encounter. Type of interaction: the category of the social event. Social roles: roles assumed between parties. Linguistic message: the words spoken. Message form: audible or visual signals. Channel: use of visual/auditory stimuli or other psychological measures. Code: verbal or non-verbal code.

An uncommon type of interaction

Choosing to provide support for a person who has lost a child or other close loved one in a sudden and unexpected fashion implies the entrance into an uncommon type of interaction in the context of Western society. Both parties lack an 'autopilot' and this is the source of great uncertainty for both. Everyday interaction norms are challenged in that the situation is unusual and extreme for the parties involved. A bereaved person's and their network's experiences of the situation show that they often lack a common understanding of the framework for communication following a sudden death. Bateson (1972) described 'frames' as the external conditions for the contexts in which a social event occurs. Such frames will function as signposts and help people to interact in order to define a given situation so that they may behave appropriately. The facts that we all learn communication frames in the society of which we are a part, and that norms for providing bereavement support are seldom in use, imply that many network members must acquire such competence when they shall for the first time provide bereavement support following a sudden death. In this way one can perceive the inexpedient and sometimes destructive forms of support as being the result of a lack of frames enabling action and interpretation of the unique encounter. Our own and others' research shows that bereaved people learn to interpret the frames of the situation through their own, painful loss, so that they become much more competent in communicating about death and grief. The same occurs with networks that have provided support over time (Dyregrov, 2003–2004, 2006c; Van Dongen, 1993).

An important explanation for the difficulties of network support can accordingly have a correlation with Western culture's lack of tradition and norms for communicating about grief and trauma. Instead of knowledge about grief stemming from traumatic loss, myths have gained prevalence. This is reflected by expressions such as 'time heals all wounds' and statements such as 'we don't want to re-open old wounds'. These statements imply to a large extent that grief is something private and lead to others steering away from grief and the bereaved. Bereaved people confirm that it is a myth when they point out that one cannot re-open a wound that has never healed. Insufficient knowledge about grief and how traumas affect people is feasibly also a contributing factor to why so many network members feel uncertain about whether and for how long their support is needed. The intensity of a bereaved person's reactions can be experienced as strange and somewhat frightening, in the event one does not understand that these are, in principle, actually normal reactions to an extreme event. A bereaved person's refusal to speak about the death, or the fact that they conceal the cause from their surroundings (e.g. with suicide), can also contribute to the parties failing to communicate constructively so that efforts to provide support hit home (Dyregrov and Dyregrov, 1999; Wertheimer, 1999). There are, however, recent developments indicating that this special form of communicative event is currently undergoing a process of redefinition in most countries in the Western world. Increased general knowledge about traumatic events and increased openness and information about crisis, grief and death will contribute to making it easier to provide social support, because the frames for the situation become more comprehensible for the parties involved. The network indicates this when they ask for more signals from the bereaved. The bereaved, on the other hand, have realized that they need to demonstrate 'openness' in order to be able to communicate the necessary signals, so that the people in their surroundings can identify and recognize the frames.

Different goals for the interaction

Usually, when people interact in familiar situations, there are goals for the interaction that are implicit or that have been expressed with relative clarity. Often one has a preconception about what the meeting between parties involved will lead to. It is in the nature of the encounter that the bereaved person's and the network's motivations and goals for entering into social support are quite different. Bereaved people are motivated by a strong wish to share and vent emotions stemming from the extreme event with their closest friends and family members. The network's goal for social support can be a wish to express compassion and comfort or provide information and advice. Some people clearly are motivated to make contact for reasons of their own curiosity. Parts of the network can be motivated to provide support out of a sense of duty. For colleagues the goal can also be the wish for a return to previous work capacity as quickly as possible. Perhaps it is particularly family members who will feel pressured to involve themselves more than they wish or can cope with. Avoidance and withdrawal can be seen as a reaction that is about a fear of encountering the pain of the bereaved or it can be a reaction based on a need to control their own anxiety about the situation or to prevent a tearful outburst (Goldsmith, 2002; Lehman *et al.*, 1986; Sarason *et al.*, 1990). It is crucial for the bereaved and the network to have the same, or to understand one another's, goals or motivations for providing and receiving support. For example, if a network member wants to help out with information, the bereaved person must have a need for it and want it. Many misunderstandings and difficulties can stem from the fact that the parties who take part in network support do not understand or know of each other's goals for the interaction. This can in turn have a connection with the parties' social roles.

Unclear social roles

The social roles that networks and the bereaved assume that they have in relation to one another will have a decisive influence on the type of support signalled, and on how the signals are interpreted. Many bereaved people and networks experience a lack of clarity with regard to roles and ask themselves: Who can I be expected to be there for? What can I expect from whom? Should *I* step in – *or are others closer?* What do the bereaved expect from *me* in this situation?, etc. We have seen that a bereaved person's disappointment over support that fails to materialize can be due to the respective parties having different perceptions regarding the 'intimacy' of their relationship (Dyregrov, 2003–2004; Van Dongen, 1993; Wagner and Calhoun, 1991–1992). When the bereaved experience disappointment over a lack of support from people whom they consider to be good friends, this can be because such people do not view the friendship as being as close as do the bereaved. In the eyes of the person in question, it is not experienced as 'natural' to step in because one perceives many others as having a much closer relation. This became evident in the Network project when people expressed surprise about being later described as close friends. Family members can experience a bit of the same thing, but in the opposite manner, when they go in as part of the support network. Because they as family members by definition have intimate roles, the bereaved themselves and those in the surroundings may perhaps expect that they will do their part. If they for various reasons fail to do so, they can experience sanctions from the people around them. Some family members fail to take on such expected roles because they have a poor or not very constructive relationship to one another, while others can be so affected by the death that the best they can manage is to hold themselves together (Brabant *et al.*, 1995; Lehman *et al.*, 1986).

This shows the importance of seeing social roles as roles connected to different situations while at the same time both bereaved people and network members have and act on the basis of many different social roles in daily life. This is clearly reflected if the social roles between the bereaved person and network members previous to the death were formalized through a hierarchical relation, such as through an employer–employee relation.

Inconstant sense of security in social situations

The type of social situation in which survivors and networks meet can, potentially, play an important part in the nature of these meetings. How the parties cope with addressing or speaking about what has happened will differ greatly, depending upon whether they meet at the funeral, in a store, at the workplace, in a public setting or in the home of the bereaved. For example, at a funeral there is, traditionally, a very clear framework for the social situation. Traditional condolence rituals as a conclusion to the ceremony and before the funeral gathering have been replaced by more individually adapted rituals and a corresponding loss of some of the more secure factors. This can lead to uncertainty in connection with that which for many is the first encounter with the bereaved. Many bereaved people experience this encounter as being more successful if there is plenty of time, few outsiders and few distractions. They would prefer to have the opportunity to influence the framework when they are to speak about and address the painful event that has just taken place. Perhaps they wish to display photos of the deceased, light a candle or even show a good friend where they found the deceased, in order that he/she will acquire the best possible understanding of that which has occurred. If the parties have a similar definition of their mutual intimacy, the network members will also frequently prefer a situation that is as calm as possible for their encounter with the bereaved. Both the bereaved and their networks can experience that this provides a basis for better support. But if the roles are unclear and they experience it as being 'unnatural' to have a private relationship with the bereaved, they will perhaps prefer meeting the bereaved in situations involving many others, so that the intimacy is less intrusive. Avoidance on the part of the network can also have a connection with a general fear of lacking control over the form of communication, codes and channels when support is to be expressed.

Difficult to adapt the form of communication

In the meeting between bereaved people and a network, a form is always selected, or a 'tool', to transmit that which is to be communicated (Briggs, 1986). This tool can be a hug, an empathetic look, a warm squeeze of the hand, a gentle touch, comforting words or advice. We have seen that networks are to a large extent uncertain with regard to which forms they should implement to express their compassion and support. The manner in which they express themselves is sometimes misunderstood by the bereaved and not understood in accordance with the intention. Bereaved people for their own part can have expectations regarding which expressions are appropriate or desirable in the situation at hand. If they anticipate a hug or a phone call but scarcely receive any attention whatsoever, this can be extremely hurtful and result in a sense of betrayal.

Studies have shown that people believe that they know approximately what they would have liked to have communicated in a given situation but have feared that they would not manage to express it correctly (Lehman et al., 1986). Researchers point out that this is particularly due to their not daring to be direct enough or being too vague, due to uncertainty in the situation. Verbal statements can be clumsy and uncertain, and frequently accompanied by ambiguous, non-verbal signals. The difficulty of the situation can be further compounded if the bereaved become vague in their manner so as not to demand too much from the network or set themselves up for disappointment. In order to avoid vicious cycles of uncertainty and disappointment it is there-fore important for the parties to be clear about the form of communication. Research shows that when the bereaved clearly inform the network of the type of support they want to receive, the network will increase the type of support that the bereaved find helpful (Dakof and Taylor, 1990).

Difficult to find appropriate communication channel and code
In general one can say that all forms of communication of social support must be transmitted either through visual, acoustic or psychological channels. Further, the message will be transmitted through verbal or non-verbal codes. The communication channels and codes can be combined in very many ways. While some types of support can only be transmitted non-verbally (such as a handshake, flowers), others are a combination of verbal messages accompanied by non-verbal components (such as an empathetic statement accompanied by a hug). Verbal consolation can be transmitted face-to-face or over the telephone. Non-verbal support can be communicated in the form of poems, letters, food, handshakes, flowers or practical assistance.

Our research shows that networks have difficulties finding appropriate channels and codes for the expression of their compassion in relation to the bereaved. There are often discrepancies between what the bereaved expect or wish for and the practice of networks. Bereaved people can experience rejec-tion and disappointment if the support is provided through other channels and codes than they had anticipated, wished or needed. Bereaved people often want a larger degree of non-verbal support, such as friends who listen and exhibit caring, and do not necessarily say so much. Nonetheless, one sees that networks often resort to mental and intellectual codes. This can be due to the fact that network members are feeling deeply affected and are afraid of losing control. Because they have difficulties expressing emotions in the situation, they turn to words instead. For others, the situation is so unusual and they feel so helpless seeing their good friend in such despair that they cannot tolerate the situation. They are willing to do anything to change it and resort to 'good advice', which is often not very helpful, and sometimes even hurtful (cf. Chap-ter 7). When bereaved people experience signals of less emotional intimacy than they had anticipated and hoped for, they can feel betrayed and as if the network is avoiding them. A bereaved person's negative reactions to anticipated support that does not materialize also confirms Watzlawick's (Watzlawick *et al.*, 1967) assertion that it is impossible not to communicate because the absence of support *in itself* is a communicative act.

Linguistic messages and meta-communication: a challenge

In the encounter between bereaved people and networks, linguistic messages are often attributed great importance by both parties. The term linguistic message refers to that which is expressed by specific choices of words. The difficulties of the encounter are often associated with the fact that network members are uncertain of what is suitable in the situation and use words that are taken badly by the bereaved. While many bereaved people experience it as virtually a mockery when network members say 'I understand how you are feeling', this can merely be a figure of speech on the part of the network, intended to demonstrate compassion. Here it would be far wiser for them to state the truth, namely that one cannot in any sense begin to imagine what it is like to be in the situation of the bereaved. Instead of finding solutions for the bereaved, the network can express their uncertainty and that they wish to be there on the terms of the bereaved. In addition, one can encourage bereaved people to help them out with this process. This would imply communicating about the difficult interaction which the meeting entails and is called meta-communication. Brabant and colleagues (1995) found in their research that the bereaved 'educated' their uncertain support network by communicating and meta-communicating, while Dakof and Taylor (1990) showed that the network will increase the type of support for which they receive positive feedback from the bereaved and inexpedient support will decrease.

Being able to communicate about communication (the support) is accordingly an important condition in order for the support to be as the bereaved wish and in line with what network members are able to provide. When bereaved people find that their important contribution to better support is openness in relation to their surroundings (cf. the Support and Care project), and networks ask bereaved people how they wish to be supported (cf. the Network project), this entails a contribution to meta-communication. In that the parties actively inform each other about how they are experiencing the situation and of the type of support they wish for or are able to provide, a mutual frame of reference is created. Bereaved people will also be able to inform the network of the nature of poor support and the network will have the chance to be open and sincere about how they feel that they can contribute. In this manner, the parties can reach an agreement on some 'basic rules' for network support.

Main themes

- Social network support is experienced as being 'the alpha and omega' for bereaved people.

- Buffer and recovery theories can explain the significance of the support.

- Networks experience great uncertainty: What are we to say? What are we to do? What is my role?

- Bereaved people ask the questions: What can we anticipate in the way of support from whom? Why did precisely this or that person fail to appear?

- Bereaved people emphasize meeting the challenges through personal openness.

- Networks maintain that they must express their uncertainty. They also want to receive signals from the bereaved.

- The support must be understood from a comprehensive communication perspective.

- It is impossible not to communicate – and social network support is communication.

- The parties' interpretation and experience of the basic elements of communication determines how 'successful' the support is.

- The key to optimizing network support lies in making it as explicit as possible by communicating about communication (meta-communication).

7

The main principles behind good network support

In this chapter, we will first outline some requisite conditions for the establishment of network support. We will subsequently discuss the main criteria for good network support by illuminating the significance of ensuring a good relation between the parties involved, of choosing a helpful form of support and of communicating the support in such a way that it is experienced as beneficial. In conclusion, the main principles are summarized through some examples of good and bad network support.

Conditions for good network support

A primary principle and point of departure is that help and support must be given on the terms of the bereaved. This entails that support is not support unless the bereaved experiences it as such. Help can be well intended but have little value if it does not correspond with the wishes and needs of the bereaved and they do not experience the support as helpful.

In order for support to be helpful it is very important for the network and the bereaved to increase their awareness of the challenges that must be addressed in this context. It is equally important to have a focus on resources and opportunities for influencing the support process in order to answer the questions: how, when and why is social network support beneficial? Paradigms and a number of tools are needed for this in order to implement measures that function in situations where social networks and bereaved people meet. The measures must function in terms of the contents and forms of consolation and conversations, practical assistance and in particular, with regard to the advice that is given to the bereaved.

There are several fundamental parameters that should be in place to ensure that social networks can provide good support for those who suffer bereavement by sudden death. The parameters are:

- the bereaved have a need for support and help (Chapters 2 and 4)
- the bereaved want support and help (Chapters 3 and 4)
- social networks have knowledge of common grief reactions and help needs (Chapters 2 and 4)
- the bereaved have a knowledge and understanding of the network's situation (Chapter 5)
- social networks know something about the challenges of and solutions for providing support (Chapter 6)
- social networks have the courage to contact the bereaved (Chapters 6, 7, 8 and 9)
- the help acquires a form and content that is suitable for the individual situation (Chapters 6, 7 and 9)
- social networks and the bereaved have some knowledge about when professional help should be brought in (Chapter 10)
- social networks acquire the necessary support and encouragement (Chapter 11).

We will not repeat or address in further detail the contents of all of the various conditions here but refer instead to the chapters where each is discussed. As we have pointed out previously, good and helpful support is not solely contingent upon the motivation to help, but also upon communication skills, and in particular, basic social skills with regard to perceiving and understanding others. Such competence is called communicative (or interactive) competence. The concept involves understanding different forms of personal interactions with an eye towards achieving a common understanding and coherence (Burleson, 2003).

Communicative competence and coherence

The interaction with the bereaved can be difficult and the best guarantee for the helpfulness of the network is in fact clarity of contact. Being able to speak with the bereaved about how one is doing as a friend, and about the support one is attempting to provide, can serve to adapt the support better to the wishes of the bereaved. For example, one can say: 'I know what you have been through and I want to give you all the support I can. But because I am unsure of the kind of support you want, you must tell me what you feel is best. Would you like me to call or stop by? How often do you want contact? Every day or every other day?', etc. In this way, communicating about support can contribute to it being helpful and good.

A high level of communicative competence is crucial for those taking part in a difficult communication situation. And, as we have seen, social network support following a sudden death is such a form of difficult communication. Communicative competence entails an understanding of how one should express oneself to convey specific messages in social situations. As we saw in the last chapter, this is related to both the form and content, and to the relation between the parties involved. (For more on this subject, see: Bateson, 1972; Millar and Rogers, 1976; Reusch and Bateson, 1951; Sarason et al., 1990; Sarason et al., 1997; Watzlawick et al., 1967.)

An important basis for successful social support is that communicative competence includes interaction with the other or others involved in the situation. It is accordingly a matter of understanding the other person with whom one is interacting, when one acts or speaks. Because communicative competence as a concept is about parties in a relationship, it is not just about bringing out the best of oneself. A high level of communicative competence is also about acting in such a way that one increases the communicative competence of others. The parties' communicative competence is accordingly dependent upon how each understands the position and perspective of the other and on how they help each other in reaching a common understanding within the encounter.

The sociologist Jürgen Habermas emphasizes that fundamental changes in social life can only be brought about through interpersonal agreement between parties through communication (intersubjectivity). Further, Habermas maintains that new norms and discourses (prevailing modes for speaking/understanding) to an increasing extent are created as the parties consciously reflect upon and discuss interpersonal problems (Habermas, 1984). By increasing the communicative competence of the bereaved and social networks following a sudden death, one will accordingly be able to contribute to creating new praxis and improving social network support for the bereaved. In this context this would imply that the bereaved by sudden death cannot be viewed as passive support recipients while the network is an active giver. Both parties play an important part in the creation of good social support. Intersubjectivity must be created.

Sociologist Daena Goldsmith (2004) distinguishes between three forms of coherence that must be achieved, in order to create a mutual understanding in a difficult communication situation. She emphasizes that parties communicating about difficulties must arrive at a common understanding of the situation and the choice of solutions that are in coherence 'internally', 'externally' and 'between the parties'. In our context, inner coherence will be a matter of the degree to which there is correspondence between the needs for support indicated by the bereaved and the forms of support the network offers. External coherence pertains to the extent to which the support is suited to improve the bereaved person's ability to cope with their difficulties, while coherence between the parties is about the degree to which the parties develop a mutual understanding of the situation. How the parties address the various basic elements expressed by the communication model, and how they coordinate the form of communication, determines whether they achieve the various forms of coherence (Goldsmith, 2004) (cf. Chapter 6).

Main criteria for good network support

Our own research and the research of others indicate three main criteria for good network support as experienced by the bereaved:

1. The support must signal and express reciprocity between the bereaved and the network.

2. The support must be helpful and useful.

3. The support must demonstrate sensitivity for emotional experiences and events.

We have previously specified the significance of viewing network support (things people do and say for/to one another) as communication between parties. Through communication processes, the parties construct a view of the situation together, along with the possible solutions, the implications for their respective self-images and what the support will mean for the relationship. If and when social support promotes mastery or facilitates the situation, it is not only because one has offered consolation, cried together, listened, given advice, informed or provided practical assistance. Helpful support is just as much due to the parties having succeeded in informing the support with the creation of mutual understanding, as a means of maintaining the respective parties' self-perception and self-respect, and preserving a good relation between them. If some acts of support are experienced as being better than others, this stems from whether or not the sum total of the above criteria has been attained.

In accordance with Goldsmith (2004), we will now discuss three central questions in connection with the main criteria for good support and indicate some general answers with regard to what makes some acts of support better than others:

- How can network support preserve a good relation between bereaved people and networks with regard to equality and a power balance?
- Which forms of support are helpful?
- How can support be communicated so that it is experienced as helpful, sensitive and supportive?

Ensuring a good relation with the network

When networks want to support those bereaved by a traumatic death, the nature of the encounter is out of the ordinary, in that the parties meet in an unusual context and assume different roles than they have done previously (cf. Chapter 6). Fundamentally, one can say that one of the parties needs support and help and the other party can and wants to offer this. This is a situation that can influence how the parties view themselves and the relationship between them. The new relationship can challenge their self-image. In principle, this is therefore a situation where different roles are involved; nonetheless, equality can and should be aspired to in the roles and in the relation between the bereaved and the network.

Goldsmith (2004) addresses in further detail various dilemmas in connection with seeking, giving and receiving support, and how the support is experienced. For the network, a potential dilemma can exist between being helpful and caregiving versus meddling, and being sincere versus being perceived as supportive. The bereaved can be perceived as independent and competent or disrespectful and ungrateful. Asymmetry in the experience of equality and power will potentially influence both the relationship and whether or not the support is experienced as helpful. How the roles are played out can in other words have a strong effect on a bereaved person's experience of the support. Through an awareness of this, the network in particular can contribute to maintaining equality and supporting the self-image of the bereaved in a situation where it is not unusual for their self-image to have been shaken.

As an example of the significance of power and equality for network support, one can envision the period immediately after an unexpected death. If friends 'move in' to the house, send the children to school, pay the bills, buy food and prepare meals, it is important that friends indicate that their 'taking over' is due to the unique nature of the situation and of course this must be in accordance with the wishes of the bereaved. The bereaved are in a unique situation due to what has happened and often feel neither particularly independent nor competent. It is therefore extremely important that good friends, to the greatest extent possible, make decisions in accordance with the bereaved, and signal respect for their difficult situation as a means of reinforcing the self-worth and self-respect of the bereaved.

Another example is when social networks give advice to the bereaved. For the bereaved this can be accompanied by an experience that the person giving the advice has expertise or influence over their life. If such advice is not grounded in a deeper understanding of the situation, the network can insult, irritate and hurt the bereaved. It is not difficult to understand that the same advice, if in principle it had been adapted to the situation, would potentially be received differently, depending upon the relation between the parties. The bereaved will possibly be irritated if the advice comes from a person who has always sought to meddle and control their life, but feel grateful if a best friend offers it. If the underlying dynamic entails that the person giving the advice has greater expertise than the bereaved, where previously their relation was that of equals, this can undermine otherwise positive reactions to the support. For the same reason, bereaved children and young people can resist advice from adults because they can experience this as a confirmation of their identity as a child, which undermines their efforts to be viewed as an adult (Cutrona and Suhr, 1994; Goldsmith and Fitch, 1997). Consolation and empathy will in the same manner have a different effect when this comes from a person to whom the bereaved feels inferior, as opposed to when this comes from someone perceived as an equal. One does not risk losing face if one receives consolation from someone perceived as an equal, or who confirms one's self-esteem and self-worth.

Support that upsets the power balance

Giving advice is a unique form of support that is well suited for illuminating the equality dilemmas of a supportive relationship. This is because advice in particular can upset equality and influences the relation of power between the parties involved. Both the bereaved and networks confirmed this in the research when they spoke of the difficulties of receiving and giving advice (cf. Chapters 2–5). When networks enter into social support by giving advice, this is most often because they care and want to help. The bereaved sense this and sometimes can feel under pressure to accept advice or express agreement in order not to appear ungrateful. At the same time, following the advice of others can upset or threaten one's own self-image as a competent and independent individual. To accept advice will in some cases also entail swallowing one's pride, admitting dependency or accepting the control of others. If the bereaved have failed to follow the advice or recommendations of a network, this can be experienced as a rejection of the network's caregiving efforts. Sometimes this will have negative consequences for the relationship between the parties involved. Advice and supportive conversations are, in other words, not only evaluated according to how correct they may be in terms of improving a situation, but also with regard to how they make one feel and what the advice implies about the power balance between the parties.

Our own and others' research also indicates that support in the form of suggestions and advice that result in the recipient losing face is experienced as being far less helpful than suggestions and advice that demonstrate respect for the individual and support their self-image (Dyregrov, 2003–2004; Goldsmith, 2004; Dakof and Taylor, 1990). It is experienced as positive when suggestions and advice communicate acceptance, thoughtfulness, solidarity and that the recipient is liked, while suggestions and advice communicated without respect for the private sphere and that do not propose choices, or that stipulate what the other should do, are usually not appreciated. Most of the bereaved therefore find it to be negative when friends or family members push, meddle, impose opinions or do not respect the right of the bereaved to make their own decisions.

Choosing a support form that helps

The most common support forms that social networks contribute are listening, providing emotional support, conversation, giving information or advice, encouraging and inviting the bereaved to take part in social activities or providing various forms of practical assistance (cf. Chapters 3–5). Some forms of support are most appropriate in specific phases following the death, while others can be implemented at any time and still others should be assessed as to whether they should be used at all and if so, when. There will frequently be uncertainty associated with which forms of support are most helpful in an individual situation and at an individual point in time. In general we can say that friends and family members talk too much and listen too little when people close to them experience a crisis situation. On the other hand, it must be said that the bereaved can have unrealistic expectations with regard to the abilities of people in their surroundings to understand how they are feeling and what they can do to help.

Networks that have provided support over time have found that emotional support, conversation and practical assistance are the most important contributions they can offer. The bereaved to a large extent confirm this and maintain that advice is more frequently given by 'beginners' and people in the network whom they experience as being more insecure and peripheral (Dyregrov, 2006c). Whether or not the crisis-stricken individual in fact experiences the intended support as such, is also related to the contents of the support and how suitable the support is in terms of alleviating a difficult situation (Goldsmith, 2004). When one evaluates the form of support, one must therefore not only evaluate the type of support but also whether the contents of the support are adapted to the situation in a broader sense. This entails that most bereaved individuals will need different forms of network support and that these needs will vary over time. In the following section the different forms of support and when they are most suitable will be discussed.

Emotional support
Emotional support comprises different verbal and non-verbal expressions. Some examples of emotional support are a comforting presence, hugs, tears, a squeeze of the hand or other expressions of sympathy and understanding. Further, emotional support can entail empathetic listening, with subsequent expressions of understanding and consolation. Such support is experienced as invaluable. When the world has fallen to pieces and the bereaved may feel as if they are losing their grip, the presence of another human being whom they can trust is perhaps the most important type of support and help. Immediately following the event, most bereaved people need someone who listens with empathy and sympathetic insight to what they have seen and heard, and currently experience or think. The support entails listening to and accepting horrible information, or just embracing the other and offering physical closeness. Some wish and need to share their experiences, over and over again, and for these people, if the network is able simply to listen to such repetitions over time, this comprises good support. Often they do not expect, and perhaps neither want, friends and family members to say very much, but instead to serve as a kind of 'receptacle'.

Emotional support is experienced as being positive when the network demonstrates calmness, patience, empathy and the will to listen and address the situation of the individual and family. In order for emotional support to be beneficial, it is crucial that the bereaved feel that they can trust the network and are certain that any private and personal information will remain so. In order for the trust between the parties to be maintained, it is an absolute condition that everything expressed in confidence in the situation is not leaked to outside parties. It can often be a good idea for the network to communicate clearly to the bereaved what they experience as confidential information and to specify what one should and is expected to pass on, with the best interests of the bereaved in mind. One of the most important factors contributing to emotional support being experienced as being truly beneficial is that it continues over time. The network must continue to ask how things are going and subsequently have the time and patience to listen. The fact that others are willing to share memories of the deceased, such as by listening to talk about the deceased or in other ways remembering the deceased over the years, is enormously supportive. The need for this type of support will naturally diminish over time, in correspondence with the diminishing intensity of the reactions of the bereaved. For someone who has lost a spouse at a young age, it can of course be inappropriate to continue to speak of the deceased if the bereaved has found a new partner. All support must entail sensitivity to the needs of the unique situation.

Encouragement

Network members will often include different forms of verbal encouragement and consolation in support conversations. As shown in previous chapters, the best consolation is often provided without the use of many words, but instead simply by signalling that one cares. Baking a cake, arriving at the door with dinner, arranging a pleasant meal for the family, delivering a bouquet of flowers or a consolatory poem are all gestures that are greatly appreciated by the bereaved. Many mention this type of thoughtfulness and sympathy as being crucial to their 'survival' during the first unreal period of time when the ground seemed to dissolve beneath their feet. Such support also feels good over time, but is replaced to a large extent by more verbal forms of comfort and encouragement on the part of the network. The difficulties of verbal encouragement entail keeping the contents at a realistic level. Because it is so intolerable to see a good friend or relative in such despair, one may want to present the opportunities and future prospects in an unrealistically positive light. The challenge lies in finding a balance, so that the encouragement is credible. Timing with regard to encouragement is also extremely important. One can overwhelm and insult the bereaved if one commences encouragement too soon after the death. If a friend uses the phrase 'time heals all wounds' immediately after a person has lost a loved one, this is usually not well received. This is a sentiment that the bereaved in some cases can concur with after a number of years have passed, but which is not experienced as a comfort while they are in the midst of a crisis. We use the expression 'time is a friend' because this better corresponds with what the bereaved experience over time. Beyond this, one must remember that it need not feel relevant for parents who have, for example, lost their child, to refer to how other parents have experienced, coped or moved on after such a loss. In the same sense that there are favourable and unfavourable ways of addressing and coping with one's own emotions, there are more and less expedient ways of reassuring others, or responding to their feelings. It is therefore important to listen to the bereaved individual and try to the greatest extent possible to identify with their situation in order to intuit what this person in particular may need in terms of encouragement.

Supportive conversations

A great deal of knowledge has been generated on the subject of how the verbalization of traumatic experiences can restore a certain sense of control (Riches and Dawson, 1996c). Discussion and conversation with others is therefore extremely important as a means of concretely specifying and reconstructing meaning in a meaningless situation (Neimeyer, 2001). By expressing pain within a community and sharing stories of the life of the deceased, the bereaved create a story through which they can explain the meaningless loss to themselves. We see that women do this to a larger degree than men and some researchers maintain that long-term problems in men can be connected with the fact that they do not succeed in the reconstruction of meaning because they do not express their grief.

Successful supportive conversations can take many different forms, dependent upon and adapted to the individual problem, the participants of the conversation and the relationship between them. Along with the emotional support, this is perhaps the most common type of support following sudden deaths. Supportive conversations are greatly appreciated by the bereaved. Good timing, sympathetic insight and wisdom are prerequisites for such conversations being beneficial. Many of the bereaved state that at the start, the less said, the better. Experienced network members confirm this when they express that there is not much that they *can* say of a constructive nature, particularly at the very start. Those who feel that they must say something often offer consolation on their own terms rather than those of the bereaved. Supportive conversations are most helpful if the bereaved indicate a need for and desire to speak about what they experience, or if they request information or advice. Further, it is important that what is said is suited to alleviate or assuage the bereaved individual's experience of chaos, pain, despair and grief. That which is said must not offend the grieving individual's self-esteem and identity, but signal care and true intimacy.

Supportive conversations must create an atmosphere of acceptance, in other words, communicate real and unreserved care and empathy in order to enable the bereaved to explore his or her feelings and find his or her own solutions. This type of support can contribute to problem solving if the network points out actions which the bereaved may not have considered or which they have begun to consider but are still unsure about. Beyond this, a good friend can encourage the bereaved to think out alternative possibilities for solving a problem and in addition demonstrate caregiving by expressing an interest in the individual's situation (Goldsmith, 2004).

Advice

As we have seen in previous chapters, experienced network members give advice to the bereaved less frequently than others. Their experience is that they can seldom give constructive advice and that the bereaved are seldom seeking advice. People who give advice are often motivated by a desire to ease their own discomfort rather than an assessment of what the other needs (Burleson and Goldsmith, 1998). Nor is advice the best type of help in terms of coping with emotions. Nonetheless, one often sees that the first and most common response from many people offering support is to give advice. Davidowitz and Myrick (1984) found that advice was the most common response in relation to bereaved people who had lost a loved one, but that this was almost always recalled as being of little help. Advice is often wrong because it is not adapted to the situation. Emotional support therefore appears to provide far more help regardless of the type of incident and crisis, while the effect of advice will be far more dependent upon specific aspects of the situation and the person giving the advice.

We know that the recipient's assessment of whether the person giving advice has knowledge of grief reactions, and of the type of advice that is beneficial in this particular type of situation, is extremely important in terms of whether the advice is considered helpful. Advice is beneficial when the recipient esteems the advice to be of a high quality, when the advice is offered in a sensitive manner, and simultaneously preserves the relationship between the parties. Dunkel-Schetter and her colleagues (1992) found that people in a life crisis sometimes consider advice to be positive social support, particularly when those giving the advice have expertise or have experienced similar problems. It is therefore a totally different situation when a professional gives advice as opposed to social networks. Recognized expertise or experience legitimates that one is qualified to give advice and knowledge is therefore an acceptable cause for giving advice. This implies that network members who are also professionals (healthcare personnel, clergymen, police, etc.), or those who have personally suffered a loss, can often provide advice that is valued. Peers (other bereaved) and professionals who have more knowledge about what the difficulties entail are therefore experienced as being better equipped to give advice than those without professional expertise or personal experience (Cutrona and Suhr, 1992; Dakof and Taylor, 1990). When the former give advice, it does not upset the individual's sense of equality and self-respect.

The bereaved can also want advice related to how they can seek help from professionals, how to locate the appropriate authorities and agencies to acquire facts and information (such as about an autopsy and distribution of the deceased's estate) or the financial rights one has as a next-of-kin. The kinds of advice that are usually least appreciated are those that are related to the individual's grief and coping process. There must be a large amount of trust on the part of the bereaved that the person offering such advice knows what he/she is speaking about or the parties must otherwise have a particularly close relationship in order for such advice to be experienced as something positive. A close and good relation is in other words an important condition for a bereaved person not experiencing such advice as meddling but rather as an expression of compassion and care. The risk of hurting or disparaging the bereaved is reduced when they personally ask for advice, because they are signalling acceptance of the asymmetry and possible shift in the relationship that the advice entails. *When* in the course of the conversation advice is given is also important. Is advice given while the bereaved is still considering a choice of action or when the bereaved has moved in the direction of an opinion or when the bereaved has already decided upon the solution to a problem? How advice and recommendations are interpreted and evaluated will differ according to whether the advice is simply introduced by 'If I am going to be completely honest, then…' as opposed to whether one concludes with a statement indicating how much one values the bereaved. Networks must be aware of the fact that by choosing the first, openness and honesty are implied, but that one also risks pointing out something that the bereaved has not considered or disagrees with. By giving the same advice, but concluding by connecting it to the strengths of the bereaved, one more frequently experiences that what is said sinks in and is more highly valued by the bereaved.

Nonetheless, we would emphasize that advice does not necessarily exclude empathy, sincerity and solidarity with the bereaved. Whether it is appropriate or not depends on the situation and who gives the advice. When advice is experienced as negative it is in particular because it is unwanted, with little credibility or is badly timed. Whether or not advice should be given also depends on whether the network can do something to solve the difficulties and/or change the situation or has expertise about similar type problems (Goldsmith, 2004).

Information

Bereaved people who experience a sudden, unexpected death have as a rule a great need for information. They usually receive many different types of information from their social networks. The information can comprise written information in the form of brochures, books and websites, or video programmes and verbal knowledge experienced or acquired by the network itself. Many bereaved, adults as well as children and young people, wish to know as much as possible about the events surrounding the death and what contributed to the passing away of their loved one in particular. The numerous, and in part extreme, reactions that the bereaved experience result in their having a need to understand whether such reactions are normal and for how long they will last. Adults want to understand the situations and reaction patterns of children and what they can do to help. This requires information and knowledge about what is available in the way of support and assistance schemes and perhaps subsequently addresses and assistance in seeking help from professionals. Telephone calls to public agencies (polyclinics, doctor's/psychologist's office, the tax authorities, the police, etc.) in order to obtain the necessary information represent valuable network support at a time when the bereaved experience a great lack of energy. There are also many who want information about relevant bereavement organizations and possibly help in acquiring contact with these.

In the short-term, information contributes to creating order in a chaotic existence, and in the long-term, information is important for the bereaved individual's reorientation in life, as the memory of the deceased is being integrated (Neimeyer, 2001). However, it is important to be aware of the fact that information in itself does not improve coping abilities and adaptation. It will only be helpful if the information is relevant and adapted to the bereaved individual's need for knowledge.

Social activities

An extremely important form of support is provided when networks motivate the bereaved to take part in social activities. There is a broad range of such possible activities – from invitations to dinner or coffee or simply to drop in, parties, walks in the woods, attending the cinema, concerts or theatre, volunteer work, company football matches, attending church, various sporting activities and forms of physical exercise, etc. It is the network alone that is able to provide this kind of support, in that social activities occur with the close or more peripheral network circles. The network is also in the unique position of having a previous history with the bereaved and being acquainted with them, so that they can take as a point of departure activities that previously were experienced as meaningful or pleasurable.

It is important to take, or create, 'time outs from grief' in order to manage to move on in life. Where the bereaved manage to do so, it is recommended to pressure them a bit to do things they formerly found to be fun and pleasant, or experienced as being good for the body and soul. There is much evidence indicating that anxiety and depression are reduced through pleasurable activity and physical activity, in that the body increases its production of endorphins (Scott and Schwenk, 2000). Our research also indicates that bereaved people who do not isolate themselves struggle less with psychosocial difficulties following a sudden death (Dyregrov et al., 2003). We also know that it is far easier to continue a normal life and take part in social events when a certain continuity is maintained. Through the network's encouragement to take part in social activities, they can contribute to the bereaved developing positive rather than negative patterns in their life.

A number of factors are of significance to the success of social motivation. In general, it entails the network having respect for and listening to the bereaved and taking greater initiative than they may have done formerly. Usually one does not think of a phone call to a friend where one asks him or her out to the movies or to go for a walk in the woods as network support. But when a friend or family member has lost a close loved one, a new dimension arises in the relationship. The friendship does not function wholly as before, where generally speaking the responsibility for contact and initiative is equally distributed. Because the bereaved is tired and lacks energy, it is important for the network to understand the situation and adapt, so that initially they assume the main responsibility and initiative for contact. Networks can easily become fence sitters, waiting in vain for an initiative on the part of the bereaved if they continue to think according to a 50–50 or give-and-take principle. It is also important that the network has knowledge about, among other things, gender and age differences in grief and respect for the fact that grieving individuals process grief differently. This means that some need to speak about the death for years, while others, perhaps in particular men and young people, to a larger extent use activity and social gatherings to create time outs from grief for themselves. The network should also be aware that some bereaved people do not find it appropriate to laugh or do fun things too soon after the death or that they are afraid that their surroundings will think that the grief has passed and forget the person they have lost. There is a risk of putting pressure on the bereaved too soon or not respecting that the individual in question is not ready or does not wish to meet with others. There is in particular a risk of undue pressure because it is hard on the network to see that a close friend is in pain and network members have such an intense wish for the situation to return to the status quo. It is therefore a matter of finding the 'traction point' together with the bereaved and carefully leading them along. If the network signals awareness and knowledge of such processes, the parties can speak about this in such a way that the bereaved derives benefits from social activities with the assurance that they are not being misunderstood.

Practical assistance

Different forms of practical assistance are a welcome blessing for most bereaved. Some bereaved people can be so run down immediately after the death that they in fact need help with basic daily functions, such as getting enough food and sleep, literally in order to stay on their feet. Some bereaved people therefore want the network virtually to move in and take over daily functions within the family. Many are gratified if the network carries out practical tasks in connection with a viewing or funeral. Friends and family can do shopping, accompany and support children and adults at a viewing or discuss important decisions with the bereaved. While some need help cooking, taking care of young children or helping out with caregiving duties in relation to elderly family members, others can have a need for their children to be seen and supported by close friends or family members. For some, help with physically demanding work such as cutting the grass or snow shovelling is also valuable during periods when physical energy is lacking. The network can also provide important assistance by contacting public agencies in connection with a funeral or autopsy, or by doing paperwork in connection with financial, legal or police matters. Last, but not least, it is appreciated when friends and family members help out in the contact with public assistance scheme workers (nurses, doctors, psychologists, etc.) where there is a need or wish for professional help. Not many bereaved people have the stamina and energy to be put on hold indefinitely when making a phone call, or to find their way to a psychologist, even long after the death. Alone, or in collaboration with the bereaved, networks can also help to inform the school and workplace about what has happened and of what is wanted with regard to measures and information in relation to the children's fellow pupils or adult's colleagues.

The most important thing about practical help is, as with all network support, that it is offered and carried out with respect in relation to the needs of the family. During the first week, many of those bereaved by a traumatic death can have a need for numerous forms of support and quite intensively. Therefore, at the start, there will most frequently be a larger need for practical assistance than when things start to fall more into place over time.

Routines

In addition to the forms of support mentioned here, it is worth noting that the preservation of ordinary routines contributes to lightening the burden of the situation for the bereaved. Daily routines are extremely important for the creation and reinstatement of a sense of order and stability in everyday life. The network can motivate the bereaved in this regard because they know what the individual family or bereaved person is accustomed to. They can assist in re-establishing ordinary daily rhythms such as getting dressed, eating and sleeping. If the bereaved is on sick leave from work responsibilities outside the home, the network can – when the bereaved is ready for this – motivate the bereaved to resume working. They can also counteract the bereaved person's tendency toward isolation and encourage them to resume exercise routines or other social activities in which they have normally taken part. Last, but not least, it is important to help children and young people to create continuity in their lives and in daily life by assisting them with an eye towards resuming kindergarten and schooling as soon as possible. For children the preservation of routines in connection with meals and bedtimes can be important factors with regard to creating security, and encouragement and help in maintaining these routines will be an important type of support on the part of family and friends.

Rituals

Rituals have always had an important significance with regard to commemorating important transitional life events, such as births, marriages and deaths. Erving Goffman (1967) pointed out the significance of rituals in terms of creating stability and order when life changes. In addition to rituals being given individual and personal features, their collective significance in a society and culture will be reflected by current grief conventions and rituals. Through ritual activities in connection with death, people are given the opportunity to express feelings and thoughts in a symbolic community. Brottveit (2003) summarizes the function of rituals as such: rituals help to make the unreal real, to alleviate grief and repair the loss ('therapeutic function'); rituals give death a meaningful frame, define the deceased person's new position and identity ('cosmological function') and rituals have a 'social function' through the redefinition of roles and the resumption of activity.

Rituals, such as funerals or memorial services, the lighting of candles or laying down of flowers, are not only important acts of support for the bereaved but also for the network. Such acts lead to friends and acquaintances acquiring guidelines for what they can say or do and knowledge about how they can fulfil support roles. In particular, collective (common) rituals make participation in grief less threatening for peripheral networks. When everyone else lights a candle, it is easier to take part in such a group than to take the initiative for one's own actions in relation to the crisis-stricken family. Collective rituals in other words have the advantage of guiding the interaction between the bereaved and the network. The collective aspect entails that many come together and create a ring of support around the bereaved. This is as a rule experienced by the bereaved as something extremely good and positive, and not only while the ritual is taking place. Many bereaved people remember for a long time afterwards that so many people attended the funeral, everyone who put flowers on the coffin, the beautiful speeches during the memorial service or all the candles that were lit by the side of the road. The network's participation in rituals has therefore not only a support function during the relatively short time during which they take place, but for a long period of time afterwards. The thoughts of all those who wanted to take part become a good memory and help in the further processing of grief (Dyregrov et al., 2000a).

Rituals in connection with death, crises and disasters have in recent years acquired new forms. In particular, it is the social network that is now more at centre stage, in the creation of new, personal variations, independent of tradition. One example here is the many young people who create their own spontaneous candlelight and memorial services when they have lost a friend, suddenly and unexpectedly, such as through a traffic accident. Memorial services can be simple and easily arranged by having parts of the network assume the primary responsibility for organization in accordance with the wishes of the bereaved. Music, simple refreshments and a few words from those who might wish to speak can be important as a means of concluding a memorial service or funeral. Very many bereaved people state later that although they beforehand actually did not believe that they would have the energy for such a gathering, they were later extremely thankful that it had been arranged. In this way, common rituals can help young as well as old in the formation of a common platform, opening up for emotional confrontation with the loss and its confirmation through concrete actions.

Close networks can also play a central role by motivating the bereaved to follow rituals, even though they perhaps would have preferred not to do so. The value of allowing close and more peripheral friends, family members and the local community to take part in both the funeral and any commemorative rituals can be crucial to their continuing to step in for the bereaved afterwards. By excluding others, the bereaved send indirect signals that they want to be left alone, that others are not to learn about or be allowed to participate in their grief. By being open and including the network in early rituals, the bereaved can contribute to the creation of a larger support network for themselves over time.

Communicating support so it is experienced as helpful

Support that is experienced as being helpful is expressed with a form and content and through a series of events that are in coherence with the existing or desired relationship between the parties. There is therefore no recipe for supportive actions or statements that are positive and applicable in all cultures. This section is about the support's form of communication (cf. the communication model in Chapter 6). The communication form reflects the verbal and non-verbal messages, the social situation the parties are in, when the support arises in the meeting between the parties, what else takes place in the meeting and where in conversation mention of the death, opinions or advice arise. How these factors are preserved is discussed under four different communication forms – the direct, indirect, solidary or deferential (Goldsmith, 2004).

As a means of illuminating the respective communication forms, we will take as a point of departure a situation where a good female friend supports a mother who has lost a child by sudden infant death. She wants to communicate that the mother should take better care of her surviving children. A direct means of saying this would be: 'You should perhaps take better care of Jonathon and George; they are not doing well.' An indirect manner would be: 'I read the other day that many bereaved children are not adequately attended to by their parents.' A manner expressing solidarity would be: 'I also found that I did not manage to take care of my children when I was feeling run down, so it helped to receive some outside assistance.' A deferential form of speech could be: 'I hope you don't mind my saying that I see that Jonathan and George are not doing well. Perhaps you might consider whether they should receive more help.' As is clear, some of these statements are more authoritative and disrespectful, while others are more tentative and inquisitive, and in particular, the examples chosen here signal the full range of positions, from an expert with a wish to direct the mother, to that of an equal peer, where one shares one's own experience and leaves it to the mother to evaluate and act according to her own judgement. Although it would be most common to combine the forms of speech, such as direct with deferential or direct with solidarity, we will first address some features of each form in particular.

Direct communication form

The direct form of communication makes it possible for the parties to understand one another because it aspires to illuminate the parties' needs and wishes – to make more explicit that which has not been formulated and is implicit. The advantage of expressing support directly through opinions or advice is that the network is clearly stating what they think that the bereaved should do. At the same time, it makes it clear that the person making the statement is of the opinion that the recipient should do something other than what he/she is doing or thinking at the time. As we have stated, this can represent a threat to the bereaved individual's independence, need for recognition or own manner of resolving a particular situation. The fact that many bereaved people ask about the network's views after they have made a decision does not make the situation any easier. Perhaps the bereaved person is fishing for confirmation regarding a decision that they have made. If friends or family then refrain from stating what they actually think is best (even where it goes against that which has been indicated by the bereaved), they risk losing credibility as a sincere friend. At the same time, they are betraying the expectation that good friends only want the very best for one another. On the other hand, if the network suggests alternative actions that the bereaved dislikes, the bereaved can question the loyalty of the friendship and whether they truly understand the situation. Such dilemmas are of course not impossible to handle, but require wisdom and empathy, particularly when there is disagreement regarding how situations should be addressed. In the case of such dilemmas, someone will start by saying 'if I am going to be honest' in order to prepare the recipients for the possibility that they may disagree with the views or advice that is coming.

Shall we be completely honest?

When a family member gives 'their honest opinion', for example regarding taking care of surviving children, the individual in question risks going against that which the bereaved does or thinks. The individual hereby runs a risk of being perceived as critical and non-supportive as opposed to compassionately supportive. Networks can therefore experience a dilemma with regard to whether they should express their honest opinion or say what they think the bereaved wants to hear, or believes to be the right thing to do – a dilemma between support or honesty. When one then also knows that many bereaved people appreciate honesty in both conversations and any advice offered, it becomes a challenge for the network to be both supportive and honest. It is important to find a balance here and attempt to discern in each individual case the form and degree of directness that is appropriate for the support, in order for it to be experienced as supportive. Support that entails agreement with a friend's irrational assessment of a situation will potentially be experienced as quite supportive but will perhaps not be helpful in any sense whatsoever. To the contrary, such support can contribute to the creation of a misguided and evasive coping style.

Goldsmith (2004) claims that for some it can even be inexpedient to make open communication and emphatic listening a standard for all social network support (see also Gottlieb, 1992). Nonetheless, she maintains, it will probably be helpful for the crisis-stricken to communicate their needs more openly with network members who have not previously supported bereaved people. For networks it will be important to listen and respond with greater empathy. This is a conclusion that, in correlation with our research, is about the fact that the situation is special, unfamiliar and unknown territory for both parties, and as such they lack guiding principles for the interaction. The less the parties know one another, the more clearly the parties must communicate about the type of support that is wanted and that can be expressed. The parties must exchange these guiding principles when they communicate social support. In order to ensure that the direct communication form does not become direct and tactless, the network must combine directness with respect or solidarity.

Communication form expressing solidarity

A friend can signal that he/she sympathizes with the bereaved with the use of a verbal style using their own confirmation to provide a sense of solidarity. This form of communication as a rule requires that the bereaved and the network are very close or that the parties have an extremely similar experiential background (for example, that both have experienced sudden, unexpected death). By connecting the support to in-group language or actions indicating that 'I have also experienced something similar', the distance between the bereaved and the network is diminished. This also explains in part why peer support holds such a special position for the bereaved. When the parties know each other well, solidarity can also be expressed through a more informal language or through more profound explanations and conversations. The bereaved will more often appreciate and accept views and advice expressed through a communication form which voices solidarity because the network is then perceived as being more credible and trustworthy. Goldsmith shows in her research that this solidarity and a direct communication form is experienced as being the most helpful by people in difficult situations (Goldsmith, 2004).

Deferential communication form

A deferential communication form ensures that neither the bereaved nor the network risk losing face. This communication form demonstrates caring attentiveness, and a more formal language is often used than when one is signalling solidarity. For the initial contact with the bereaved one can, for example, excuse oneself and ask for assurances that one is not imposing. Or one can choose a deferential and careful verbal style to express opinions such as: 'I hope that you don't mind my saying so, but it might be an idea to…' A deferential mindset can also be signalled through informal actions offering practical help in a careful fashion or by simply being present while the bereaved weeps or by squeezing their hand.

Indirect communication form

An indirect message can be communicated with or without words because the context in which it is taking place is clear. Tears, a squeeze of the hand or sending flowers to the funeral are examples of forms of support that employ an indirect communication form. Such actions are often experienced as empathetic, showing solidarity and deference. Indirect verbal messages can, however, easily be veiled, vague or tactless and are exactly what bereaved people often dislike. Nonetheless, it can sometimes be useful for networks to go out of their way to provide the kind of support experienced as helpful by the bereaved. In order to avoid hurting the bereaved or behaving inconsiderately, friends will sometimes need to sound out the situation carefully before acting. For example, a more indirect and deferential style is used when the person one wants to give advice to does not define a problem or ask for advice. Advice given in an indirect manner allows space for the bereaved to interpret this as something other than advice, which to a lesser extent threatens self-respect or the relationship between the parties. Such advice can be understood as a milder form of recommended action and imposes less pressure to follow the advice.

Combination of communication and support forms

In practice the communication forms are usually combined, for example so that support is communicated directly and tactlessly, directly and with solidarity, directly and deferentially, indirectly and deferentially, etc. Goldsmith (2004) explored different ways of combining the communication forms outlined here with three forms of support (advice, offers of practical help, expressions of compassion/empathy). In correlation with our research findings, she found that some language styles were preferred over others. In our research both the bereaved and the network maintained that openness, clarity and directness are the most important factors for good network support following a traumatic death – and they point out that support must be extended deferentially and with empathy (Dyregrov *et al.*, 2000a; Dyregrov, 2003–2004). It is, however, fundamental that the choice of language style and forms of support are based on the parties' primary and respective experiences in their encounter. The bereaved find that network support is improved if they personally manage to inform others about what has happened, how they are feeling, the support needs that they have and how others can best support them. Social networks indicate the same – they wish to be guided, informed and educated by the bereaved in order to succeed in providing support on their terms (Dyregrov, 2006c).

Main themes
Basis for good network support

- The bereaved person(s) must have a need and wish for support and help and have some understanding of the network's situation.

- The network must have knowledge of common grief reactions and help needs, know something about the challenges and solutions connected with providing support and the courage to contact the grief-stricken party.

- Social networks and the bereaved should have/acquire knowledge regarding when professional help should be brought in.

- Social networks should receive the necessary support and encouragement.

Main criteria for good network support

- The support must signal and express reciprocity between the bereaved and the network. This is communicated through acts and thoughts, the willingness to provide support, loyalty, agreement, availability, encouragement and forms of providing consolation.

- The support must be helpful and useful. This implies that it contributes to problem solving, makes things easier or clarifies the thoughts of the bereaved.

- The support must demonstrate sensitivity with regard to emotional experiences and events. Support that is sensitive is gentle, cautious, observant, considerate, understanding and compassionate.

Principles of a good relation with network support

- The point of departure is asymmetrical: one of the parties needs support and help; the other party can and wishes to offer this.
- Self-image is supported when the bereaved feels respected, accepted, liked and not criticized.
- It is negative if the network 'pushes', meddles, imposes opinions or does not respect the bereaved person's right to own decisions.
- A potential dilemma exists between being helpful and caring vs. meddling and being honest vs. being perceived as supportive.
- There is less risk of losing face when consolation comes from an equal friend or family member or when the network confirms equality.
- When the bereaved ask for advice, an acceptance of asymmetry and a power shift is signalled.
- The bereaved can feel pressured to express agreement with the network's views so as not to appear to be ungrateful.
- The bereaved accept more easily advice from recognized expertise (friends who are also professionals) or experience (other bereaved people).
- The degree of directness and the form of support must be adapted so that it is also experienced as being empathetic.
- The bereaved must feel secure about the network's trustworthiness and confidentiality.

Helpful forms of support

- Emotional support – empathy and sympathetic insight, 'receptacle' function.
- Conversations – more listening than talk, 'follow the lead' of the bereaved.
- Advice – focus on the needs of the bereaved, the network's competency and equality between the parties.

- Information – about the nature of the death, normal reactions of bereaved, addresses, knowledge about support and help measures, literature, peer organizations.
- Social activities – activities to allow breathing space from grief based on things that were formerly pleasurable.
- Practical help – a broad range in correlation with the family's needs (housing, food, children, economy, legal/police, funeral home, contact with assistance scheme/school/workplace, etc.).
- Routines – help in maintaining ordinary daily activities (eating, drinking, sleeping, housework, work, school, etc.).
- Rituals – motivate for and participate in memorial gatherings, funeral and other collective acts in connection with the death or deceased.

Communicating support so that it is helpful

- The support must be respectfully adapted to the bereaved person's need for support.
- The support must address different needs.
- The support must not violate the bereaved person's feelings and identity.
- The support must demonstrate respect for the thoughts and decisions of the bereaved.
- The support must show respect for the bereaved person's private sphere.
- The support must vary and if necessary continue over time.

8

What kinds of support can family and friends give?

This chapter contains practical and concrete advice for family members or friends regarding how they can provide helpful support. In order to adapt advice as required to individual situations, we would recommend that readers also brief themselves on the basic conditions for network support described in previous chapters. Important key phrases for this understanding include the bereaved person's and the network's experience of the situation, a perception of network support as communication, and the significance of respect and empathy and giving support on the terms of the bereaved. With the point of departure being the bereaved and their networks' advice regarding helpful support, this chapter presents general advice, the kind of support that family, friends and other bereaved people can provide, support for young people, what one should not say or do and what networks wishing to provide support can do in the event that they are rejected in their attempts.

General advice for family and friends

We have previously specified that no two situations will be alike because relations between the bereaved and the network and what comprises helpful support in any given situation will vary. Nonetheless, we would like to point out some fundamental features of network support that make possible a certain degree of generalization.

The first contact

Many family members and friends experience the first contact subsequent to the death as the most difficult time to make contact. They fear the emotional intensity and tension that the situation may entail and unsure about their own reactions, as well as those of the bereaved. Many are so uncertain about what to say and do that they avoid the bereaved or refrain from speaking about the deceased with them. This is experienced as a rule as very hurtful. It is difficult to know what to say to someone who has lost a loved one suddenly and unexpectedly. But it is not necessary to say very much; there are often no adequate words of comfort. That family members and friends actively make contact and go out of their way in their efforts to help, in spite of the fact that it can be uncomfortable to make contact, is often more important than words. Although family and friends may wish to 'do' something, they must remember that this may not necessarily be what the bereaved need in the initial period. The most important thing is to show the newly bereaved family and the individual bereaved person that one is there and that one would like to help. Having the courage to be physically and psychologically present, without the need for so many words, can be the best kind of support in the initial phase following a death.

Network members can say that they do not know what they should say, but want the bereaved to know that they are there for them. The most important thing is that those wishing to provide support are honest. They can tell it like it is, in a simple fashion: 'I don't know what I should say. I have thought through the words many times, but they are so empty.' Give a hug or a warm embrace and take the conversation as it comes. It is good for the bereaved to see that friends and family share their grief with them. If one starts to cry, it does not matter, but one should not expect that the bereaved will necessarily do the same. They can still be protected by shock or simply have no tears left. One can also ask about how the loved one died. It is possible that one's inquiries will be rejected, but it is important to ask nonetheless. In the days immediately after the death it can be a good idea to wait to make contact until later in the day, in that sleep is often late in coming and the bereaved can need whatever sleep they can get when they finally do manage to fall asleep. Right after a death as a rule there are so many who make contact that a certain amount of coordination is sometimes required. The network should be aware of this and address it with the bereaved and if no others have assumed such a 'coordinator function' perhaps *you* can do so?

Networks can organize their efforts: who does what?

There are a number of reasons why within a family or group of friends coordination and organization of the network support can serve to economize on resources. Not everyone needs to, or can, give all the different forms of support that the bereaved need. It will always be the case that some feel they are best suited to a role where they provide some forms of support, others take on other roles, while some can fill all. As discussed above, it is crucial that the support does not just materialize during the first days, but continues over time. 'Over time' in this context can be years, though certainly not with the same amount of effort and intensity. Support is usually needed for much longer than most in the network believe. It can also be expedient and important for friends and family to collaborate their efforts in order to economize on time and energy. This is because there is always a risk that friends and family may 'burn out' if they provide support with too great an intensity and put all their own needs and considerations aside over a long period of time. When many close friends or family members surround the grief-stricken and there is a huge need for support, it can be wise to speak together and possibly 'allocate' tasks among those involved, designating times for physical presence, practical tasks, or other types of support. In this way some can regain their strength, while others assist the bereaved and the support can be stabilized and made consistently available over time.

Giving support on the terms of the bereaved

Although friends and family can never completely understand grief that they have never experienced personally, they can accept the experiences of the bereaved regarding how they are feeling and the type of support that they need. On the basis of this one can put oneself at their disposal and support them on their own terms. The main rule of thumb should be to allow the wishes and needs of the grief-stricken to determine the content, form and duration of the support. Friends and family must attempt to communicate with the bereaved about support. They must ask questions such as: What can we do? How shall we do it? Who can help out with what? How often would you like us to drop by? Who would you like to come to see you? Are we fussing too much now? Are there other things you would like me to help out with? Such questions can make individual and adapted support possible, clear up any misunderstandings between the parties, and reduce the network's uncertainty. By listening to 'those who know where the shoe pinches', the foundation is laid for the best possible use of the good support resources found in close family and friends.

The only exception from the main rule of providing support on the conditions of the bereaved is when the type of support requested is not in their best interests. The Support and Care project showed that those who isolate themselves the most after traumatic deaths are those who also experience the greatest difficulties physically, psychologically and socially. Family and friends should therefore re-examine the wishes of the bereaved in the event that they notice that they are struggling, wish to be left completely alone and that nobody can reach them. If after having gently applied pressure the network still does not achieve contact, it can be the case that professional help should be brought in (see Chapter 10).

Support over time

Continual attentiveness and interest on the part of family and friends is even more important than a large amount of availability and assistance on their part just after the death. The 'invasion' of the home that takes place during the initial days following a traumatic death gives the bereaved a good feeling of many people thinking about them, but can also be overwhelming and contrast greatly with the loneliness they can experience after some time has passed, when fewer people come to visit and the telephone does not ring. It is often after some time has passed that the sense of loss is most acutely felt, when everyday life returns, when the surreal sensations evaporate, and it is not possible to fool oneself by saying 'this did not happen'.

Although the intensity of reactions diminishes gradually over time, we know that the bereaved have a need to verbalize and try to understand what has happened, and to reminisce about the deceased with others over time. Often it is sufficient to listen to what the bereaved have experienced, seen, thought and felt. One should allow them to speak without interrupting and signal that one is willing to listen to whatever they have to say and perhaps over and over again. It is a good idea to refrain from giving advice or saying that you understand how they are feeling. One cannot understand such extreme events without having personally experienced something similar. Help of a practical nature and over time can prove necessary if the network sees that the bereaved is so exhausted that basic tasks are not being done in the home. This type of help can entail housework, cooking, snow shovelling or helping out with caregiving responsibilities, but one should also remember that once in a while it is good for a person struggling with painful thoughts to be able to do something practical. Help with parenting duties is an often lacking and extremely welcome type of help in periods where adult caregivers are too exhausted to carry out the parenting role. An adult whom the children trust can then temporarily perform duties such as helping out with homework, driving children to school or recreational activities and provide care and intimacy for the children. Gradually, and depending upon what the individual has been through, friends and family will have an important function in contributing social stimulus. Then it is important to propose activities that the grief-stricken has previously enjoyed: going to the movies, trips to the mountains, listening to music, exercising or getting out with friends again. It is often a good experience to meet with 'greater society' again for the first time after the event in the company of good friends. Help in acquiring information from public agencies or in filling out forms can be invaluable during a time period when a lack of energy can be a key problem for many bereaved people. Precisely because close friends and family have the important position of being *close to* the bereaved, an important task will also be that of intercepting signals that they may be in need of assistance beyond that which the network should or can give. Such signals can include persistent concentration and sleep problems, nightmares or intrusive images and memories from the event or a complete refusal to speak about the event. If such symptoms last beyond the time of the first month following the death and the person in question does not gradually resume participation in their ordinary life, the network's encouragement for the bereaved to contact a physician, or personally contacting an assistance scheme in the public sector for the bereaved, would provide an important form of support (see also Chapter 10).

We will here summarize some general advice that can be useful for family and friends. The context for the advice is the relation between the bereaved and the network, and relates to the types of support that can be appropriate and the form of support. As research has shown (cf. previous chapters), the bereaved and the networks are in agreement regarding the basis for the advice, which they maintain can contribute to better support from social networks. Nonetheless, we would specify again that the advice must always be adapted to each individual situation.

Advice regarding the relation surrounding the support

- Make active and early contact – do not avoid the grief-stricken person but be prepared for the possibility that you may be rejected.

- Find out whether the bereaved has a need for support from you in particular.

- State that you are there for the bereaved and wish to provide support.

- Be direct and honest about your uncertainty in connection with giving support and tell the bereaved that it is important that they speak of how they wish to be approached.

- Find out what you can do and what the 'expectations' of you are.

- Remember that there is a broad range of grief reactions and that which you have personally experienced as being important and correct about grief is not necessarily true for others.

- Show respect for the broad scope of reactions and patience with those who struggle for a long time.

- Forgive the bereaved if they are angry or say something hurtful to you.

Advice regarding types of support

- Find out the type of support that the bereaved need through communication and by acquiring knowledge.
- It is not always so important to say much; just show that you care.
- A letter, a flower or a small greeting, or bringing some food, such as a cake, warms the heart – and a hug warms even more.
- Inquire as to whether the bereaved wish to speak about what has happened and remember that some have a need for repeated offers.
- Be particularly attentive to children in the family.
- Give support that shows that you commemorate the deceased over time (e.g. contact on red-letter days).
- Encourage participation in social activities (things they appreciated previously), so that the bereaved do not isolate themselves and their social life does not disappear.
- Practical assistance, such as helping out with childcare, gardening and housework, can be invaluable.
- Contribute to contact with other bereaved people, bereavement support groups or peer organizations if the bereaved so wish, but remember that they are usually not ready to take in the situations and pain of others until about a month after the death.

Advice regarding forms of support

- Be present and available.
- Listen sincerely and in earnest – show empathy.
- Show respect and patience for the way in which the bereaved need to grieve.
- Take the initiative and make suggestions (e.g. for pleasant activities), without expecting as much initiative in return.
- Offer help with practical things but do not take over unless the bereaved request that you do so.
- Mention the name of the deceased in conversation where it is natural to do so.

- Show that you care and step in to help over time – where relevant let them know if you for whatever reason must pull out for a while or for good.

In addition to this advice to the social network, what follows are some simple suggestions for the bereaved that will provide the necessary foundation for enabling family and friends to provide helpful support:

- Remember that the network finds openness, honesty and directness from the bereaved to be the most important in terms of improving and ensuring helpful support.

- Let family and friends understand that you tolerate and wish for openness about the death.

- If you wish and have a need for it – accept help and support.

- Explain to others about the help and support you want.

- Give good, clear feedback on good support and comment on support that could have been different/better. Networks want to learn how they can best support you.

- Remember that the network often does the best it can, but is uncertain about the situation.

Support from the family

For many the family represents the most natural source of support and one that can help in many ways. Immediately following the death the family can assist in contact with the clergyman, funeral home and in relation to the police or public health service. Also later this can prove a welcome form of help. It is also the family who would most naturally live in the home of the bereaved as a support during the first period, but here the needs of the bereaved can differ greatly. Family members should be particularly attentive to any children in the home of the bereaved family, in that many adults can need help performing caregiving roles. It is important to allow young people to speak about the deceased as much and as often as they like, to give them the opportunity to express as much and as intense a grief as they may need and are willing to share with adults. If they do not want to speak, this must be respected. If they do not want to speak this is usually not a cause for concern and it is only if this continues over time, and they simultaneously pull away from friends and their school performance begins to suffer, that there is cause for concern.

If family members live with the crisis-stricken (nuclear) family they will in particular be able to provide support in terms of re-establishing routines for any children involved. These will be familiar and beloved people, who are trusted and who can provide support in terms of relief from caregiving duties. Because adults' grief can be all-consuming, we know that many children as a matter of course receive less attention than they otherwise would. In addition to children's own grief, the 'unavailability' of adults can cause them to feel vulnerable and afraid. Some children are afraid to speak with their parents because they feel that they thereby will only compound their sadness. In order to prevent communication difficulties within the family, it is extremely important to establish a good informative climate for everyone, where difficulties and questions are addressed in an open and direct manner. Adults should remember that in such a difficult situation they can be perceived as good role models for how children and young people will come to address life crises later in life. Here grandparents, aunts and uncles, etc. can be good confidantes and they can in particular help out in taking children to recreational activities and other events, so that the children's daily routines to the greatest extent possible can be maintained. Practical assistance with other caregiving duties that adults may have, such as responsibility for elderly parents, can also be an invaluable form of help.

Family members can help children and young people

- by encouraging parents to allow children to take part in the rituals in connection with the death (to see the deceased, help out in choosing the clothes the deceased shall wear or choosing music for the funeral, etc.). It can also be good for the parents to be relieved of childcare duties during these ceremonies
- by helping out in picking children up from school and day care, or by taking them to or attending children's recreational activities and other things which parents for a period can experience as a burden
- by being a confidante for the children when they have a need to speak to someone with some distance to what has happened
- by helping parents to 'notice' the children in the family if they are only interested in the deceased and the grief becomes all-consuming.

Grandparents as a network

When grandparents lose a grandchild, they are an important source of support in many ways, while at the same time, they personally experience grief over the grandchild they have lost. Perhaps this is the type of grief that is little recognized but which can be experienced as an extremely heavy burden. Not only is one grieving over one's grandchild, but also the loss that one's own child has experienced. If grandparents personally experience the loss as an enormous strain, it is important that they can find someone who can support them. This will also prevent their grief from becoming an added strain for the parents. Most are able to find this balance and are there as a support for their children, whether in the form of practical or emotional support. It is important to remember that the manner in which one understands the loss or 'the meaning' of that which has happened will not necessarily correspond with the thoughts of the next generation, so that one should refrain from making categorical statements, such as 'God works in mysterious ways'. This widens the generation gap. Grandparents should also remember that young people often seek out others their own age for support and help. This does not mean that grandparents are insignificant but rather that they are helpful in other ways. It can be the case that parents who lose a child wish in fact to spare the grandparents. Then it is important to communicate about this and find an appropriate balance.

The role of parents of bereaved parents is sometimes difficult and it is easy to assume the parenting role for one's children again and take over much of the organization of that which is taking place. This can be helpful, but at the same time, bereaved parents may feel even more helpless if they are pushed to the side and lose control. They can feel invaded and can react in a negative manner to their parents (or parents-in-law). The advice is therefore to pick up on the signals from children and daughter- or son-in-law and offer help according to their wishes. One should be careful about the relation not becoming so close that it becomes suffocating. The grandparents must accept that the parents at times can seem unreasonable and perhaps do things differently to what they personally might have wished. They are adults and must take responsibility themselves and do things in their own way. The most important thing that grandparents can do is to show that they are thinking about and miss their grandchild, that he/she has not been forgotten and that they are there if the parents need to talk.

Shall we ask how things are going?

Many in the network wonder whether one should ask the bereaved how they are feeling or how things are going. Many believe that the answer is 'No', at least when some time has passed – based on the myth that one should not reopen old wounds. Our research shows that this is wrong. Most bereaved people state that their most important strategy for coping with the difficult situation is openness. They want conversation about the deceased to be open and direct, and to be able to include the deceased in conversations, even long after the death has occurred. When we asked the bereaved what is important for them, they always reply 'that others do not pull away'. But as mentioned previously, here the needs of men and women can differ. To start with, however, both genders have a wish to speak about what has happened but men are more selective in their conversations over time. They choose confidantes with care and sometimes they prefer only to speak with their partner and not with people in their surroundings. Family members can ask directly about what the bereaved want in this regard and can ask the same at a later point in time in order to be sure that they can converse about the deceased should they wish to do so. Many appreciate being asked how they want things to be, if they would like to take the initiative for conversations, or if they want the family to do so. Of course, the bereaved also appreciate being able to speak about subjects other than the death. It is the stiff and evasive conversation that is most difficult for them, where the most important event of their life is never mentioned. When one has first spoken about what has happened and a type of mutual understanding is established, the bereaved can with greater ease speak about other things. But some become also understandably tired of the question: 'How are you doing?' It can therefore be a good idea for family members to vary the ways in which they inquire. One can perhaps say:

- I am sure that many are asking you how things are going and that you get tired of it.

- I think about how different daily life must be for you now when John is not in the house.

- I have heard that things get worse after a while, not better. Is that how it is for you?

- How is work going when your head is certainly full of thoughts about John?

Support from friends

Friends have become more important in contemporary society. This implies that as a friend one has a particularly important role as a support and caregiving person. Many adults have experienced that some friendships lose their meaning following a traumatic death. This occurs because friends refrain from making contact or where conversations become 'meaningless' or if the bereaved find that the distance with regard to personal values becomes too great to bridge after a death. Many bereaved people find that their priorities undergo a change. Material things become less important while intimate, human values are emphasized. Old topics of conversation are no longer suitable. The bereaved are more demanding in terms of the time they spend with others and can dissociate themselves from those they feel to be solely concerned about material matters and not about what they experience as the more important aspects of life. Perhaps one as a friend must expect that the friendship will be subject to reassessment after a traumatic death, where the depth of the friendship changes, either in a positive or sometimes negative fashion. It is not always easy to accept help and some find it difficult to accept more than they give. One must then remember that friends and family that provide support over time experience for their own part that the friendship acquires new and extremely meaningful dimensions (Dyregrov, 2005b, 2006c).

Friends can, like family members, step in with practical assistance and participate in mobilizing the support of other friends. Early after the loss, it is important to send signals that one is thinking of the bereaved, appreciates them and will be there for them. Some bereaved people feel that all the attention becomes so much of a strain that they need someone to coordinate information to be passed on to the network of friends. It can be exhausting to receive 15 telephone calls every evening during the first week, when one is already both worn out and run down from the loss one has suffered. The network should therefore proceed with caution and not be overly zealous in their efforts to help, so that the network's own desire to help does not acquire the upper hand. One should perhaps instead help the bereaved in setting up 'dosages' of contact if in the beginning the onslaught is too overwhelming. Many bereaved people also confide in family and friends, so as to give them an awareness of how bad they are feeling. Friends can, with the permission of the bereaved, investigate how they might like to receive additional help, such as by taking part in a bereavement support group or by receiving help from a psychologist.

As a friend one can also gently encourage the bereaved to take part in social activities, suggest taking them out for a walk, or possibly to the movies, or to a party, etc. One can speak with them about the fact that nobody expects them to be all smiles and that they need not be in great form in order to participate, because the most important thing is to experience surroundings other than their own living room. If there are many people present, they can greatly appreciate it if a friend takes a little extra care of them, because the contrast between the outer joy in their surroundings and the inner emptiness and grief they are feeling can be enormous. We know from our studies that social isolation is part of that which is most strongly associated with problems over time. The point in time at which a bereaved person feels ready for more participation in social activities can vary. As a friend, patience and repeated invitations are necessary in order to help the bereaved along. After a while it is also good to speak about other things, to be like others. If the network has understanding for the fact that it is possible to laugh and joke even while struggling with grief, it becomes easier for the bereaved to come along without having to worry about what others think of them. When friends and family do motivate the bereaved person to do pleasurable things, they can implement the tactics which those bereaved by traumatic death personally refer to as important advice on self-mastery.

The advice of the bereaved on self-mastery

- Spend time with friends ('take a time out', have some fun, 'forget').
- Let others see that you tolerate and want openness.
- Write (poems, diary, letters/commemorative words/songs to the deceased, create a scrapbook of memories, find a release for obsessive thoughts).
- 'Speak with' the deceased (e.g. at their grave).
- Listen to/play music (preferably music which the deceased liked).
- Commemorate the deceased on red-letter days (e.g. celebrate his/her birthday, light a candle, visit the grave, etc.).
- Remember positive experiences with the deceased, reminisce and cry.
- Read poetry or literature about the cause of death (loss of a child, sudden infant death, suicide, etc.).
- Go for walks to think or speak about the deceased, or for distraction (alone/with a companion).
- Take part in demanding physical activity (increases energy and offers time away from thoughts).
- Take part in religious activities.
- Work.

Support from other bereaved people

There are many different reasons why bereaved people of all age groups appreciate meeting others in the 'same situation'. They encounter people who can confirm and share reactions with them. There will often be someone in their close or peripheral network who has experienced a sudden, unexpected death and in a way can be called 'other bereaved' or they can meet with peers in a bereavement support group. In bereavement support groups one can listen to what helps others and try out some of these things personally. Because other bereaved people have experienced many of the same reactions, they are in many ways the 'experts' when it comes to support. We can therefore not give peers very much advice. The most important thing of all for anyone part of such a peer group will be to be themselves and to seek to make the most of their own experience in order to identify with the situation of the other. As is the case for other types of networks, other bereaved people must adapt their support to the person they are seeking to support and to the situation, whilst never forgetting that one's own grief will never be like another person's. The greatest 'danger' of this type of relationship is that those who have experienced loss will impose their coping techniques on others, accordingly, and that they have only minimally reflected upon how different the situation can be for other bereaved people. We will here summarize the experience of the bereaved with regard to the significance of peer support, as important guidelines for the support from other bereaved people.

The significance of peer support
The bereaved person is able to:

- meet others and see that they are in the same situation as them
- receive confirmation for their own struggles and that they are completely normal
- take the opportunity to speak about thoughts and feelings, be seriously heard, and feel truly understood by others
- take the opportunity to express thoughts and feelings one seldom airs with others
- feel that they are 'not obliged to say so much', will be truly understood, and that the peer group 'can stand hearing about it'
- receive advice and information (self-mastery, offers of help, literature)
- gain hope and faith that it is possible to move on (by meeting others with longer 'service time')
- benefit from the chance of a 'time out', to do pleasurable things or dare to show joy in the company of others because one need not at the same time shake off seriousness
- have the opportunity to support others – that is meaningful
- continue to give and receive support over time (when everyone else has forgotten).

A special focus on supporting children and young people

Like adults, the young bereaved also appreciate that neighbours and family friends are there for the family and beyond having a certain need to speak with and lean on their parents, young people want support and comfort and to 'have fun', 'be normal', and 'do ordinary things' with friends.

Because few teenagers consider their parents to be their closest confidantes and because they more frequently open up to close friends of their own age group, it is of great significance that friends stand by them after a sudden death and particularly over time. First and foremost it is important that friends are present and listen when young people have a need to speak about what has happened. It is important if friends indicate that young people can ring them up or come to visit them at any time and that they are there for them and do not back away. The most important friend is the one to whom a young person can tell 'everything'. Because many young people experience 'abrupt maturity' in connection with the death of a loved one, they become 'adults' prematurely. For friends who are to provide support, this becomes a great challenge. They must be willing to take part in conversations with a depth for which they perhaps, in terms of their age, are not particularly motivated. Here friendship can be put to the test. Professionals can prepare young people for this, and perhaps meet with the closest of those from the network to build bridges in this area.

All friends, however, need not be in the inner circle where one addresses the grief of the bereaved. Young people to a larger extent than adults use some friends to address the need for intimacy and to share painful thoughts, while others in their circle of friends are good to have when they want a 'recess from grief' and to have fun. It is therefore important that somewhat more peripheral friends do not pull away because they do not find it natural to address the grief and crisis of another person intimately. Perhaps they are one of the 'party friends', who are also important, although in another way than the best friend. In order to gain clarity about this, friends can ask directly if the crisis-stricken wants to speak about what has happened or wants to spend time together without bringing up the subject. If one is told the latter, one can rest easy in the knowledge that perhaps one serves as a 'party friend' for the person in question (cf. Chapter 4).

Among young people who lose a sibling there are many who find it a positive experience to have contact with the sister or brother's friends afterwards, even if they were not previously part of the same circle of friends. That such friends knew the deceased is often of great importance because the young bereaved and these former friends can then share memories, grief and feelings of loss, and function as a support for one another because they are 'in the same boat'. A young boy says: 'I had already "adopted" my brother's friends before it happened. But I "adopted" them *even more* afterwards and they had me as well.'

Young people, like adults, want the support of friends on their own terms and most of the advice presented here about adult support also applies to young people. This implies that the support must be adapted to their daily state of mind, so that young bereaved people can speak when they wish, receive comfort when they need it, and have fun when they need a time out from grief. Hurtful comments can be cleared away and friends can clarify wishes for support by bringing up and speaking about how the young people would prefer to be approached/supported. As one young person says: 'They came home to me and asked: "James, how should we go about this process here? I thought that was very good."

Young bereaved people's advice to friends

- Express that you do not have words for the situation or do not know what to say.
- Do not believe/say that you understand how your friend is feeling.
- Don't try to say the 'right' words or give advice.
- Speak with and ask your friend how you can support him/her in their grief.
- Respect his/her wishes regarding how you should behave and after a while ask if what you are doing is ok.
- Remember that speaking about the deceased in a natural way does not re-open old wounds. Your friend thinks about the deceased often.
- Create a recess from grief, have fun – when and if your friend manages to.
- Avoid hurtful 'throwaway' comments such as, 'Why don't you just go hang yourself and get it over with' and correct others on this point.
- Take the initiative and support your friend over time.

Parents and the family's support of young bereaved people

Many young people have mentioned having difficulties in accepting support at home because they feel that their parents are worse off than they are and they want to protect their parents from seeing just how much pain they are actually in. Some young people say that speaking with parents and family about the things they are struggling with is 'wrong', 'daft', 'a strain', etc. On other occasions, family support is made difficult by the fact that parents have previously not been in the habit of speaking openly with them, the young people are hindered by detachment processes, or they have taken on parents' caregiving roles. Parents or other caregivers are for their part worried about the young bereaved and wish to support them or get them professional help.

When young people under pressure give in and tell their parents how they are feeling, they frequently make light of the situation and say that things are going better than they actually are. This occurs both because they are then hoping to hereby avoid any further 'fussing' and because they want to protect their parents from understanding just how much pain they are in. For parents and other close adults it is therefore extremely important to approach young people gradually and with care. The most important thing is to signal a willingness to be open about what has happened and to speak with the young people when they are ready to do so (Dyregrov, A., 2006b and Dyregrov, K., 2006b). Pressuring or forcing young people to speak about how they are feeling can lead to their virtually shutting adults completely out of their experiences. One must neither pressure young people to behave or grieve in a certain manner. In contradistinction to adults, children can cry and grieve one minute, and take part in games and be totally indifferent in the next. Many children and young people also spend a long period of time on beginning to address the loss of a close loved one, and particularly boys can wish to avoid having to speak about what has happened. If children and young people are functioning well in school, are not pulling away from friends and do not demonstrate significant personal changes, the family should be patient and speak about what has happened when natural opportunities to do so arise.

It is also extremely important that the adults do not hold back information about the incident even if this is done to spare the young people. When young people find out that they have been excluded or lied to, this can do irreparable damage. The things young people may be imagining about the contents of an autopsy report or a suicide note can be far worse than the reality. Beyond this, young people are at risk of developing a long-term inability to trust if they are lied to or shut out from what is otherwise common knowledge for the rest of the family. It can be important to share information about decisions in the family after the death and also include them in making some decisions, such as about what one shall do with (some of) the deceased's possessions. Young people can often have opinions well worth listening to, while at the same time being included is a good experience. A good dialogue and openness where one can share the facts about what has taken place, their situation and how one might alleviate it is often the ideal solution. Communication about the event must of course be adapted to the age and maturity level of the child and be repeated over time, since children and young people can come to understand the event in a different light as they grow older. In the following we summarize some advice for parents and adult network members based on the young people's positive and negative experiences with support from them.

This is how family members can support children and young people:

- Help parents to 'see' the children in the family.

- Encourage and support parents to allow children to take part in rituals.

- Help parents by picking children up from school, day care, or recreational activities.

- Mobilize other adults as 'support people' for children and young people if the closest caregivers for a period of time have reduced capacity for caregiving duties. Do not impose too much of the adults' despair on young people or allow them to assume adult roles.

- Be a confidante for the children when they need to speak about what has happened.

- Give correct and honest information adapted to the age and maturity level – do not hold back important information that young people want to receive or will hear from others.

- Allow young people to grieve in their own way – do not pressure them to grieve like parents/adults. Allow them also to be young and carefree in their grief.

- Encourage young people to take a 'time out' to do fun things and relax with friends, even at an early point in time when the adults cannot envision doing so.

- Make sure that young people are functioning well in their daily lives after the first chaotic months (sleeping well vs. nightmares and problems sleeping, eating normally vs. change in eating patterns, meeting with friends vs. isolating themselves, school performance as before vs. overachievement or a drop in marks). If not, it can be a sign that they need professional help.

- Speak with young people about the importance of maintaining contact with friends, even if friends for a time can seem very 'childish'.

- Speak with the school about how the young person is doing and inquire whether the necessary support measures have been implemented. Let the young person know about this or allow him or her to accompany you when you do so.
- Signal to the young person that speaking about the deceased, the event and how one is feeling over time is permitted.

What should you not do or say?

One should never overlook grief and loss by changing the subject, for example, when the bereaved mention the deceased. One should not try to console parents over the loss of a child by pointing out that it is a good thing that they have other children or that they can have more children. A child can never be replaced. Family and friends should not pressurize the bereaved into packing away the clothes and possessions of the deceased or do this for them. One sometimes sees that a family member wants to clear away the possessions of the deceased quickly, while others need to have them around for a longer period of time. If as a friend one speaks with the deceased about such things, it is important to signal respect for the fact that the close bereaved must resolve this as they see fit. A friend can communicate that there is no right or wrong way of doing things and strive not to take sides in the event of any disagreements between family members. The network must also not pressurize the bereaved into starting work again too soon. A grief process takes a long time and requires a lot of energy.

The most important thing is not what you say but that you are there and make an effort. Nonetheless, many bereaved unfortunately experience that various things are said that hurt them deeply. We will therefore give some advice concerning what one should refrain from doing or saying. Usually it is not only a lack of knowledge that leads someone to say the wrong thing or pull away but also the tension in the situation when one is face to face with the bereaved. 'I know what I want to say but then when I open my mouth the words come out differently.' Many resort then to phrases that definitely do not have a large supportive value – but unfortunately have the opposite effect.

Refrain therefore from saying:

- Put it behind you and move on with your life.
- You still have the other children.
- You can have more children.
- I know how you are feeling.

- Imagine if she had survived with all the extensive injuries.
- Think of everything that he has been spared.
- It could have been worse.
- Everything happens for a reason. It is God's will.
- It must be getting better now.
- Time heals all wounds.
- Now you must be sure not to bury yourself in grief.
- Fortunately you did not have enough time to get to know the child very well (with infant deaths).

One can say instead:

- I cannot even begin to imagine how it must be for you.
- Some say that you have the other children, but that does not help, we have none to lose.
- There is not so much that I can do but I can listen to you and be there for you if you wish.
- I know that losing a child is the worst thing that can happen to parents and that the grief is long-term, but remember that you have me and many others who want to support you.

Although one has experienced grief personally and found one's own manner of coping with it, or one's life experience and knowledge entail that one believes that one has good advice to give the bereaved, one should exercise restraint in terms of giving advice about how they should grieve or move on with their lives, because this is something one cannot know. If they ask directly, one should of course tell them what one thinks would be useful, but be careful about forcing opinions down their throats. In one's eagerness for them to feel better, one can risk pushing them even further away. Sensing the pain of a good friend can make one overly zealous about relieving that pain, but in that case we are not showing respect for the depth of the loss the bereaved have suffered. Being present, even if one feels helpless, can sometimes be the best kind of help one can give. Some of the most painful experiences the bereaved have involve being avoided, acquaintances who hide behind the shelves of the local store, look in another direction to avoid eye-contact or in other ways seek to avoid them. This type of 'social helplessness' is often a reflection of the fact that people in the surroundings do not know how to handle the situation and choose avoidance – seemingly the easiest way out.

Refrain therefore from:

- making contact out of curiosity
- believing or expressing that you understand how they are feeling. Instead express that you lack words for the situation
- giving advice about how they should react or handle the situation or about how they should grieve (clear away the deceased's things, take pictures down off the walls, etc.)
- asking the father how the mother is doing – he will then feel that he is of less importance than her.

When one is rejected

Some of the bereaved are so defeated by the death that they do not manage to relate to many people and they can bluntly reject family and friends' compassion or attempts to provide support. It is very upsetting to feel that the bereaved do not want one's support and help. There are however many reasons why the bereaved can, for a period of time, reject support and help:

- There can be too many who want to help at the same time.
- They are so exhausted that they do not have the energy to accept help.
- They are so angry or in another way so emotionally distraught that they do not want the people in their surroundings to see them this way.
- They can have lost their trust in others and are sceptical of the idea that others want what is best for them.
- They feel that others cannot understand.

Some family members and friends feel rejected and hurt if the help they offer is not accepted with open arms. It is here important to tolerate rejection, not to take it personally and for that reason refrain from making contact later. Friends can send a greeting, saying they are thinking about the bereaved and will be in touch later. If they are rejected, they can say that they understand that it is perhaps not the right time to make contact but that they will be there for them in the time ahead. Such gestures are greatly appreciated by the bereaved and make it easier to resume contact later on. If as a friend one signals that one will make contact again later, it is then extremely important to do so. The bereaved will often remember 'the extended hand' and appreciate this at a later point in time when most have forgotten. One of the very things that is the most greatly appreciated is the friends and family who are there 'when daily life returns'.

Main themes
General advice for network support

- Make contact actively and soon.
- Find out if the bereaved have a need for your support.
- Tell them that you are there for them and want to provide support.
- Be direct and honest about your uncertainty regarding how to give support.
- Find out what you can do – ask them what they want.
- Show respect, be patient and be prepared for possible rejection.
- It is not so important to say much – but show that you care.
- Send a flower, a letter, a small greeting – a hug warms the heart!
- Inquire whether the bereaved want to speak about what has happened, and repeat the inquiry.
- Be particularly attentive to children in the family.
- Provide support that shows that you remember/commemorate the deceased over time.
- Encourage participation in social activities.
- Offer help with practical things, but do not take over unless the bereaved want you to do so, e.g. help with childcare, gardening and housework.
- Contribute to establishing contact with other bereaved people, bereavement support groups or peer organizations.
- Be present and available.
- Listen honestly and earnestly – show empathy.
- Show respect and patience for the bereaved person's way of grieving.
- Take the initiative and make suggestions without expecting much initiative in return.
- Speak the name of the deceased in conversation where natural.
- Show that you care and step in over time.
- Be prepared for and tolerate rejection.

Avoid

- making contact out of curiosity
- believing or expressing that you understand how they are feeling. Instead state that you have no words for the situation
- giving advice about how they should react or handle the situation.

How family members can support children and young people

- Give correct and honest information, adapted to age and maturity level.
- Help parents to 'wake up' and notice the children in the family.
- Encourage and support parents in allowing children to take part in rituals.
- Help parents by picking up children from school, day care or recreational activities.
- Mobilize other adults as 'support people' for children and young people.
- Be a conversation partner for children when they need to talk.
- Let the young people grieve in their own way – also allow them to be young and carefree in their grief.
- Motivate young people to take 'time outs' to do fun things and relax with friends.
- Check up on whether the young people are functioning well in daily life after the initial chaotic months – if not it can be a sign that they need professional help.
- Speak with the young people about the importance of maintaining contact with friends.
- Speak with the school in agreement with the young person about how he/she is functioning and about necessary support measures.
- Signal to the young person over time that speaking about the deceased, about the event and about how they are feeling is permitted.

9

What kind of support can the school and workplace provide?

The school and the workplace are situated in the middle, between social network support and professional help. These arenas will subsequently have both functions simultaneously. While pupils and colleagues have an important opportunity to provide support and comfort directly, teachers and work supervisors have an important function with regard to adapting the frames of the school and the work situation. Because the school is the place where children and young people spend the most organized time and meet many in their social network, the school is in a unique position for young people after a sudden death. Here many of them also have the greatest number of acquaintances outside of the family. In the same fashion, the workplace has a unique opportunity to support adults. In this chapter we will address the important opportunities that first the school, and second the workplace possess, with regard to providing support for people who have experienced the traumatic death of a close loved one.

The school

The school is a central arena of support for crisis-stricken children and young people, but also for the bereaved family as a whole. The school's objectives regarding a close relation between the home and school to attend to the well-being and environment of children will as a matter of course also imply its involvement if the family of a pupil experiences a traumatic death. By giving fellow pupils time and possibilities for empathetic insight during the school day, the school personnel can become a good source of support for crisis-stricken children/young people and other pupils who are more indirectly affected. It is therefore important that emergency plans and follow-up strategies for young bereaved in the schools have been established (see

Childhood Bereavement Network, 2008). The plans should attend to the interests of children/young people, peers, fellow pupils and the members of the school community. The plans' objectives, measures and support forms must be discussed with all school staff members in order for the routines to function (DfES and DoH, 2005; Dyregrov, A., 1989, 2004, 2006b; Health Development Agency, 2004).

The teacher will potentially be an important support person for children and young people, due to their influence and position. One important task is to help young people back to school as soon as possible, particularly if they can be there somewhat on their own terms during the initial period. In this way one helps to give them continuity in an otherwise chaotic everyday existence and a 'psychological recess' from the sad atmosphere at home. At the same time, the school, teachers and fellow pupils will be able to provide them with important support. The extent to which children and young people will need to be taken care of at school will vary. The most important point is to adapt the situation as best as possible for the individual pupil and family. The school will also, in addition to providing caregiving for individuals, potentially have an important responsibility in terms of creating frames for collective processing. The objective of support for young bereaved people should be to provide individual attention and considerations, to create good frames for collective processing of what has occurred and to help the crisis-stricken to activate social support from schoolmates. Such measures will otherwise benefit the overall atmosphere of the class. The most important condition for the successful functioning of help measures is the presence of trust, empathy and contact between pupils and teacher. In addition, a good collaboration between home and school is important.

Measures
The traumatic death and the circumstances surrounding it will of course determine the scope and focus of support measures. In order to adapt the school day it is important for teachers to communicate care and understanding for the situation by first investigating how the bereaved pupil is doing. Subsequent to this, measures based on the individual's support needs are implemented. The school should have responsibility for contacting the pupil and the home for necessary adaptations and plans for attending to the pupil's needs, and involve the other pupils in a three-way dynamic between the school and the parents. Just after the death, some relevant support measures could entail lowering the flag, a memorial service (in some cases also a viewing), home visits, drawings from classmates, greetings to the home and attendance at the funeral.

Older and younger children greatly appreciate it if the class makes a considerate gesture such as by sending flowers after the death or to the funeral. Further, it will be important to provide information about the event and to discuss the subjects of grief, loss and crisis reactions with the class. How the school informs fellow pupils and talks about what has happened is of particular importance and must be done with understanding and in collaboration with the families of those pupil(s) who are the most personally affected. As time passes, the commemoration of red-letter days (flowers on the grave on holidays, visits to the parents, etc.) will be of great significance to the family.

It is crucial for young people that teachers show that they care through sincere participation in their unique situation. The teacher must make it clear to the pupil that they personally and the school as a whole will do their utmost to make the necessary accommodations in order to prevent the situation from disrupting school attendance. The teacher must send a clear message that someone, whether it is them personally or someone else, will be there for the pupil over time and an agreement should be formed regarding how the teachers can be updated on a regular basis about how things are going and adjust any measures for attending to the needs of the young bereaved person. The involvement must be based on knowledge about what happens to children and young people who experience losing close loved ones suddenly and unexpectedly, and the knowledge must be correlated daily with the young person's changing state of mind, grief and crisis reactions, and concentration and learning difficulties. Such knowledge should be assured through basic and continuing education for teachers. One hereby avoids the formation of suspicions regarding the pupil's motives if he or she does not always manage to keep up with his or her schoolwork. Knowledge will also serve to ensure a realistic time perspective with regard to the child's grief and crisis reactions, where it will not be expected that everything will return to normal after a few months.

Information

Information about what has happened is a crucial tool towards mobilizing social support along with professionally designed adaptations on the part of the school. It is important that the teachers take the initiative and signal that this can be accomplished. An obvious condition for this is that the bereaved pupil and the family in fact want this. Teachers can ask bereaved pupils if they want to inform the class and subsequently help them or in collaboration with them or their family inform the class of what has happened. Some pupils take the initiative for this themselves but most will need support and encouragement to dare to do so. Such information gives fellow pupils the opportunity to ask questions and express their own reactions together with adults. In this way, the school can contribute to preventing the spreading of rumours and pushy questions from fellow pupils. At the same time, fellow pupils are given permission to support the bereaved pupil and acquire the opportunity to do so according to his or her express wishes. Teachers can make a meaningful contribution by making the necessary arrangements to ensure that schoolmates understand the situation and provide support based on what the young bereaved person wants and can manage to accept. For younger children it can sometimes be necessary for teachers to protect them from being excluded from the games of classmates, or from teasing or intrusive questions in connection with the death. Basic knowledge that the (head) teacher receives about the death must be passed on to the pupil's other teachers so that they also show consideration during the school day. Because young people experience not knowing whether the teachers know as a strain, it will give them added security if the head teacher tells them who knows about the death. Another important point is that if pupils change schools during the first period following the death the new school must also be informed. Children experience it as a problem if this is not done because the people in their surroundings forget long before they have ceased struggling with what has happened. The new teachers must subsequently make it known that they have been informed of what has happened and of the situation in general. The young person must be spared having to relate this over and over again.

Practical arrangements for the school day

Young people often experience difficulties in school after a traumatic death in the family or circle of friends. Many experience fatigue and have concentration problems, while some struggle to achieve the same school performance as previously. They do not want to impose further strain on their guardians and after a while some become completely exhausted. Some young people experience a lack of understanding for the need to postpone tests and similar type trials, and particularly if they have been previously judged as unmotivated, requests for postponements are interpreted as excuses and attempts to get out of doing their schoolwork. This has an effect on their schoolwork and social participation and the young people request help in this regard from teachers and the school (Dyregrov, 2005a, 2006d).

It is first and foremost important to alleviate young people's sense of the pressure in terms of external expectations to perform, attend and continue school as before when they have been through such an ordeal. For most, flexibility in connection with absence and performance evaluation will comprise an important form of support. The school and the teachers must expect that pupils can often need to return somewhat gradually after the funeral and some will perhaps need a short-term 'sick leave'. For young people in secondary school it can prove decisive to their school progression and in fact, for their entire future, to be granted dispensation from absenteeism rules for a period following a traumatic death (Dyregrov, 2006d). Although returning to fixed school routines and following the ordinary school schedule comprises a good form of crisis help, it is very important that signals are also given regarding more flexible absenteeism rules. Young people that have problems falling asleep will benefit more from being allowed to arrive a bit later and attend fewer classes, rather than having to struggle through an entire school day from which they have little or no benefit.

Small adaptive measures can make learning possible if children and young people are struggling with concentration and learning problems. Just subsequent to the death some will have a need for time outs, such as being permitted to leave class or simply to be more passive in classes without this having consequences for their marks. In some cases there can also be a need for pupil outplacement or leave from school for short periods. Some young people can be so disturbed by what has happened that they need to sit in a separate room or find distraction from their thoughts through alternative-type learning methods, such as by working at a PC. Others can have a need for exemption from (some) tests and exams, for an extended exam time or an adapted type of exam, dependent upon whether they manage to concentrate best on written or oral tests. Teachers can also alleviate the pressure for marks for young people by having the school view the new tests in correlation with the pupil's previous performance when marks are awarded. Understanding and empathy in the school day are also important forms of support. If themes such as grief, crisis and suicide are addressed in class, it is a good idea if teachers prepare pupils who have just experienced such things for the fact that these subjects will be addressed and that they are given the option of not attending the class.

The all-important empathy

Due to the extreme nature of what has taken place, young bereaved people are extremely vulnerable and overly sensitive in relation to their surroundings. An extremely sensitive issue for young people is empathy from teachers and how it should or can be expressed. The interaction between the teacher and pupils in crisis can therefore be extremely challenging and there can be a fine line between support and care that is experienced as good versus intrusive fussing. Good support will be dependent upon the existing relationship between the pupil and the teacher, how what is said and done influences the young person's identity and self-esteem, the pupil's subjective experience of the support and not least, the unstable nature of the young person's state of mind from day to day. It is important for the pupil that teachers proceed with caution and show that they understand their situation. It can therefore be important for teachers to explore the young person's situation carefully and not expect to acquire a complete understanding immediately. Young bereaved people do not like to be 'surprised by sympathy'. While they want true empathy from teachers, it also must be such that they are able to accept it. It is important to sit down and speak with the pupil and allow an adequate amount of time, in surroundings where one will not be disturbed. Teachers must not 'fall all over' the pupil with empathy and physical contact if they have not previously had a close relationship. Unless they personally have been in a situation that was very similar and at the same age, it is therefore neither a good idea to say that one understands how they are feeling, but listen instead, be present and show that one cares. If the teacher implicitly and explicitly indicates that they are there for the young person when they are ready to speak about or receive support, and repeats this over time, it will be easier for those in need of support to accept it. It is a matter of finding the 'traction point', as the young people themselves put it (Dyregrov, K., 2006b). Some of the best support takes place when teachers demonstrate that they care over time by asking on a regular basis how the young person is doing. This is experienced as being very positive and particularly if it is done in private or at parent–teacher meetings and in such a way that others do not overhear.

The need for an outreach programme
(Head) teachers, social teachers and nurses especially will be the most significant and ideal helpers in a school context. Beyond the fact that for this group, a support and care perspective constitutes a part of their professional background, all have the necessary parameters to enable them to function as an outreach programme for young people who are struggling. Our research has shown that if one is to support young people in crisis, this help must be in the form of an outreach programme. This entails in particular that the support and help is offered and repeated over time and that young people can accept the support when they feel ready to do so, that the 'chemistry' with the helper is right, that the helpers are easily accessible, that they address that which is found to be difficult or, if necessary, provide contact with other professionals (Dyregrov, K., 2006a, 2006d; Heltne and Dyregrov, 2006). Routine contact with social teachers, form teachers or nurses offering a fixed schedule of

appointments for contact throughout the school year will serve to ensure this. Offers of adapted parameters and help should be repeated if pupils who are clearly falling behind reject this. Teachers in the same school must also have the same practice with regard to attending to the needs of one and the same pupil and coordinate their efforts in terms of how they behave in relation to him or her. It is extremely important that the help for young people to the greatest possible extent is carried out in collaboration with them, by asking them simple and direct questions such as 'What would you like help with?' 'What do you need?' or 'What are you struggling with?' Because there will be a large variation in the needs for support and care on the part of vulnerable young people, one must adapt the overall situation with both heart and mind for the individual pupil.

The workplace

> Work contributes to accelerating necessary processes. A workplace provides a structure between free time and work, between working and resting.

The workplace is an extremely important arena in the lives of many people, because it fulfils an important need for social belonging. As the above quote shows, the workplace also contributes to creating order and structure in the lives of crisis-stricken individuals. Because a large portion of our identity is connected with work, the workplace has an important function in terms of creating and preserving identity. The workplace is also a key arena for social support. Since one spends the greater portion of the day at the workplace, for many it is the most important meeting place with society outside of the family. How one is met at the workplace is therefore of decisive significance with regard to how one copes with a loss. In addition, a symbolic gesture of condolence or information from the deceased's workplace can play an important role with regard to helping the bereaved move forward in processes for the reconstruction of meaning.

The significance of support and care at the workplace

Many bereaved people praise colleagues for their fantastic support while others experience disappointment in relation to colleagues and understanding at the workplace. The Support and Care study indicated that bereaved people who had received support at the workplace appreciated this very much. They had experienced that the goodwill and understanding both from management and colleagues were prerequisites to their returning to 'a normal life' (Dyregrov *et al.*, 2000a; Nordanger *et al.*, 2000). A constantly recurring theme is how the workplace is either a help and support in the grief process of the bereaved or how insufficient attentiveness, understanding and accommodation contribute to longer periods on sick leave and a more complicated grief process.

For many of those bereaved by a traumatic death it is extremely important to have a job to go to, so that one is not 'locked up at home with one's own thoughts', while it is at the same time essential to be greeted with understanding for the fact that one does not have a full working capacity (for a long time) afterwards. This awareness is in the interests of both the bereaved and the workplace but also important from a social economic perspective. In order to ensure that the bereaved can be met in a beneficial manner within their work arena, supervisors and workplaces must receive concrete information about what grief does to people, and about how to go about greeting a grieving colleague in an appropriate fashion. Knowledge must be acquired and a tradition developed in connection with the fact that it is advantageous to take care of colleagues who are having a difficult time. As addressed in previous chapters, the bereaved miss contact with the network, and in many cases they find that friends and colleagues do not understand them or pull away. As a rule the reason why others pull away is because they do not know what or how they should communicate with the bereaved.

Insufficient support from the workplace appears to be a disappointment similar to that experienced with insufficient support from friends and family and is associated with psychosocial difficulties (Dyregrov *et al.*, 2000b). Thuen (1997b) concludes that social support from friends and professionals after infant death, in the sense of information, practical and emotional support, correlates with better psychological adaptation in a long-term perspective. In Atle Dyregrov's doctorate research (1988) mothers who returned to work early were compared with mothers who remained at home. Here the findings indicated that those who returned to work managed much better than those who did not. Although support and care first and foremost benefit the bereaved and their family, they are, as shown by Boscarino and colleagues (2005), also consistent with a corporate profitability mindset. The studies of the latter showed that in the aftermath of crisis events employees at workplaces with an active strategy for helping staff members did better health-wise with regard to somatic and psychological ailments and alcohol consumption than did those at workplaces without such a strategy (Boscarino, Adams and Figley, 2005).

There is today much greater openness about sudden death, grief and crisis reactions than there was only a few decades ago. There is a general understanding that this subject must be taken seriously, and that this, in the long run, will provide social gains. Nonetheless, the Support and Care project revealed obvious inadequacies in the level of knowledge about grief and crisis reactions among colleagues and supervisors at the workplace. In order to prevent bereaved people from the experience of being misunderstood, rendered suspect ('they are cultivating their grief') or being met with ignorance in connection with absenteeism and extended sick leave, it is important that knowledge about the situation of the bereaved and the significance of support is circulated in working life. It is highly significant that supervisors and managers are attentive to and acquire an increased awareness of how grief affects people's lives and daily existence. We hope to contribute to a greater sense of security on the part of supervisors, so as to facilitate their approaching the bereaved.

What type of support can management and colleagues provide?

The most important thing that colleagues and the workplace can do is to develop a working environment that allows the bereaved to have reactions and allows the possibility for an unstable working capacity: 'An employer must have understanding for what a natural grief process entails, that there are weeks and months of chaos, and then come the years with feelings of loss and emotional ups and downs.'

Supervisors and colleagues can provide different and/or overlapping types of support for the bereaved by sudden death. While management will have the primary responsibility for leading and implementing measures, the effect of the measures will be dependent upon the participation of colleagues. While some measures will be more formal and be implemented at an early point in time, others will be more informal in nature, integrated into daily social conventions, and (ideally) continue over time. The objective of good support should be to create a focus on, and correspondingly adapt and accommodate, the working situation of the bereaved employee, to attend to colleagues in relation to the event and the creation of good frames for a collective processing of what has occurred. Support measures should entail making the necessary arrangements so as to give the bereaved the chance to 'think about something else' or to speak about what has happened, by management and colleagues demonstrating empathy, humanity, understanding, thoughtfulness and respect. Further, it will be important to provide colleagues with information about the death and the situation of the bereaved, information about flexible work schemes and the company health service. Other relevant support measures on the part of a company/organization can be lowering the flag, taking part in memorial services, funeral attendance, paying visits and sending greetings to the home and the implementation of colleague support programmes. In collaboration with the bereaved, possibly through group forums, discussions on the subjects of grief, loss and crisis reactions, and creating opportunities for employees to talk through things, are key measures.

The bereaved experience it as particularly important that managers demonstrate symbolic leadership and make contact in order to show their support. Managers' support is of particular importance as a signal to the bereaved indicating that their loss has been recognized and that there is space for their grief at such time when they are able to return to work. It can be expedient for colleagues to coordinate their contact through one staff representative during the initial period. The workplace should assist in acquiring professional help in the event that the bereaved person is having a particularly difficult time and here the company health service can be of inestimable value. At a time when energy levels have been significantly reduced, help in finding a psychologist, for example, will be extremely valuable.

Information to and from the workplace

In order to be able to mobilize support at the workplace, information about what has happened is crucial. Information should first of all pass from the bereaved to management, and then be further passed on to staff. It is important that supervisors consult the bereaved and ask how they would like the workplace to be informed and thereafter to make the necessary arrangements in accordance with the wishes of the bereaved. Some bereaved people wish and manage on their own to express and present information to their colleagues. Others are grateful if management, for example in a group forum, informs the workplace on the basis of what the bereaved wishes to have made public knowledge. The most important thing is that management takes the initiative for information at the workplace and asks how the individual wants this to be communicated. This does not occur to many bereaved just after the death or they find that they do not have the energy to take the initiative to organize it.

The collective support at the workplace is mobilized by providing information to staff members about what has happened, how the family is doing, and how they wish to be greeted when they return to work. Such information will, beyond permitting one to speak about and address the event, give signals regarding what one can do to provide support. In addition, one hinders the spreading of rumours and false information within the miniature society that a company represents. In particular with deaths that arouse the attention of the local community (e.g. murder) it can for the same reason be important to provide information beyond the scope of the particular department in the company where the bereaved works.

Understanding and caring support over time

There are many forms of empathy and caring support from the workplace that are experienced as beneficial just after the death. Telephone calls, flowers, or management and colleagues attending the funeral are all gestures that are appreciated. Baking a cake for the gathering after the funeral, collecting money for a gift or greetings to the family are other good expressions of support. A warm hug or silent squeeze of the hand are also heart-warming gestures. After the bereaved person has returned to work, it is also a kind gesture if colleagues stop by to say 'Hello' to the bereaved and ask 'How are you feeling?' or say: 'We are thinking of you a lot.' An sms greeting or email are other signs that one sees the bereaved and wants to express one's compassion. If for various reasons it is difficult to touch on the subject of the death and the situation of the bereaved at work, colleagues can make a phone call after working hours. The bereaved greatly appreciate colleagues who manage to balance between being a supportive friend on the one hand and a professional colleague on the other. This contributes to normalizing the working day and life for the bereaved.

Colleagues can encourage participation in social activities outside of working hours, invite the bereaved out to dinner (possibly with the entire family) or motivate them to take part in activities at the company. One should not wait too long, but start out with small things, possibly one-to-one, and not be deterred by a rejection in the initial period after the death. There is support in a gentle prodding, whereupon one then withdraws, stating that the invitation will be re-issued if the bereaved clearly explains that it is too early. If attempts at social motivation are made in a respectful manner, the bereaved will appreciate this, even though they may not always have the energy to take part. The bereaved request that colleagues seek them out and take the initiative, exercise gentle pressure and persuasion, and in particular that colleagues provide support over time.

As with all forms of support following a sudden death, a longer-term timeframe is requested from colleagues and management at the workplace. Many experience that support and caring gestures last for a half-year, at the most. Afterwards it appears as if most, also at the workplace, believe that the period of grief has come to an end or that one has forgotten. The bereaved can hide their grief if they notice that there is no room for feelings at the workplace. It is therefore perhaps even more important that there is room for the grief over time, that the bereaved do not feel obliged to hide their reactions because they understand that their colleagues only want to hear that things are going better, while the truth is that they are now struggling even more than previously. The bereaved can feel relatively well one day while on the following day they hardly manage to get through it. The mood swings can be great on the inside even if they cannot be noticed on the outside.

Although many bereaved people want the workplace to serve as a neutral space where they can concentrate on work tasks, a few small hints that one remembers the death over time are of enormous significance to them. This need not be more than that colleagues sometimes ask whether he/she thinks a lot about what has happened, mention the deceased by name where it is natural to do so or provide some caring support in the event that they notice that the bereaved is having a difficult day. After the first year has passed, many of the bereaved appreciate it very much if others take the initiative and ask how things are going. Management and colleagues should do this and not be afraid of reopening old wounds – as a rule the wound is still open and it is good to receive confirmation of the fact that others also remember the deceased. Over time there is of course a difference between having lost a spouse and having lost a child, where in the latter case the grief can be a heavy burden for years afterwards. If the bereaved colleague has begun to date others, it will of course not be natural to begin to ask about or mention the deceased.

Openness and verbal support

Many bereaved people have a need to speak about and share their thoughts about the subject that preoccupies them for the greater portion of the day. If they go to work at an early point in time after the death, the need will often be great to have someone to speak with in the course of the working day. Nonetheless, there are many who do not manage to take the initiative to start such a conversation, and they are unsure about whether they are putting too much strain on outsiders. Many bereaved therefore feel less that they are being a bother if the initiative to speak about the deceased comes from a colleague and not from them personally. The most important thing of all is to be met according to one's own needs and on one's own terms. The greatest form of help for the bereaved is therefore to be permitted to 'be at work and use colleagues according to need'. Even though colleagues can know one another reasonably well, the needs of the individual can be difficult to discern, because the reactions following a traumatic death create difficult and unknown territory for all parties. As mentioned previously, the bereaved in the Support and Care project found that openness was the most important coping strategy in terms of mobilizing network support. By communicating their needs regarding how they wish to be approached, the bereaved also make their colleagues more secure and competent with regard to providing support. Feedback such as 'thank you for caring' can be an important means of eliciting or reinforcing the desired support from colleagues. A mother who lost her 19-year-old daughter by suicide says the following about the information she gave at her workplace: 'Openness means that people participate in my grief! I give them the chance to do so.'

If the bereaved individual is able to do so, we would recommend that upon their return to the workplace a meeting be arranged for (close) colleagues. Here the bereaved can, together with the manager, inform those present of the circumstances of the death and of how the bereaved wishes to be approached and how much the person in question wants to speak about the death at work. The scope and the bereaved person's role at the meeting can be adapted to what they manage and want.

How much the bereaved opens up to colleagues is often connected with the type of workplace and the relation the bereaved has had to colleagues and management before the death. Work in a small, family-based company can be extremely different from office work in a hectic, open-plan office. Regardless, it is often the attitude and the level of understanding among colleagues and management that determines how comfortable the bereaved feels about talking. In addition, some bereaved people will have an easier time opening up than others and the degree to which they feel a need to speak with colleagues about what has happened will vary. One should also respect the fact that some do not have a need or will not manage to speak about what has happened. In that case the best recourse, if the relationship is close enough, is to clarify this by offering one's support and asking whether the bereaved wishes to speak about what has happened.

Work or sick leave?

To grieve subsequent to having suffered a significant loss is a natural and healthy reaction. In such a perspective, extended or regular use of sick leave will be inexpedient. Sick leave requires a diagnosis and in the situations we are describing, a psychological diagnosis is often given. Such a psychological diagnosis puts a stamp of illness on the condition that is not real and which many find follows them for the rest of their lives. We also know that it is sensible to try to resume work again relatively quickly, in spite of the fact that many dread returning to the workplace after a sudden death. Through a quick return one spends less time in isolation with one's own thoughts, while there is at the same time the possibility for support from colleagues.

Our research shows that very many people are for a period away from working life after a sudden death. This can take different forms and be for different lengths of time. While some are away from working life during the week of the funeral, many will have a need for a bit more time or repeated breaks from work. Some are put on full- or part-time sick leave while others are on active sick leave or have compassionate leave. There is no uniform practice in working life following sudden deaths; whether or not management understands and implements measures in response to the life crisis appears to be quite random. While some bereaved people are seen and attended to in relation to their needs, others are expected to show up fit-for-fight a couple of days after the funeral.

When weighing the pros and cons of work vs. sick leave, the objective must be to find a balance between taking into consideration the individual's need for a time out in the crisis, while simultaneously encouraging the quickest possible return to working life. The workplace must accept and make the necessary arrangements for the fact that the bereaved does not have full working capacity when they return to work, although they may try to conceal at work that their days are a strain. With the need for a time out, the form of absenteeism must be adapted and discussed with the individual in order to take into consideration his or her unique situation. We will address in further detail how the different kinds of leave schemes can have benefits and advantages for the crisis-stricken.

Absenteeism and the return to the workplace

Active sick leave gives the bereaved the opportunity to take advantage of the resources that being at a workplace entails and to receive support and care, while at the same time the working capacity of the individual is taken into consideration. The distraction which the work entails can also help prevent destructive brooding and complicated grief reactions. As one bereaved person put it: 'There is after all a lot more to dispel one's thoughts at the workplace than when one is just sitting at home.' For some men, whose social network to a larger extent than women is connected with the workplace, active sick leave will ensure important contact with the network. At the same time the flexibility of this form of sick leave allows the possibility for contact with the loss, the grief and the crisis, taking into consideration mood swings and the need for time out. For some bereaved people an active sick leave must function in a highly flexible fashion if it is to be utilized. Some can be so unstable in periods that they from time to time must leave work in the middle of a workday. It is difficult to know in advance whether or not one will manage a full workday and something can suddenly trigger a flood of despair, loss and grief causing the individual to break down.

Practical arrangements with regard to active sick leave can also be important in terms of this form functioning well. Colleagues can help with reducing the work pressure and volume of work tasks or by taking over some of these. One need not be afraid that the bereaved will take advantage of this. What they usually want most of all is to be able to be at work as they were before, but this is very difficult and can take a long time. If some work tasks prove to be impossible to carry out, it can be important to replace these with others, so as to avoid full-time sick leave. Such tasks can be connected with something that awakens intense memories of the deceased, triggering flashbacks from the moment when one found the deceased, or work with children, if one personally has lost a child, etc. Redefining the contents of the workday is another approach to accommodations at the workplace. By including a long commute to work in working hours, one can reduce the length of the workday so that the bereaved can manage it without a more extensive sick leave.

But even a flexible, active sick leave will not be exclusively positive for everyone. Sometimes the type of work combined with the personality of those bereaved by a traumatic death will entail that it is advantageous to find other types of relief from working life. If one has a job that is extremely dependent on the individual in question, making it difficult for others to take over, a conscientious employee can easily push him/herself to overwork. The demarcation of one's own needs in relation others can be full of conflict, and if the bereaved too frequently set aside their own needs, they can suddenly 'hit the wall'. In such cases it can be easier to be completely away from the workplace in order to spare oneself, or others, the extra pressure.

Part- or full-time sick leave is therefore expedient for some people and/or for some types of jobs. Some bereaved people simply have no business being at work because they are so beside themselves that it can constitute a risk for themselves or others. Problems concentrating, sleep deprivation and lack of energy can make precision-demanding work tasks impossible for a period of time, so that the most reasonable solution is to be removed from the job or given other work tasks for a while. Examples of such demanding work tasks can be the handling of machinery, therapeutic treatment of other people, responsibility for young children, etc. An evaluation of full-time sick leave should always be balanced against knowledge of an intensified focus on other tasks that can offer a helpful 'time out', and which in turn contributes to helping the crisis-stricken to move on with their life.

Compassionate leave is another form of workload reduction that some workplaces offer their employees subsequent to a traumatic death. For some bereaved people this can be a beneficial offer in that it sends other signals than that one is sick – one is on leave to take care of one's personal welfare. In principle, one is not sick but the serious life crisis and pursuant strong reactions can result in a need for quiet and relief from the responsibilities of daily life so that one has the chance to recuperate one's forces.

When it is a matter of a need for absence from the workplace, care and attendance on the part of supervisors can be signalled in many ways. 'You can be away for as long as you need' and 'take all the time you need' are messages from supervisors that are greatly appreciated by the bereaved. This is emphasized over and over again by the bereaved in the Support and Care study. Through such statements, understanding for the extreme situation is indicated, along with acceptance for the individual experience, and care and support for the employee by the workplace. Such a point of departure need not imply that all bereaved people have a need for full sick leave or take advantage of this, but it puts them in a position where they are much freer to do what is best for them, in collaboration with the workplace. While it is accepted that most need understanding for their somewhat reduced work capacity during the initial period after the death, it is important that the employer also has an awareness of the fact that many bereaved people can be quite out of sorts and need a day or two away from work in connection with red-letter days, such as the deceased's birthday or the day of their death. For many this will be the case on the red-letter days of the first subsequent year, but one should also keep in mind that difficulties with such days can also arise at a later point in time.

One sees now and then that those who use work to cope with grief can be setting themselves up for an ugly fall somewhere down the line, while others use the job situation to create good patterns on the way back to a good life. Supervisors can be attentive to bereaved people who are overly productive and who should perhaps be reigned in. While some need offers of flexible working arrangements or contact with the company health service for special difficulties, others will only need encouragement and ordinary compassion. For many, it is easier to be at work and possibly on an active sick leave, in a supportive environment that sees and makes the necessary accommodations for the crisis-stricken, than just to sit and stare at the four walls of their living room. For some, simply reduced expectations with regard to work performance will be sufficient support. Other bereaved people can have a need for a gentle push in order to get started again, in that serious life crises can also drain away self-confidence and the faith that life can go on. A female public health service employee says:

> I believed that I would never work again. But in May one of my colleagues called and said: 'Now we are in such a pinch, can't you come in and help us out, even if it is only for two to three hours?' I said, 'Sure, I will come.' And it was fine. But if it had been up to me to decide when I felt ready, I am not

sure whether I would have begun. So they tricked me, in a way. They have confirmed that they did it on purpose. But it just shows how thoughtful they are. They were extremely aware of the importance of my returning to work.

After a period on sick leave, it can be particularly helpful if someone from the workplace makes contact and asks how the bereaved person wishes to be greeted when he or she returns. This can be done in consultation with the personnel department or immediate superior, so that colleagues can be informed of how the bereaved wishes to be greeted. Contact during a sick leave period shows that the workplace cares, increases the motivation to return to work and can also contribute to making the return easier. Clear supportive words stating 'we will be there for you', 'you will resume work again at your own pace' and 'we hope you will be back soon' warm the heart and facilitate the return. Many bereaved people find that confronting the workplace as soon as possible serves to lance the boil, as it were, while others will need more time. Returning to work does not mean, however, full working capacity and many struggle for a long time with a lack of initiative, little joy in their work and reduced motivation for work. It is a myth that some cultivate their grief, but the bereaved differ greatly in terms of the amount of time they need before they can manage to find any joy in their work. Managers and colleagues should therefore have a dialogue with the bereaved to clarify when they can again begin imposing 'production' requirements.

It is of extremely great importance that the workplace understands that the fluctuations in working capacity can last for a very long period of time, in fact long after the first year following the death. There are also great differences here, such as between men who often use the job and activity as an aid in their grief and women who struggle more with unwanted thoughts throughout much of the workday. Most bereaved people want to get back to work as soon as they can, because they personally experience this as the most important step back to a 'normal' daily life and if there is one thing the crisis-stricken wants, it is precisely to return to normality and ordinary life. It is therefore important that the supervisor and the bereaved together find out when it is right to apply pressure carefully and when one must take time outs. Nobody is served by the bereaved later saying, as did a father in the Support and Care study: 'I can't even remember that I was at work.'

Guidelines and plans for psychosocial follow-up
Some workplaces have thought through and created plans for psychosocial care of employees that experience crises and disasters at and outside of the

workplace. While some connect the guidelines to the existing company health service, others allow the routines to function in tandem. Others, particularly large workplaces, also have a colleague support scheme. Here the responsibility for care is connected to specific colleagues who are also responsible for mobilizing employees at the workplace. Colleagues who have experienced similar type deaths can potentially serve as a unique resource in such a system. In the work of formulating, evaluating and revising routines for psychosocial follow-up after a sudden death and other crises, the bereaved and crisis-stricken will in the long-term also comprise an important resource.

An enhanced focus and increased knowledge about grief and how grief affects a person physically and psychologically, along with the development of guidelines and written routines for the workplace with respect to deaths and other experiences of bereavement, will lead to improved psychosocial health on the part of the bereaved. This will in turn influence the level of well-being and the performance of a grief-stricken employee. But written routines for psychosocial follow-up at the workplace are not enough. In order for such initiatives to work, the human factor must also be included in the manner of sincere interest and care for the bereaved – both from management and colleagues. On the other hand, the crisis and the psychosocial strain can be intensified by avoidance, weakness and insufficient understanding and accommodation, which can create a large additional burden in the working situation.

With good crisis leadership, employees feel taken care of and it provides a sense of personal security that oneself or one's family will be taken care of if something should happen (Dyregrov, 2000). In addition to the fact that the bereaved will receive help to return to work more quickly, a caring environment will have a positive effect on the other employees, who can also be hard hit by their colleague's personal crisis, while at the same time everyone experiences a safer, more compassionate workplace (Nordanger *et al.*, 2000). It is important that local governments acquire an overview of the type of psychosocial care that is provided by the crisis-stricken person's workplace (possibly also from the company health service), so that one can collaborate on assistance measures and overlapping can be avoided. For a number of bereaved people the workplace represents the most important and sometimes the only place where they are taken care of. The bereaved have no doubts about the fact that adequate care on the part of the workplace saves society money, spares them from having to take medication and from long-term sick leave, and colleagues from increased work pressure during their sickness absence.

Main themes
The school
OBJECTIVES

- Give the bereaved child/young person individual attention and individual consideration.
- Organize network support for the bereaved child/young person.
- Where appropriate, create good frames for a collective processing of the incident.

RELEVANT SUPPORT MEASURES

- lowering the flag, memorial service (in some cases also viewing), possibly attendance of the funeral
- home visits, drawings, greetings to the home
- information to the class/school and between home and school
- flexible and adapted measures (exams, marks, attendance)
- empathy, thoughtfulness and care in the school day
- accommodation measures for social support from fellow pupils
- discussions of the themes of grief, loss, crisis reactions, etc.
- commemoration of red-letter days (e.g. on holidays: flowers on the grave, visits to the parents).

THE MEASURES PAVE THE WAY FOR:

- open and direct information to the bereaved person's fellow pupils about what has happened
- the opportunity for fellow pupils to ask questions, express their own reactions and empathy in relation to the bereaved (drawings, flowers, participation in the funeral (possibly a viewing) in collaboration with the family of the bereaved)
- an opportunity for the bereaved to speak about and process what has happened
- an opportunity to resume schooling as soon as possible
- accommodation measures to help overcome learning and concentration problems
- empathy and support that the young bereaved person can accept and needs.

The workplace

OBJECTIVES

- Find a balance between showing consideration for the individual's need for a break from work and at the same time motivate for the quickest possible return to working life.
- Focus on, adapt and accommodate the working situation for the bereaved employee.
- Take care of colleagues in relation to the event.
- Create good frames for a collective processing of what has happened.
- Possibly create the opportunity for colleagues to talk through the issue.

RELEVANT SUPPORT MEASURES

- lowering the flag, memorial service, possibly funeral attendance
- visits and greetings to the home
- colleagues' empathy, understanding, willingness to talk and openness in connection with the death
- discussion of the themes of grief, loss, crisis reactions
- implement colleague support schemes, company health service
- evaluate the need for sick leave and flexible and adapted work programmes.

THE MEASURES PAVE THE WAY FOR:

- open and direct information to colleagues about what has happened
- the opportunity for colleagues to ask questions, express their own reactions and empathy in relation to the bereaved (flowers, funeral attendance (possibly the viewing) in collaboration with the family of the bereaved)
- an opportunity for the bereaved to speak about and process what has happened
- an opportunity to resume work as soon as possible
- an adaptation of the work situation to enable functioning throughout the workday
- the use of colleague support schemes, company health service, etc. in a family perspective.

10

When should professional help be brought in?

Even with the best possible support from a network, the strongest human being or the most well-functioning family can be confronted with so many complex issues that professional help proves necessary. In this chapter we will address in further detail a number of factors that can be indications that more help should be brought in. Before we give any concrete advice, we will describe some factors that can help determine who will experience particular difficulties after a sudden death.

Grief: important contributing factors

Many different factors contribute to influencing reactions in the short- and long-term. Many of the factors mentioned in the following can have different ramifications in different periods during the time following the death. Because the interplay between the various factors is complex and the reactions vary both in type and intensity over time, no advice can ever be wholly precise. A friend or family member in a support position should rely on common sense combined with the information presented in this chapter to determine whether or not one should advise the bereaved to seek professional help.

Among the factors that influence the subsequent development are:

- Situational factors

  - How did the death occur? What was the degree of drama?

  - Were family members present when the death occurred? Were they subjected to powerful sense impressions?

- ○ Was it a sudden or expected death (murder, accident, suicide, illness)? Was the death precipitated by a long-term period of illness?

- ○ Was there time for preparation before the death?

- ○ Ritual design and participation – was a peaceful parting possible?

- ○ Did the bereaved receive adequate information about what happened? Was the chain of events or the background for the death clarified?

- Factors pertaining to and the relation to the deceased

  - ○ How old was the deceased when he/she died?

  - ○ What was the nature of the relation to the deceased? Was the bereaved closely attached to or dependent upon the deceased?

- Factors about the bereaved individual and family matters

  - ○ Family members' individual histories (e.g. previous losses, psychological problems, coping strategies) and couple/family history

  - ○ Gender

  - ○ Openness and directness of communication

  - ○ Other family dynamic patterns (secrecy, stability, conflict, etc.)

- Support and reactions from the surroundings

  - ○ Support from family and friends

  - ○ Support from professionals

  - ○ Support from the workplace

  - ○ Support from bereavement support groups or peers.

The fact that so many factors must be taken into consideration provides an indication of the complex range of reactions that individuals and families can exhibit in the aftermath of a death.

Risk and protection factors

As stated earlier, sudden death can trigger both loss and trauma reactions. To a large extent, the same factors will comprise both the risk of, and a protection from, the development of problems following situations of loss and trauma. We will therefore not distinguish between these factors in the following. There are a number of factors in connection with both the death itself and the bereaved as individuals that can represent a risk entailing that some bereaved people will struggle more than others. Those who have been subjected to powerful sense impressions in connection with the death can more easily develop complicated grief reactions that are posttraumatic in nature. This can also be the case if the death is wrapped up in speculation and rumours or if the bereaved was the one to find the deceased, witnessed a lot of bloodshed, experienced strong unpleasant odours, unpleasant sounds or other powerful sense impressions. A lack of preparation for the death is also a risk factor with regard to the development of complicated grief. In many cases a lack of preparation is combined with a death that is dramatic.

Women appear to have a greater tendency to develop problems than men (Breslau *et al.*, 1997; Stroebe, 1998). Further, previous traumas or losses will potentially increase vulnerability in relation to new losses, particularly if previous losses were not handled in an expedient manner. Those who have previously suffered from psychological disorders, or have few resources for coping with stress, are usually also among the most vulnerable. Nonetheless, it must be said that in a comprehensive study of risk factors in connection with traumas, Brewin, Andrews and Valentine (2000) found that factors stemming from the time previous to the trauma had less effect on the development of problems in the long-term than did factors that arose during or after the trauma. Included in the latter are the severity of the trauma, lack of social support and other additional stress factors.

Those who have experienced extensive support from, and intimacy and dependence in relation to the deceased, will often struggle more than others. In recent years a better understanding has emerged of the significance of having developed what is referred to as a secure attachment to one's caregivers in childhood. Children who grow up in homes where there is a lot of instability, violence, or with parents who for various reasons are not sensitive to the children's psychological and physical needs, are at risk of developing what is called an insecure attachment. Those who have such a history of insecure attachment are particularly vulnerable when they later lose close family members (Stroebe, Schut and Stroebe, 2005). When people with this type of attachment history prove to be more vulnerable in subsequent situations of loss, this is presumed to reflect both the fact that previous losses can be activated and also that such people have an extremely strong attachment to those who become stable individuals in their immediate surroundings.

When a bereaved person does not succeed in integrating a traumatic event into their personal system of meaning and struggles to reach an understanding of what has happened, complications can easily develop in grief. The psychologist Robert Neimeyer has put a particular focus on the illumination of such factors, and indicated the significance of the reconstruction of meaning and use of narratives in work with helping the bereaved (Neimeyer, Baldwin and Gillies, 2006).

If the family's climate of communication is not open and important information is not shared with family members, this can increase the chance of problems, particularly in the long-term. This is the case when children are not well informed and family secrets are created, about which only a select few are allowed knowledge. The establishment of family secrets is not uncommon after a dramatic death, where important information can be held back to spare the children. Good follow-up from the public health system after the death can be an important source of help, with an eye towards enabling the family to cope adequately over time. This will be the case if the family encounters role models here that are capable of speaking openly about difficult things and who hereby give the family members, including the children, the possibility to speak about what has happened and the altered situation within the family (Dyregrov, A., 2001). Family and friends can make a positive contribution if they point out to the parents that they should not seek to conceal important matters from their children and help the parents to speak openly and directly about that which has happened.

Last but not least, one knows that little support or the absence of support in social networks implies a risk of more problems after the death. This need not be due to the fact that the network does not wish to provide support, but, for example, can be because the family has just relocated, making it more difficult to mobilize network resources from the previous place of residence, while a new network has not yet been built up in the family's new home.

There are also good protective factors that strengthen the possibilities for a healthy grief process. First and foremost, one ought to have avoided most of the above-mentioned risk factors. Beyond this, research has shown that a person's social resources, such as support from family and friends, and support in the work situation from superiors and colleagues, are all positive factors (cf. previous chapters). Some also find help in their religious affiliation or in community organizations that provide support. People who are extroverted and optimistic will often manage better than those who are less sociable by nature. The former find it easier to activate their social networks and through their optimism they also produce a more positive atmosphere in their surroundings.

Previously in this section we have indicated some family circumstances that would entail an increased risk of problems in the grief process. A logical consequence of this is that those families that are able to speak openly and directly about what has happened and about the consequences of the death usually cope with the death better as a family unit. When communication is direct, family members can open up to one another, and when time is set aside, providing an opportunity for the creation of understanding with regard to how individual family members are doing, everyday life is experienced as more simple. In families with children it is important that children experience a safe environment with space for their questions, thoughts and feelings. A so-called inquisitive or elaborative style, involving conversations over time about the deceased, enables better coping than when such conversations are not permitted. The chances for good individual coping are also improved when a single individual in the family does not have hegemony or otherwise dominate the narrative (Bohanek *et al.*, 2006; Harley and Reese, 1999).

For many years the common belief was that those who held on to the deceased, keeping them close at hand in their thoughts and behaviour after a death and who did not loosen the ties with the deceased to reinvest these in others, would struggle over time. However, more recent knowledge about grief now shows that it is in fact helpful to be able to maintain an inner connection with the deceased (inner representation) (Field, Gao and Paderna, 2006). Using the deceased as an inner helper or guide, with whom one can speak or ask for strength, can have a positive effect for the bereaved. At the same time, clinging to a lost relationship or being so obsessed with the deceased that it obstructs the ability to function on a daily basis will be more of an indication of complicated grief than of a natural connection to the deceased.

Complicated grief reactions

In Chapter 2 we touched upon complicated grief reactions. In this chapter, complicated grief reactions are described in further detail in order to enable the network and other assistance workers to assess to a certain extent whether or not the bereaved should receive a referral for professional follow-up by a doctor and/or psychologist.

How many experience complicated grief?

In Great Britain more than 500,000 people die each year. Some 10 to 20 per cent of all those who lose a loved one, regardless of their age and the type of death, develop complicated grief reactions like the types described below. If one estimates that for each person who dies, there are on average six close bereaved people, this will correspond with approximately 300,000 people. As mentioned earlier, some types of death pose a greater risk of complicated grief reactions. This is particularly the case for sudden, dramatic deaths that occur at a point in time in the life of the individual where it could not have been foreseen, while such reactions are less common for grief following death by natural causes at a 'normal' age. In addition to complicated grief reactions, people can develop other psychological problems (depression, anxiety, etc.). In sum, this means that there are many who suffer extreme difficulties following a sudden, unexpected death, where professional help at an early stage can be important. In the following we will distinguish between various forms of complicated grief.

Complicated grief: with a core of separation distress

Within the context of international grief research, work is being done to develop a new grief diagnosis: prolonged grief disorder, where separation distress holds a central position. This diagnosis is predominantly connected with a strong sense of loss and longing, of an intensity and duration beyond that which would characterize normal grief reactions. The person who has lost a loved one suffers on a daily basis with various separation distress symptoms, such as an intense sense of longing and yearning, avoidance of reminders of the deceased, numbness, difficulties reconciling themselves with what has happened, bitterness, difficulties trusting others, emptiness and meaninglessness in life and feelings that a part of oneself has died. These disturbances are to have been persistent for at least six months, and constitute an impairment to daily functions. Fixed criteria are established to determine whether or not one qualifies for such a diagnosis, but it is simultaneously clear that many can benefit from professional follow-up even though they may not satisfy all the stipulated requirements for the diagnosis of prolonged grief disorder.

It is this complicated variety of grief that is sometimes referred to as heartache or chronic grief. It entails a psychological protest against reality, is characterized by an intense longing and sense of loss, informed with the desire to preserve the world as it was. People with such complicated grief will often be bitter and pessimistic about the future and have difficulties forming social relations and carrying out daily activities.

Posttraumatic stress disorder

The other variety of complicated grief is connected with traumatic death. Here it is the situational factors or drama in connection with having been a witness to, or intrusive images in connection with, the death that trigger specific long-term reactions. In recent years the traumatic aspects of unexpected and violent death have received a lot of attention because they can lead to that which is referred to in the field as posttraumatic stress disorder, or PTSD (Amaya-Jackson *et al.*, 1999; Figley, Bride and Mazza, 1997; Murphy *et al.*, 1999; Murphy *et al.*, 2002; Stewart, 1999; Winje, 1997).

Beyond having been a witness to or having been confronted with an event or events that involved death, the threat of an imminent death or serious injury, or which otherwise threatened to one's own or others' physical safety, the situation triggers feelings of fear, helplessness or terror. There are three groups of symptoms specific to this disorder: 1) intrusive memories, thoughts or experiences in connection with the event; recurring and distressing dreams about the event; that one acts or feels as if the traumatic event is recurring; intense psychological distress when one is exposed to events that symbolize or resemble an aspect of the event; 2) persistent avoidance of anything that is associated with the event or emotional numbing as a means of avoiding thoughts, feelings or conversations associated with the event; avoidance of activities, places or people that arouse recollections about the event; difficulties remembering what happened; a marked diminished interest in significant activities, such as holiday or leisure pursuits; feelings of detachment or estrangement from others; restricted range of effect; sense of foreshortened future; 3) persistent symptoms of increased arousal, manifested through difficulties falling or remaining asleep; irritability or outbursts of anger; difficulties concentrating, hyper-vigilance (always on guard); exaggerated startle response (strong reaction to anything new); physiological reactivity with exposure to events that resemble an aspect of the traumatic event. In order to fulfil the diagnosis of PTSD, one of the symptoms from the first group, three from the second and two from the third are required. The symptoms are to have lasted for a month and as for the first grief variant, the ailments shall result in a reduction in the ability to carry out ordinary daily functions.

Some bereaved, particularly those who were involved in finding the deceased, or who were subjected to powerful impressions in connection with the death, can experience 'intrusive flashbacks', where visual and auditory memories or other sense impression continue to enter their consciousness long after the event has occurred. Others can experience difficulties concentrating or difficulties sleeping or they have nightmares. For very many people, these types of trauma reactions lead to exhaustion and lethargy. Research has shown that 50 to 60 per cent of those whose bereavement is caused by murder, suicide or accidents develop posttraumatic reactions on a scale that entails the risk of developing PTSD (Brent *et al.*, 1993; Dyregrov *et al.*, 2003; Joseph and Williams, 2005; Murphy *et al.*, 2002; Winje, 1997). Although it is most common for such trauma reactions to subside on their own, some bereaved people continue to struggle with them over time. For these individuals, social network support is important, but not sufficient. The network will potentially provide important assistance if they help put the bereaved in contact with professionals, something many bereaved people cannot manage to do personally, because their grief has weakened their initiative. With help from psychologists or other therapists, the troublesome reactions can be alleviated through good treatment methods.

A number of bereaved people do not have the strength to approach any positive memories in connection with the death, because the memories or images of the traumatic nature of the death arise each time they begin to approach the positive memories. Our own and others' experience has been that it is first necessary to help the bereaved to mitigate the posttraumatic reactions in order for them to move on in their grief process. We have in another context described different aspects of the treatment of such complicated grief (Dyregrov, A., 2006a) and came to the following conclusion (p. 785):

> Our increased knowledge about grief and grief therapy makes better professional help possible for those who struggle to an unnecessary extent after a death. For those suffering with complicated grief reactions, it is now, dependent upon the specific nature of their difficulties, possible to tailor-design a programme that will help them live with the loss in a way that to a lesser extent diminishes their quality of life.

Complicated grief: abbreviated or postponed variant
In those cases where the bereaved stops grieving prematurely and focuses on moving on in their life, this represents a less common variant of complicated grief. It is easy to believe that all those who appear to be coping well and who do not display any reactions are suffering from this response, but that need not be the case. There are both adults and children who never have serious grief reactions, neither immediately following the death nor down the road, and who virtually shake off the event, and concentrate on everyday life without developing any subsequent problems. Such individuals can have a more difficult time if they start in therapy and here the network should simply support their good coping mechanisms. Recent research indicates that

approximately 20 per cent experience grief in this way, even following that which is commonly viewed as an extremely painful death, such as the loss of a child (Wortman and Silver, 2001).

On the other hand, there are those who push aside all of their reactions and resume daily activities without their having had much contact with feelings in connection with their loss. These must either invest a large amount of energy in keeping what has happened at bay, or they find that they are debilitated in their daily functions or schooling. It is not easy to distinguish between those who have pushed grief aside and those who manage well due to good coping skills. It is in fact their daily ability to function in their free time, at home and on the job/at school that must be used as a sign indicating how well in fact they are managing.

It is in particular with regard to young people that it can be difficult to know when it is advisable for them to seek help. It is not unusual to see them push away their grief in connection with the loss of parents and siblings and in periods manage to function at home and in school in a normal fashion. Some tolerate very little or no talk whatsoever about what has happened, while others can speak about what has happened but do not allow themselves to feel their sense of loss and longing. Usually it is not possible to carry out any form of therapy in such cases and it is only when the individual ceases to function in everyday life or when their school performance suffers that they can be motivated to accept more assistance. Good advice to the network would be not to pressure the young person into contact with a psychologist or others before they are personally motivated or it is clear that their ability to function on a daily basis is coming undone. Sometimes we must unfortunately accept that they perhaps will not want to accept help until after a long period of time has passed, in some case not for a number of years.

Complicated grief: family problems

The problems that have been described up to this point have been related to individuals. Sometimes professional help is necessary due to family problems. As a rule this bears a connection to a lack of communication between the parties involved, in particular after the loss of a child. We have previously pointed out that it is a myth that parents who lose a child separate or divorce more frequently than is the case for other parents, and that to the contrary, most in fact grow closer after having experienced such a loss. Nonetheless, there is also a relatively large number who struggle in their interactions.

There can be a number of reasons why bereaved parents struggle in their interactions after having lost a child. A common combination of factors is that the two parties react differently, with reactions of different intensity and duration, and simultaneously do not succeed in speaking about what has happened and the resulting reactions. It is a well-known fact, confirmed by studies, that men speak less about their feelings than women (Goldschmidt and Weller, 2000; Samuelsson, Rådestad and Segesten, 2001), and a good qualitative study (Cook, 1988) has also shown that the way men handle their feelings after the loss of a child differs from women. Men block out the thoughts of what has happened by thinking about something else, often practical, concrete activities (distraction) when unpleasant memories or emotions arise. They can also think about the loss systematically, approaching it in a rational manner. When they do address painful issues, this frequently occurs in solitude or through non-verbal expressions (Cook, 1988).

After a child's death, it is usually the case that women claim that they must take the initiative to speak and that they have the greatest need to speak. It is therefore important for their male partner to meet them halfway and at least have an understanding of their needs, even if they do not always manage to say very much. If women experience respect and support for their needs, this in itself contributes to a positive experience of the relationship. When this does not take place, the relationship becomes silent and empty. In those cases where parents experience that their relationship is debilitated, what is stressed is that this is precisely due to a lack of understanding, communication and caring along with differences in grief reactions. Networks that witness that parents, and thereby often the entire family, are struggling can tactfully suggest that they seek a kind of help that can assist in their taking care of the relationship and the family. This could be, as an example, a best friend who speaks with a mother and proposes exploring the type of assistance resources available, and subsequently reports her findings to the mother.

Among other family problems that can develop is a poor interaction between the generations where parents hold back information from their children or misinform them. An example of this would be if adults tell a child that a suicide was in fact a death due to cardiac arrest, or in other ways create the basis for family secrets, which can later divide the family. Sometimes it is clear that only one of the family members' versions of what took place at the time of death is given credence, while the stories or perceptions of others are discredited. Regardless of the background of the situation, other family members and friends can understand that the couple or family is struggling with negative or destructive processes and can be in need of help towards learning how to improve communication. It cannot be expected that the network can or should take responsibility for clearing up such problems directly, but they can contribute to motivating the bereaved to seek help before the problems solidify into fixed patterns.

Normal versus complicated grief

The description of the different complicated grief reactions in this chapter may have been a bit theoretical for some. Perhaps it will be easier if we provide a list of what normal grief does not entail. It is not normal grief if:

- intrusive memories or delusions stemming from the death continue to disturb the bereaved
- the bereaved continuously blames him/herself for what he/she could have done, thought or said or refrained from doing, thinking or saying
- the bereaved has a strong sense of their own worthlessness
- the fear of another 'disaster' is strong and persistent
- the bereaved is not able to function at work or in their free time, cannot speak about the deceased at all or must avoid everything that reminds them of the deceased or the death
- the bereaved continues to brood and think about the death without room for other thoughts
- bitterness, anger or other vengeful thoughts continue with undiminished intensity
- all talk about what has happened or about the deceased has ceased within the family
- after a child's death the parents are overly preoccupied with the deceased and to such an extent that they do not manage to see the surviving children.

If such signs are observed there is every reason to believe that the person one is trying to support needs professional help.

Some simple advice regarding when professional help should be brought in

Grief, feelings of loss and longing are common but some bereaved people struggle with intense flashbacks, self-reproach, anxiety and other reactions indicating the necessity of additional help. If friends and family members observe that the bereaved is struggling and know that they are not receiving any help from the public health service, it can be important to motivate them to find such help, or with their consent, make the necessary arrangements so that they can receive such help. There can be cause to seek help when:

- reactions do not pass but continue with undiminished intensity
- the bereaved does not function at work, school or in their free time
- the bereaved isolates him/herself from the surroundings
- the family struggles with the allocation of roles, internal conflicts or other 'family landmines'
- one notices other danger signals (increased alcohol consumption or abuse of medication)
- the grief continues beyond the period of the initial months without change, no grieving is evident, or other signs of complicated grief
- parents are in need of advice with regard to handling the situations of children and/or young people
- the interaction with the social network has reached a 'deadlock'; the bereaved pull away completely from other people or they need help managing 'social ineptitude' in their surroundings.

One should remember that the bereaved can have different reasons for not wanting help from their social network or from professionals. This can be because they lack the energy, resources or initiative, or because they do not believe that others will understand the situation. They can also have a lack of confidence in the ability of others to help them; they may not want to bother others or they may have had such a negative encounter with the public healthcare system that their anger or distrust inhibits contact. Sometimes disappointment over promises that were not kept results in their not wanting any more help. In such a case, family and friends can gently motivate them to seek help, despite the scepticism the bereaved may be feeling.

What type of help can one receive from professionals?

Because sudden death results in long-term afflictions for so many people, we would recommend bringing in professional help early and automatically for dramatic deaths such as accidents, suicide and murder. While in the case of illness there is often a scheduled, systematic contact with the public healthcare system, which also enables the opportunity for an evaluation of the need for follow-up after a death, this is less often the case with a sudden death. Parents who lose children are also in a unique position because as a rule this leads to extensive problems afterwards. Here professional help should go hand-in-hand with the help provided by the network. The emergency assistance, so-called psychological first aid, is provided either at a hospital, by paramedics, a clergyman or a local crisis team that is mobilized for the family. With this type of emergency help there are two factors that are extremely important: a) to obtain information about what has happened, b) to ensure that the information is passed on and that the bereaved (family) is taken care of in a compassionate manner.

Help in the critical phase

Already in the course of the first days following the death it can be appropriate to give the bereaved more information so that they can make the right decisions, such as about bringing children along to the viewing and the funeral, how one should speak to the children, the use of sleeping pills, sick leave, etc. Further, at an early point in time information about the following will be beneficial:

- common emotional, cognitive and behavioural reactions after a loss
- differences in reactions within the family (family dynamic) and possible gender and age differences
- children's reactions
- coping advice with regard to traumatic flashbacks, insomnia, etc.
- reactions and different progressions over time and preparation for the passing of anniversaries and red-letter days
- anticipated social network reactions
- preparations for rituals, return to the scene of the event, accident or hospital ward
- offers of public assistance, economic support schemes and legal help, bereavement support groups and support organizations such as the Foundation for the Study of Infant Death (FSED), Stillbirth and Neonatal Death Support (SANDS), Roadpeace, and Cruse.

In the context of early help, it is important that help routines are made systematic and that they function. On the basis of the knowledge available about grief and crises, existing local government routines for emergency help and parents' experiences following a death, we have systematically organized the elements that should be included in good routines for taking care of the bereaved by sudden death (Dyregrov et al., 2000a; Dyregrov et al., 2002; Dyregrov and Dyregrov, 2005a; Nordanger, Dyregrov and Dyregrov, 2003).

Professional help for adults

While emergency care should be given to everyone, the need for more specific help will imply contact with psychologists and others who can provide help in relation to the complicated grief reactions described above. We will describe some of the ways in which the bereaved can be helped by psychologists or other healthcare personnel with therapeutic experience, in order to enable the network (and the bereaved) to understand better what professionals can contribute.

Help for complicated grief with separation distress

When someone is overly preoccupied with the deceased, exhibits an intense sense of loss or longing and this reaction has continued with an undiminished intensity for many months, it is important to investigate what can be done to alleviate the grief reaction. An important part of the treatment then entails speaking about the significance of the deceased in the life of the bereaved and creating some perspective with regard to what has happened, preferably parallel to a discussion and exploration of the individual's attachment history. The bereaved is asked to begin delimiting the amount of time he or she spends on thoughts and memories of the deceased. This can be done by setting aside a specific period of time each day, for example a half hour or an hour, for thinking and/or writing about the deceased. For some this is combined with their being encouraged to clear away clothing and personal objects, putting them aside in a specific place in the home, disciplining themselves to spend less time at the burial site, etc. In order to help reduce the amount of time spent on thoughts and activities connected with the deceased, they learn different methods that allow greater control over their thought processes, such as thought stopping methods, distraction methods, different sleep inducement methods, etc.

The 'reconstruction of meaning' approach to the bereaved emphasizes grief as an active process, where the bereaved is deemed capable of choosing whether they would prefer to focus on the loss (and grief work) or on the reinstatement of their life, through a practical focus instead on those things that are necessary in terms of their resuming their professional activity and social life (Stroebe and Schut, 1999). Both aspects are normally required in mastering life after a loss. The narrative tradition emphasizes how we create and reconstruct our experience and thereby can reconstruct the loss in ways that will enable us to live better after the fact. Neimeyer (1999, 2000) had the bereaved spend time creating meaning by having them write prologues and keep diaries about how the deceased influenced them while they were alive, etc.

Some of those who experience this type of chronic grief benefit from so-called therapeutic rituals. Especially following a sudden death that has precluded the possibility for a proper farewell, ritual acts can provide an opportunity to say good-bye after the fact. The rituals can be designed differently, and can be anything from writing a letter to the deceased, which one symbolically burns at their graveside, to planting a tree or other type of ritual act commemorating the importance of the deceased and which simultaneously can be used as an important site for subsequent rituals. The rituals can also entail writing a book of memories, creating a website, etc. Another variant used to help is to 'visit' the deceased at the moment of their passing. 'Imagine that you are there now, what would you say?' Such activities enable the closure of processes that have not yet received a proper conclusion.

Different forms of writing activity can play an important part in the processing of complicated grief reactions. Beyond writing down profound thoughts and feelings in connection with the loss, the bereaved can be asked to write about the significance that the person has had in their life, how the death has affected their development as a human being or way of being in the world, the positive and negative sides of the deceased, what they have learned, etc. Bereaved people can also be asked to imagine themselves ten years from now and to look back from there on to the present, in order to reflect about what they have learned. The purpose of such activities is to create reflection and a certain distance, in order to make movement possible when the bereaved appears to be locked into feelings of loss and longing. The loss is processed in delimited time periods during which the bereaved approaches what has happened, while they simultaneously receive advice and concrete methods for distancing themselves from their longing and sense of loss for the greater portion of the day.

Some bereaved people are asked to write down everything they did not have the opportunity to say to the deceased, perhaps because the death happened so quickly. This can be writing done individually, but the family can also be asked to collaborate in the formulation of the letter to the deceased with specific instructions about why it is important to listen to one another. In such letters or journals, the bereaved can be asked to write about:

- What has happened lately?
- What do I miss the most?
- What did XX mean to me?
- What am I angry or disappointed about (after suicide, death by overdose, etc.)?

- What will I always carry with me in terms of what XX has meant to me?

For many bereaved people who experience complicated grief connected with separation distress it is also important to resume ordinary activities, such as going back to work, resuming daily tasks and recreational pursuits, and in particular, to find the courage to take part in enjoyable social occasions. For some it is important to develop new routines and skills. For those who experience this type of grief, participation in bereavement support groups can in fact serve to perpetuate their feelings of loss and longing. It can therefore be important to encourage resumption of the social contacts they had before the death more than those connected with a common experience of being bereaved.

If there is intense self-reproach or guilt in connection with this type of grief, that which is known as cognitive methods can be used to counteract this. As a rule it is not actual guilt that is the cause of such feelings and with the help of specific questions and a systematic review of the knowledge the person had at specific points in time, they can receive help in deconstructing the emotional logic from within. Cognitive methods entail techniques for changing thoughts, feelings and behaviour, such as by practising the confrontation of situations which one otherwise would prefer to avoid, or learning to control undesired thoughts and feelings. Specific treatment methods, such as Eye Movement Desensitization and Reprocessing (EMDR) and cognitive behaviour therapy can also be used.

Help with posttraumatic stress disorder

For those struggling with complicated grief of the posttraumatic variant, posttraumatic therapy is used. The form this takes will depend upon that which is most profoundly disturbing for the bereaved. If it is a matter of intrusive flashbacks, there are some simple visualization techniques that can be tried as self-help techniques to help acquire control over disturbing memories. If these methods do not provide results, one must implement more extensive trauma-therapy methods. There are a number of effective treatment methods for posttraumatic problems (Bisson et al., 2007; Bradley et al., 2005). For avoidance reactions, reviewing the series of events, retrieval of factual information, conversations with or writing to the deceased and the confrontation of memories and situations that have been avoided are important elements of this type of therapy. Although acquiring control over intrusive memories or thoughts can diminish physical agitation, some must also learn methods to reduce this directly, which can simultaneously enable deeper sleep.

In recent years specific therapeutic methods have been developed for grief, methods which draw from cognitive behaviour therapy and exposure methods, such as 'Traumatic Grief Disorder Treatment' (Shear *et al.*, 2005). Grief therapy has progressed from being 'just' talking to a systematic use of a series of methods, the aim of which is to alleviate the problems with which the bereaved are struggling.

Different methods developed within exposure therapy and cognitive behaviour therapy will also be used. Here the bereaved individual is gradually exposed to the types of stimuli that are the most common traumatic triggers and thereby learns to control memories and thoughts. Thought stopping methods, distraction methods and writing methods can be used that focus on compulsive thoughts, etc. This type of grief can also be accompanied by intense feelings of guilt, where methods from cognitive therapy are particularly effective in alleviating guilt and hindsight, reducing cognitive errors and for counteracting self-reproach and brooding.

Help for complicated grief of the abbreviated or postponed variant

Many of the same methods mentioned above are also used for this type. The problem with regard to this grief variant is that it is difficult to come to a position where help can be offered because the bereaved has little sense of discomfort. With this group one must in fact wait until they are receptive to help, and with some young people this can imply waiting until they reach young adulthood. We have elsewhere (Dyregrov, K., 2006a) through a case study described the nature of the help provided when the grief of a young woman was put on hold after her mother's suicide. It was not until a year after the death that she wanted help. With this type of therapy different methods and techniques can be involved:

- relation building to strengthen the client's motivation for carrying out a series of unpleasant tasks
- psycho-pedagogical measures involving information about common grief reactions, what others have done to improve their state of mind, and what must be done in therapy in order to feel better
- exposure to memory-related materials, situations, conversations and places that are avoided
- work to counter guilt and shame so as to alleviate brooding and intrusive thoughts
- role-play to facilitate carrying out difficult activities (such as speaking about one's situation at the workplace or school)

- systematic desensitization (gradual approach), which moderates reactions to painful memory triggers
- use of self-help methods and use of trauma-focused treatment, including the EMDR method, to moderate traumatic memory material.

Among the bereaved suffering from abbreviated or postponed grief there are some who are afraid of what will happen if they should allow their feelings to surface. These individuals can be helped by reducing their fear of losing control. It is important to allow the necessary time, to take one thing at a time, to redefine the loss of control as a necessary expression of feelings and to show that although they release control just a bit, they can subsequently regain it anew. Often people struggling with abbreviated grief are asked to bring along items of an emotional significance (objects, pictures, albums, video films) to the sessions and to visit places of symbolic significance to help make the loss real and to enable them gradually to allow feelings that they have blocked off to surface. Homework can consist in allowing the bereaved to approach the loss for delimited time periods, or to begin in a bereavement support group. Also here the therapist adapts what is done to the situation of the bereaved.

Help for complicated grief with family problems

The range of problems specific to this area is broad and the methods used will take as a point of departure the issues in the couple or family relation that represent the greatest difficulties. Nadeau (1997) and others have given us terms that have helped us to grasp the complex family dynamic frequently initiated by a loss, terms that pave the way for family interventions which can help the family to evolve and heal over time. This includes terms that enable us to understand how information is distributed within the family and what takes place within the family interaction. Questions that provide insight to such matters are: 'How are facts and feelings distributed within the family? How rigid is the family and to what degree are different interpretations of the loss allowed? How flexible are they with regard to re-allocating roles? How strict are their behavioural codes? How is meaning attributed to what has happened? Who defines the story told about what has happened? Are some members cut off from others? How is the family's capacity for listening?'

When the reason for seeking help is poor family communication and togetherness, different family therapeutic approaches will be used. By making the discussion of communication, allocation of roles, emotional well-being and conflicts into a part of the conversations with the family, it is possible to work directly for the establishment of a good grief-management climate in the family. If a family member is overly preoccupied with their own grief situation, loses interest in the family and intimate activities or becomes increasingly angry and irritable, other family members can pull away from or become overly protective of this person. Open discussion about such topics can lead to more conscious choices about how this can be handled within the family. In family work after a death it is important to address information that is not distributed within the family, different wishes regarding the pace at which possessions are handled and cleared away, traumatic triggers, 'grief competition' and any lack of synchronicity in reactions. Through conversations, the sense of togetherness can be strengthened and new conflicts avoided. In family work it is important to create an open, sincere and inclusive kind of communication where children are involved, so that when they later return to the subject of the death at various phases in their childhood and youth they will have a good factual basis for their evolving understanding.

When parents lose a child and one or both parents experience complicated grief reactions or are overly preoccupied with the person they have lost, it is important to help them to return as soon as possible to being able to be good caregivers for their surviving children. The assistance will then comprise helping the parents to process and handle grief reactions in such a way that they manage to maintain open and direct communication with their children, are able to be emotionally present for them and to help the children to establish the connection with the person they have lost over time (Dyregrov, K., 2006a).

Balance between network support and professional help
If the bereaved are struggling with complicated grief reactions, such problems will seldom pass if one 'only' speaks with one's network. In the professional contact, the conversation is often carried out in a structured fashion, and combined with tasks that the bereaved must carry out between sessions. More recent trauma therapy methods can be very helpful, for example, in moderating recurring intrusive images where one envisions what has happened to one's loved one. The methods can also provide control over memories in connection with finding the deceased or of what one saw as the witness of a fatal accident. When the bereaved receive professional help, this of course does not mean that they no longer need good support from their network – to the contrary. For many bereaved people the therapeutic process is difficult because they are forced to confront difficult situations and carry out tasks associated with both feelings of loss and anxiety. This makes it particularly necessary for those around the bereaved to be there in the capacity of support people.

It is important that those who struggle over time receive good professional help to supplement the support they receive from their network. Our increasing knowledge about grief and grief therapy makes possible better professional help for those who struggle to an unnecessary extent after a death. For those who have complicated grief reactions, it is now, dependent upon what they are struggling most with, possible to tailor-design a programme which can help them to live with the loss in a way that is less detrimental to their quality of life. A prerequisite for this is that professionals expand their repertoires of methods, so that the bereaved can be helped in the best possible fashion. Network members play an important role in motivating the bereaved to seek help, and based on what has been outlined in this chapter, we hope to have contributed to the knowledge regarding when there is cause to bring in professional help. Although some of the advice given is relatively precise, in individual cases it is not always so easy to know whether the situation is serious enough to require a professional investment. Our advice is that it is better to bring in professional help too early and once too often, than to postpone this type of contact. Then the family or the individual bereaved can in consultation with professionals determine what can be done, or alternatively, decide that there is no need for further contact.

Main themes
Factors that affect the grief process

- Situational factors

  - How did the death occur? What was the degree of drama involved?

  - Were family members present when the death occurred? Were they subjected to powerful sense impressions?

  - Was it a sudden or unexpected death (murder, accident, suicide, illness)? Was the period of hospitalization long-term?

  - Was there any sort of preparation for what happened?

  - Ritual design and participation: was a peaceful farewell possible?

  - Did the bereaved receive adequate information about what happened? Was the series of events or cause of the death clarified?

  - How old was the deceased?

- ○ What was the nature of the relation to the deceased? Was the bereaved very attached to or dependent upon the deceased?
- Factors regarding the bereaved individual and family circumstances
  - ○ Family members' individual histories (e.g. previous losses, psychological problems, coping strategies) and couple's and family history
  - ○ Gender
  - ○ Openness and directness of communication
  - ○ Other family dynamic patterns
- Support and reactions from the surroundings
  - ○ Support from family and friends
  - ○ Support from professionals
  - ○ Support from the workplace
  - ○ Participation in bereavement support groups.

Three types of complicated grief

- Complicated grief: with core of separation distress.
- Complicated grief: posttraumatic stress disorder.
- Complicated grief: abbreviated or postponed variant (less common).

It is complicated grief if

- intrusive memories or images from the death continue to disturb the bereaved
- the bereaved continues to blame him/herself for what he/she could have done, thought or said or failed to do, think or say
- the bereaved has a strong sense of personal worthlessness
- the fear of another 'disaster' is strong and persistent
- the bereaved is not able to function at work or in their free time, cannot speak about the deceased or must avoid everything that reminds them of the deceased or the death
- the bereaved continues to brood and think about the death without room for other thoughts

- bitterness, anger or thoughts of revenge continue with undiminished intensity
- all conversation about what has happened or about the deceased has ceased within the family
- after the death of a child the parents are so preoccupied with the deceased that they do not manage to care for their surviving children.

When should professional help be brought in?

- When the reactions do not pass but continue with undiminished intensity.
- When the person is not functioning at work or in time off.
- When the person isolates him/herself from the surroundings.
- When the family struggles with the allocation of roles, internal conflicts or other types of 'family landmines'.
- When one becomes aware of other danger signs in the individual (increased alcohol consumption or abuse of medication).
- When the grief continues beyond the initial months without change, does not commence or there are other indications of complicated grief.
- When parents need counselling with regard to handling of children and/or young people's situation.
- When the interaction with the social network has 'fallen into a rut', the bereaved pull away from other people entirely, or when they need help handling 'social ineptitude' in their surroundings.

11

Support for the social network

In this chapter we address the need for supporting social support networks and what can be done in concrete terms.

The support network's need for support

We have previously in this book discussed the network's experience of their situation when they support the bereaved by sudden death (cf. Chapter 5). We have seen that close networks in particular make a large and important contribution. Almost everyone who provides support finds that it gives them valuable learning experiences and life knowledge. They find that they develop as human beings and that their friendship with the bereaved acquires greater depth. Sometimes families and groups of friends organize their efforts and distribute responsibility for various tasks at different points of time after the death. In spite of these positive experiences, friends and family members also find that it is exhausting, challenging and difficult to stand by a crisis-stricken person and provide support, especially over time. They feel a great sense of uncertainty about how to approach the bereaved and some state that they must pull out in order to avoid 'burnout'.

Members of support networks request knowledge and information so as to avoid becoming run down and to enable them to provide the best possible support. By providing social networks with greater security in the act of meeting fellow human beings who have experienced the sudden death of a close loved one, social resources will potentially also be liberated, in that the public assistance scheme will be relieved of carrying the entire responsibility. In order to reach this objective, the existing knowledge about burnout processes will comprise an important basis for supporting social networks and increasing their expertise. The most important thing is that the networks feel the need for such a type of support.

Compassion fatigue and burnout: issues of relevance

The term 'burnout' has become common vernacular for people who have reached the limit of their emotional and mental energies for a particular activity due to demanding tasks and a long-term stress load. We frequently hear of burnout among top executives, politicians or healthcare and assistance personnel. A series of concepts have been developed to describe the kinds of work-related stress and the types of strain healthcare personnel are subjected to when they work with traumatized individuals. The consequences of such work-related stress are described by terms such as 'secondary traumatic stress' (Stamm, 1995), 'compassion fatigue' (Figley, 1995) and 'burnout' (Rothschild and Rand 2006). These terms can also be applied to support networks that struggle with compassion and support tasks. One speaks of secondary traumatic stress when people who are in the surroundings of the crisis-stricken also suffer, due to the close relationship they have with the affected individuals. It will, for example, be painful to experience that someone whom one cares for deeply is having a difficult time due to a traumatic death. In addition, friends and family members can experience secondary trauma from things they hear or see in connection with the death (Rothschild and Rand, 2006). The term 'compassion fatigue' is used when people develop personal difficulties as a result of providing care and support for others in need (Figley, 1995). 'Burnout', which is perhaps the most well-known term, will in this context be reserved for more extreme cases of compassion fatigue (Figley, 1995; Rothschild and Rand, 2006). This term can be applied to members of the social network whose health is influenced in an extremely negative way due to an experience of excessive strain in their role as support people.

Professional assistance providers and work-related strain

A lot of research is done on the subject of trained and untrained individuals whom through their work have functioned as assistance workers in connection with traumatic crises and disasters. On the other hand, little research has been done about what supporting the crisis-stricken after such events involves for social networks. Rothschild and Rand (2006) summarize some of the research that has been carried out in recent years on the consequences of working with traumatized people for professional assistance providers. We will here illustrate some parallels from this research to the social network in its encounter with sudden death.

Different studies show that personnel providing practical and emotional support for the bereaved are subjected to a critical stress load (Bartone *et al.*, 1989; Berah, Jones and Valent, 1984; Dyregrov and Solomon, 1991; Johnston,

1993; Raphael *et al.*, 1983–1984). Research also indicates that exposure to violent death is clearly connected with posttraumatic stress and that there is a direct relation between the degree of exposure and degree of stress (McCarroll *et al.*, 1996, 2001). Being the recipient of crisis-stricken people's stories and intense emotional reactions or meeting with anxious peers are particularly critical aspects. In a study done following an explosion accident on board a naval ship, 10 per cent of the volunteers who took part in the handling of the deceased experienced posttraumatic stress disorder (PTSD) four months after the work was concluded. After 13 months, only 2 per cent satisfied the criteria for PTSD, possibly thanks to there having been a great emphasis on preparations, a delimitation of working hours and an adherence to routines during the course of the work and subsequent to this for the assistance teams (Ursano *et al.*, 1995). Studies also show that when assistance workers are volunteers and simultaneously members of the same 'society' in crisis, stronger emotional and physical disorders are experienced after conclusion of the crisis work. One study (Bartone *et al.*, 1989) showed that assistance workers without education in psychosocial work (officers) who had provided support for the bereaved after a military air accident were greatly at risk of developing illness and psychological symptoms. The longer their exposure to the work situation, the more they suffered from symptoms and illness after a year had passed. One risk factor was having had relatively limited experience with such work before the event in question (Bartone *et al.*, 1989). Other studies also document that more experienced volunteers show fewer stress reactions subsequent to assistance work than volunteers with less experience (McCarroll, Ursano and Fullerton, 1993).

The main tendencies in the studies are nonetheless that relatively few of the personnel in question develop long-term problems after a disaster-response effort (Dyregrov and Mitchell, 1992; Leffler and Dembert, 1998; Marmar *et al.*, 1996). This is attributed to good debriefing routines (structured, comprehensive group discussions the first week and follow-up meetings over time) and good colleague and management support. Most professional assistance workers function well while working or in contact with the bereaved, so that few develop serious problems down the road. However, the risk increases for long-term reactions and delayed responses if the assistance worker in question has had little experience and little training for the tasks, is a volunteer and not a professional assistance worker (Dyregrov and Mitchell, 1992). Large portions of the social network will belong to this category. But even if the stress load for personnel in crisis work and social networks is not identical, there are common features regarding the things to which the two groups are exposed. This is particularly the case for close network members who are present at or arrive just after the death and who provide support throughout the funeral, viewing and over time. These individuals are exposed to strain through their own observations or through hearing repeated accounts of the event and can eventually come to experience a sense of powerlessness and inadequacy. This corresponds with how close social networks describe the risk of burnout (cf. Chapter 5).

A strain providing support after a traumatic death

All those who provide support over time will be confronted with people in crisis and be witnesses to human suffering. As a close friend, this involves meeting the bereaved person's intense crisis reactions, vulnerability, sensitivity, anxiety and despair. The crisis-stricken person's unique needs for compassion are in themselves a source of strain for the network. The need to have someone beside them during the first period is great and the close network frequently meets this need. This is not only time-consuming but imposes great demands on the psychological strength and stamina of those carrying out such tasks. During the first period following the death help is needed to organize the chaos while the network must simultaneously take into consideration the enormous vulnerability of the bereaved. The network must offer acceptance and understanding, in conjunction with their efforts to orient the bereaved towards reality. As an aid in the reality orientation process, information is needed – something the network does not always have access to without collaboration with professionals. Sometimes the bereaved have support and help needs that are so great that nobody, or nothing, can relieve them. The networks will then experience a sense of powerlessness.

Supporting crisis-stricken people can also entail personal challenges. One is obliged to address one's own fear of death, relation to death or fears about losing a loved one. Some only discover that they have not clearly addressed such issues upon finding themselves in close contact with a traumatic death. A close friend or family member is not only extremely close to the bereaved in their difficult situation, but they have also often known the person who has suddenly lost his or her life. They will therefore in addition potentially experience their own personal grief. When the deceased is a child or young person, many adults will be able to identify with the situation of the bereaved as a parent who loses a child. For that reason they also feel some of the pain felt by the bereaved.

Network members will be subjected to strong sense impressions if they arrive at the scene of the death or support the close bereaved during a viewing or other rituals (such as in connection with dressing the deceased). In the Network project we saw that some network members for their own part can develop disaster anxiety and fears about losing loved ones. We know that it is quite challenging and demanding to handle personal anxiety in addition to the pain of close loved ones. Further, the one providing the support might also have to cope with their own feelings of loss in relation to the deceased. Sometimes the situation can lead to conflicts, and friends and family often experience feelings of inadequacy with regard to the suffering and distress of the bereaved. Some situations and choices will without a doubt also result in ethical dilemmas for close networks. Beyond this, one knows that those who have had a positive experience with providing support will take on such roles more frequently than others and can be involved with supporting several people who are having difficulties at the same time. A large capacity for compassion can also result in a heavier stress load. On the whole, the strain is then enormous. It is then all the more important to find a balance for one's personal engagement and involvement so as not to fall into the kind of over-involvement resulting in burnout.

What are the characteristics of burnout?

There are a number of signs and danger signals that are normally observed in people referred to as 'burned out'. Caregivers may progress from involvement to over-involvement and from compassion fatigue to burnout. Because these are processes that occur gradually, while one is personally engrossed in one's duties, other network members can sometimes pick up on signs of burnout before the affected individual. People marked by compassion fatigue will have a lower tolerance for frustration and people in their surroundings will witness clear behavioural and humour changes, such as withdrawal and passivity. Simultaneously, the person in question can be restless and have difficulties setting limits for their own level of commitment and involvement in that which is wearing them out. The person in question does not manage to set aside their involvement, even though for outsiders that appears to be the only correct means of resolving the situation. A person on the verge of burnout feels extremely tired and taking short breaks does not help. The motivation and engagement in what one is doing is diminished or completely lacking, and although the person is doing a great deal, they will have a constant feeling of 'never' managing to do things well enough. Reduced self-esteem is not unusual. In the end one becomes more and more vulnerable, and takes in 'everything'. Many do not stop until somatic disorders become pronounced or anxiety and depression are a fact.

The person who *is* burned out experiences losing energy, initiative and idealism, often in connection with previous requirements to give of themselves over a long period of time. This is often a reaction to taxing work-related requirements, combined with a great capacity for compassion and empathy. Burnout is characterized by emotional exhaustion, extreme fatigue, emptiness and an experience of the meaninglessness of life. Individuals suffering from burnout can experience physical pains in their musculature, headaches or more vague physical ailments. Digestive difficulties, with pyrosis or reduced appetite and nausea, are not unusual. Many experience problems sleeping, such as problems falling asleep, early awakening or nightmares. In some cases, people experience trouble breathing, such as hyperventilation, in connection with panic or anxiety attacks. Mood swings and a more rigid and negative attitude towards others can also develop. That means that while some become extremely tired and worn out by the caring and support work and constantly feel that they are not doing enough, others can react by withdrawing and avoiding all contact and actually begin to develop a negative attitude towards those whom they are trying to help. Those who were previously relatively patient and stable become irritable and unstable. In order to compensate for the discomfort and unfamiliar changes in their daily life, some resort to excessive smoking or an increase in the consumption of alcohol or medication. Because many of the same processes are activated when the network supports the bereaved after a traumatic death, compassion fatigue and burnout are relevant issues also in this context. But that does not mean that all those who offer support following a sudden death become burned out. By illuminating the risk factors and implementing preventive measures, it is possible to prevent burnout while at the same time making the most of network support.

When does the risk of compassion fatigue and burnout increase?

There are a number of common features for assistance providers and care and support workers who are exposed to an increased risk of compassion fatigue and burnout (Dyregrov, A., 2002). This applies to people who:

- have a strong wish to contribute something meaningful in relation to others
- take on helper roles because they 'can't help themselves'
- are committed and take action
- have an ideal of being a strong, resourceful individual
- have a great capacity for empathy in relation to the needs of others and a great capacity to put aside their own needs

- are preoccupied with taking and having control and have a low level of tolerance for their own mistakes
- have few and poor self-care routines
- often have or take on great responsibility
- have great expectations with regard to their own ability to 'set things right' or 'fix problems'
- often find themselves in complex situations involving large professional and human challenges that can be impossible to solve or mitigate.

People will have different risk levels with regard to developing compassion fatigue or burnout and the paradox is that people who in principle are the most competent and suitable can be at the greatest risk for developing burnout. Those who have the greatest facility for taking on helper roles have many positive and common characteristics. The capacity for empathy and compassion for the suffering of others is one of the most important qualities. Empathetic people have an intuition of what others feel, see experiences from the perspectives of others and have a great ability for understanding in relation to the needs of others, while at the same time they put aside their own needs. The bereaved by traumatic death experience that people with a large capacity for empathy are the best support people.

People who easily assume helper roles have in common the fact that they demonstrate a strong wish to contribute something meaningful in relation to others and some 'can't help themselves'. They are often committed individuals who like to take action and have an ideal of being a strong, capable person. At the same time, they can be preoccupied with taking and being in control and have a low level of tolerance for their own mistakes, combined with great expectations with regard to their ability to set things right. As such, the typical helper often acquires a large amount of responsibility and finds themselves in difficult situations involving large challenges that can be impossible to solve or mend. The Network project shows that the stipulated common features of assistance providers also apply to close and dedicated family members and friends who step in for fellow human beings in crisis (cf. Chapter 5). Friends and family members state that the motives for providing support include a sense of common humanity (94 per cent), because they feel sorry for the bereaved (84 per cent), or they knew that the bereaved would have been there for them had the situation been reversed (80 per cent) (Dyregrov, 2006c). Only 37 per cent gave as a reason for their involvement the fact that they had personally received help from the crisis-stricken person previously. As we have seen, close network members are also committed, take action and have a great capacity for empathy along with the ability to set aside their own needs. Many assume a great deal of responsibility in complex situations involving huge professional and human challenges and have high expectations with regard to their own abilities to set things right for good friends. At the same time, it is clear that many elements in the difficult situation of the bereaved are impossible to solve because one cannot bring back the person who is gone. Many in the closest network also struggle with a poor conscience for not doing enough. A woman in the Network project describes how network members experience this and how it can finally lead to paralysis in the situation:

> I believe that you also can grow worse after a while, because you can reach a point where you must protect yourself. I have experienced it. It became so intense and there was so much grief and you never finish with it. In order to take into consideration the needs of the family, the children and yourself you must create distance and live life now. One cannot only think back or about all the horrible things that can occur in the future. So one has a little bit of a need to protect oneself if it becomes long-term, even though I am the sister. My sister is struggling somewhat psychologically and has anxiety and I have a niece who is struggling, so it all becomes a bit much. We are called out during the night sometimes as well. I feel now and then burned out and must pull back to recover my strength.

Our research confirms that many friends and family members who provide support following traumatic death have the qualities of the typical assistance provider or 'helper' (the Network project and the Support and Care project). These are qualities that, according to the bereaved, result in the best support. But we have also seen that these same qualities result in an increased risk of compassion fatigue and burnout, because special strains are involved in supporting someone after a traumatic death.

It is easy to become overly involved

In addition to personal qualities that can increase the chance of a positive involvement, or possibly over-involvement in others' lives, come factors in connection with the relation between oneself and the person in need of support. When networks support the bereaved this will often be based on friends and family being fond of or caring about the person who is struggling. Some people are motivated also to help out of a sense of obligation. Others are mobilized to provide an extra investment if they recognize the bereaved person's intense pain and emotions because they have experienced something similar. Increased involvement will also potentially be conditional to one's identifying with the crisis-stricken because the person in question resembles oneself at their age, is of the same gender or in a similar life situation. Others give more of themselves than would be expected, because a fellow human being makes a strong appeal to their need to help, while others have essentially unclear boundaries between themselves and others. In some cases, making sacrifices for other people can serve to bolster one's own self-esteem and as such be part of the drive to help.

The danger of over-involvement on the part of the network increases if one has limited access to feedback from others or lacks experience or frames of reference for what takes place. Over-involvement can more easily arise if one is personally tired or in crisis, because one does not have one's head enough above water to be able to recognize how one is functioning personally. In such a case the helper is also unable to add new perspectives to the situation; one sees 'only' what the other sees. The result becomes that the person who should help experiences increasing levels of exhaustion and pain and feels the need to withdraw because it is too painful to relate to the person struggling. If one is alone as a support person over time and has nobody to discuss the situation with, the chance of burnout also increases.

How can social networks be supported?

We have knowledge about networks' willingness to provide support and the extremely positive effects of this. Simultaneously, we know that the situation of the bereaved subjects close friends and family members to a great strain, which in turn leads to an increased risk of compassion fatigue and burnout. In order to make the most of social network support following a sudden death, it is therefore extremely important to outline support measures for the network.

In the event of crisis and disaster, emergency personnel have experienced that long-term effects and burnout can be reduced by training and preparation before and good follow-up after such work (Dyregrov, A., 2002). There are good reasons to presume that the same holds true for close social networks following traumatic death. They will need knowledge and information and to have a focus on processing their own experiences. In order to prevent over-involvement and burnout, networks will also have a need to develop coping strategies in order to be able to confront the crises of others. A combination of such measures will comprise important support. Network members can receive such support from one another, from the bereaved, from a local government's public assistance scheme and through their own coping skills. In accordance with social networks' wishes for support, we would specify that they can be supported by receiving:

- the opportunity to reflect upon and summarize strong impressions and thoughts
- knowledge about encountering the bereaved following a traumatic death
- advice, guidance, counselling and emotional support from professionals.

Networks as support for other networks

It is important that the person supporting the bereaved by sudden death be seen and supported within their own family and among their own friends. The network can support other network members by:

- sharing thoughts, experiences and impressions
- gaining acceptance and support to spend time and energy on the bereaved
- learning and reflecting on their own initiative by listening to what others do
- speaking of inadequacy and uncertainty and about possibly needing to take breaks
- receiving inspiration to support the bereaved over time.

Members of support networks need to be able to reflect on and summarize the strong impressions and thoughts that arise in the encounter with people in crisis. Beyond sharing this with their own family and network of friends, it can be shared with others who are supporting the crisis-stricken family. Because of the risk of secondary trauma, one should nonetheless consider carefully which impressions one passes on and to whom. In the Network project there was a large consensus regarding the benefits of speaking together as a group when many friends and family members had supported a crisis-stricken family. They greatly appreciated having the opportunity to speak together about their personal experiences as support people. For most this occurred for the first time in the focus group interview. It was important for them to hear about what others had experienced and thought, to learn from this and to be able to move forward in terms of their own processes. Many wished to listen to others' experiences or they wanted answers to questions while others wanted advice.

They found that the community of others from the support network gave them a 'refill' and the inspiration to provide support over time (Dyregrov, 2006c).

Together with a spouse/partner or close friends, support persons can allow themselves to react, while at the same time they can clarify their own reactions in certain situations. Often it will be helpful to receive feedback from others who know the same affected parties, in order to acquire perspectives on how others have helped out or on something one has said or done. Others need support for things that one does not dare or wish to do, such as when one finds it difficult to ring up the bereaved. It can be good to know that one is not alone in such experiences of 'being a coward' or in hesitating to take the initiative when this feels cumbersome and difficult. Such an understanding need not serve to rationalize avoidance, but rather as an incitement to be a bit more courageous, by speaking together about the reasons why one pulls away from crisis-stricken individuals. It will also be important to acquire understanding from the immediate family for the fact that a commitment to the bereaved requires time and a rearrangement of priorities that, at least at the start, can be to the detriment of time for one's own family.

Many friends and family members need to speak together about what they are feeling without the affected parties present. It is easier to speak openly and to support one another when one need not be afraid of upsetting the bereaved with an eye towards the extremely sensitive situation that they are in. If the bereaved are not present, network members will also find it easier to speak together about feeling tired and to consider withdrawing for a while from the situation. While the support network can benefit from discussing their experiences with others who support the same bereaved individuals, it is crucial that such conversations are held in such a way that one does not betray or expose the people one is supporting. As long as it is expedient and in the best interests of the bereaved, they should be included in such conversations. At the same time, the network members must impose stringent requirements upon their own integrity and ethics when the bereaved are discussed in their absence.

Some bereaved people can have a need for the presence of physical companionship to such a great extent that it will not be possible for a good friend to meet this need on their own and then it can be extremely practical to coordinate the support so that not everyone is present simultaneously, but rather that several share the burden. We know that distributing the support investment over time by coordinating what various friends or family groups do early after the death is also something the bereaved want. In addition, such coordination of support will potentially create an experience of a shared responsibility and less of a guilty conscience, something that greatly reduces the danger of burnout in social networks. Beyond this it will be helpful to learn what others in the network do in concrete terms to provide support, to avoid unnecessary overlapping. For coordination, an exchange of information and experiences is needed, which in turn requires that time is set aside for interaction and that the members of the network are accessible for one another. The more peripheral networks that want to step in can receive valuable support and suggestions from those who are closer, so that they dare to take part in supporting. In the longer-term, it can be extremely fruitful for the network of friends and the bereaved to focus together on the beneficial experiences they have had. In this way groups of support networks can summarize and pass on important lessons for possible later use. This creates a type of ballast that makes people more secure about confronting their own and others' life crises.

While many friends and family members that support bereaved people speak with and acquire the support they need from their own family or other network members, others wish to discuss things with professionals, or they want both.

Local government as a support network resource

Following crises and disasters, an increased awareness of the significance of the mobilization of social network support for the crisis-stricken is a key task for local government assistance schemes. It has been observed that there are various reasons why crisis help should as a matter of course ensure or mobilize social network support after crisis and disaster events:

- to prevent problems that do not require professional help from becoming ones that do
- network support has qualities that professional help can never replace
- network support is needed quickly
- the crisis-stricken are not always personally able or do not think about mobilizing the network.

Before a member of the clergy, a physician or other assistance personnel leaves a crisis-stricken person, they often ask the person in question whether they have any good friends or family they might contact who can stay with them. In some cases the bereaved personally take the initiative, while on other occasions they receive help with this and sometimes the local government's assistance scheme must provide supervision if the crisis-stricken has no network to turn to. As a rule, some individuals close to the bereaved step in, at least during the very first period. As we have seen previously in this book, some close social networks become more involved with crisis-stricken people than one would usually expect, and clearly exceed what they can manage and have the resources to do. They make a brilliant investment, sometimes even around the clock, which to a certain extent relieves local government of its responsibility for the crisis-stricken. Although the network's need for support has been little known until now, it would be expedient if public assistance schemes viewed support for the social network as a task in keeping with the fulfilment of their work tasks.

In Norway, according to the Act of 23 June 2000 No. 56 relating to health and psychological follow-up after crises and catastrophes, local government shall in its healthcare services offer 'necessary healthcare assistance and social services to the population during war and with crises and disasters in peace-time' (§ 1.1). Further, local government in Norway is directed through the Act of November 1982 No. 66 relating to municipal health services to 'promote public health and well-being and good social and environmental conditions and to seek to prevent and treat illness, injury or defect. It shall disseminate information about and increase the interest in what the individual personally and the public in general can do to promote their own well-being and health and public health' (§ 1.2). By providing information and support for support networks, local government will be able to contribute to family and friends providing better support, and support over a longer period of time. The result of such an investment will quite probably relieve public health agencies of care and support tasks. The local government's support measures for social networks could comprise:

- individual support and relief counselling
- guidance and information
- help in organizing short-term and long-term network support
- community courses and written information (about crisis reactions, the significance of network support, prevention and management of stress, etc.).

Social networks request advice, guidance and counselling from professionals who know something about meeting the needs of the bereaved following a traumatic death. This can be done by professionals who come into contact with networks through the bereaved family or through professionals whom network members have contacted, or make contact with. Local government crisis teams can assemble groups of networks when these clearly make up a 'team' surrounding the affected families. They can come together and receive the chance to reflect upon their experiences, with an outsider who has knowledge about crises and who structures the discussion, making connections between the experiences of the network members. This can be a one-time event or be organized as a resource base for both parties. Professionals can support them in the knowledge that the contribution they are making is good, listen to any traumatic experiences they may have had and give advice. At the same time, networks can make suggestions to professionals in the form of observations or thoughts about the needs of the bereaved. After an accident where the father of two preschool children died, the widow asked for a psychologist with experience of grief and crisis work to come to a meeting with the social network. Fifteen people met for three hours in the widow's home. Here the psychologist could first say a little about common grief reactions in the short- and long-term, so those present could then discuss how they might best provide support and help. Naturally enough, they were concerned about how they could assist the widow, how they could distribute the tasks and in particular, how they could help the children. It was proposed that male network members could volunteer to do things with the children so as to provide them with male role models. The meeting took place some time after the death and it became evident that several of the network members at that time had a greater sense of their own grief than they had been able to manage previously, when they had only been concerned about how they could help the widow and the children. In the group they could speak about the strain giving support entailed and their own impressions; they could receive praise for what they had done and be motivated to provide continued support. The response indicated that this was extremely important to them, particularly the confirmation they received that the support was useful and important.

Many close friends and family members who are in the midst of the worst following a traumatic death relate that they have felt a need for individual counselling from professionals. The clergy, family physician or other trusted individuals have helped them and often a single counselling session has been sufficient. Such a session can be about the network member's own reactions to what they have heard, seen or thought in their encounter with the crisis-stricken. The counselling session can address guilt stemming from feelings of inadequacy or of not doing enough, or because one's own children are still alive when a girlfriend has lost hers. Professionals can also provide confirmation for the fact that the support they are giving seems reasonable and that one is relating to the bereaved and what has happened in an appropriate manner. This can be sufficient to enable the network, despite its uncertainty, to dare to continue and trust its instincts regarding what constitutes good support. For some networks it can be a challenge to balance considerations for the close bereaved with taking care of one's own family. Many close network members with their own family and children need to discuss their caregiving responsibilities, and their reactions to the death. This is particularly the case if the young people personally had a close relation to the deceased. Networks that provide support following sudden deaths of children and young people can, like the bereaved, experience an increased fear that something will happen to their own children. It can be good to speak with professionals about such fears, so as to avoid being unnecessarily drained of energy by them.

Professionals know that good professional frames of reference along with knowledge and experience within the area of crisis management can act as important ballast in terms of preventing burnout in connection with crisis work. If most networks lack this in their encounter with sudden death, it will be all the more important for them to acquire knowledge about crisis events in order to create a frame of reference for their encounters with the bereaved. For example, it will be useful to be able to understand the reactions of the bereaved as normal reactions to an extreme event, something to which knowledge about common crisis reactions will contribute.

Such knowledge results in those giving support feeling less overwhelmed or anxious about the bereaved, while at the same time it provides a better understanding and support in the situation at hand. Support networks want advice and guidance about why the relation to the bereaved can go wrong, why the bereaved choose to isolate themselves, and about how active they personally can or should be. Professionals with knowledge about communication processes will therefore be an important resource for the network.

Local community professionals that support the bereaved by traumatic death can make helpful suggestions to members of social networks regarding how they can best organize long-term and short-term support. Through advice stipulating the wisdom of allocating tasks and time so that not all friends and family members arrive at the same time or only come in the beginning, it can be made possible for the support to continue over time. Close friends who have not previously been close to the bereaved in a deep crisis can misjudge how it affects them personally. Advice to take care of oneself, to get enough sleep and seek out external distractions is important in terms of preventing the support person from wearing him- or herself out completely, together with the bereaved. Crisis teams, other healthcare personnel or the clergy can inform groups of friends about general reactions to sudden death and evaluate whether their own reactions to the situation are common or a cause for concern. Others have a need to discuss whether they could have done things differently or if they should be more or less 'pushy'. We would however emphasize that professional helpers should only function as assistance for support networks and that this must never be to the detriment of their obligations in relation to the bereaved. A member of the clergy or a healthcare professional can of course not take part in or discuss concrete information that they have learned about the bereaved in the act of carrying out their professional duties. In such a case this must be done in agreement with the bereaved.

Local community courses will potentially be a means of making the most of network support following sudden death in general. Education about crisis reactions, the significance of network support and prevention and management of stress will better prepare people to support close and more peripheral fellow human beings when the day comes that they have a need to do so. Open courses in the local community will meet the need for knowledge and raise the consciousness of 'the man on the street' as a contribution to a more humane society. The courses can be based on the same framework as courses for emergency personnel for crisis situations (Dyregrov, A., 2002). Nonetheless, it is perhaps more realistic for such 'courses' to be held following concrete incidents. Some key topics could be:

- general information about stress (causes and effects on ordinary people)
- stress factors in connection with critical events and disasters
- the difference between stress load in everyday life and critical stress in crisis and disaster situations
- reactions and symptoms that can occur during and after support (physical, emotional and behavioural)
- about the importance of empathy and involvement, viewed in light of the possibilities for over-involvement and burnout
- about communication/support processes between the crisis-stricken and the social network
- about the interaction and organization of support networks
- general advice for coping with stress.

The bereaved as a support network resource
In addition to the possibilities support people and professionals have for supporting social networks, the bereaved themselves are also a resource. Feedback and open communication between the bereaved and the network is one of the most important means of improving network support following a sudden death. Through clear communication uncertainty is reduced and thereby also the danger of the network wearing itself out. The bereaved can be

a resource for the network through their conduct, particularly by giving the network feedback. As we have discussed earlier, openness on the part of the bereaved allows the support network to take part in the grief process. This means that the bereaved must not keep those from whom they want to receive support away from the funeral or apart from their struggles. They must also communicate about how they wish to be approached, what the support network does that is good, beneficial, etc. If excluded from this, the network cannot address what is happening and be there on the terms of the bereaved. Close friends and family members become uncertain and at worst, completely paralysed with regard to what they can do. Good, clear signals and responses from the bereaved make good and clear network support possible. In this sense the bereaved have an important 'educator role' (cf. Chapters 5–7).

Bereaved people who are members of peer organizations such as the Foundation for the Study of Infant Death (FSED), Stillbirth and Neonatal Death Support (SANDS), Roadpeace, or Cruse will also potentially provide helpful resources for social networks in their encounter with the bereaved. When organizations bring the experiences of the bereaved into the public sphere, through brochures, research or projects, they make important contributions towards increasing the security and knowledge of support networks.

What can the network do?

Last but not least, members of social networks can personally contribute to preventing their own over-involvement or burnout when they support crisis-stricken people. An important rule of thumb is that the lesser the scope of one's actual capacity to live up to the standards one sets for oneself, the greater the strain one will experience. We just want to mention a few general strategies for coping with stress, and, for the interested reader, make references to the wealth of specialist literature in this field (e.g. Benson, 1975; Maslach and Leitner, 1997; Williams and Poijula, 2002). Advice for self-mastery in meeting with crisis-stricken people includes:

- attempt to implement clear communication and clear responses
- adjust your personal goals and standards
- be clear about personal boundaries
- get support and possibly guidance from others
- take responsibility for knowledge and information refills
- have a life outside; do not allow the support relation to consume you
- give yourself time outs, breaks and relaxation

- carry out physical and pleasurable activities
- practise inner dialogues that create distance if the intimacy becomes overwhelming (e.g. 'this is not my child', 'this is not me')
- take care of one's own family and own social relationships
- protect one's own self-esteem
- stop – or take a break before you are exhausted.

In the following we will address some of this advice in greater detail. First and foremost: be sure to have someone to talk to. As we have discussed previously, it is tiring to support people in grief and that means that it can be important for the one providing the support to speak with someone about how this feels. If one was also present when the death occurred or when the deceased was found, or has listened to detailed and painful accounts about this, it can be helpful to put this into words. Here writing about the situation can be helpful. If one writes, one should not only put into words the events that actually took place, but also one's inner experiences during and after the death. This helps to get the events out of one's system. If one writes in detail about one's experiences, and not just about what happened, but also thoughts, impressions and reactions one has had during and after the death, this gives the incident a context and structure. This type of writing has been shown to help reduce the possibility of health ailments following critical situations.

Most people have over the years learned what best helps them to modify stress and tension. One should take advantage of this knowledge if one is in a long-term position of support. Whether it is aromatherapy, massage, yoga, meditation or something else that helps one to relax, one should continue with this in the time after the death. It is important for network members' support-providing abilities, and for their bodies and souls that they take good care of themselves. If one has learned a relaxation technique previously, it will be helpful to implement this, if one notices that one is becoming stressed or tense. Controlled breathing is one method that can help to gain control and relax quickly. One does the following: inhale gently through the nose, hold your breath for five seconds (count calmly to seven to eight) and then exhale through the mouth. When you exhale, you say to yourself either 'easy' or 're-lax'. Wait about five seconds, and then repeat the procedure. If you do this a few times, it will help in gaining control over the body and help you to feel calmer.

Listening to calm music also has a soothing effect on body and soul. In the case of long-term support work, it can be good to calm down in such a way or to set aside time to recuperate. Physical activity through exercise has also been shown to be a good stress management method, which decreases tension and physical discomfort, in addition to counteracting depression. For some, calm forms of exercise, such as yoga or Pilates, are good methods for reducing stress, while others prefer to achieve relaxation and renew their energy through more strenuous forms of exercise.

If one is feeling physically agitated it is a good idea not to drink more coffee, tea or cola than usual because this increases the agitation in the nervous system. For some, the agitation in body and soul is so intense that they have difficulties falling asleep. If one does not sleep at all for several nights in a row, one should consult a physician about acquiring sleeping pills in order to break the vicious cycle.

Other good advice for insomnia can be found in self-help books. One can also calm physical agitation by thinking in specific ways, such as by summoning up thoughts of a place where one feels exceptional well-being. It can be a place that one has visited or it can be imaginary. Create an image of this in your head and make the image as calm and comfortable as possible. Try to make the image as real as possible. One can, for instance, think about:

- the sound of waves rolling up on the beach
- the wind whispering in the trees
- the scent of the ocean or of pine or spruce trees
- warm sunlight shining down on one's face
- a breeze lightly blowing through one's hair.

If one begins to sense agitation or discomfort, the images can be used to create a comfortable situation. One can concentrate on creating and experiencing the comfortable place and see if it does indeed help one to relax.

For those who are both support people and were also present when the death occurred or found the deceased, memories of the event can be disturbing. We want to offer some advice for gaining control over such memories. One can try the following: if it is a matter of disturbing images, one can summon them up and envision them as they appear when they arise against one's will. One can subsequently attempt to push them away a little at a time, so that they gradually diminish in clarity. If this does not help, one can try to imagine that one is viewing them on a TV screen. When the image is in place, one turns off the TV with the remote control. If this is difficult, then change the channel. One can also allow the image or images to change as one views them, such as from colour to black and white, or in shape, size, etc. In this way one gains control over the images, instead of the images having control over oneself.

If the source of disturbance is auditory impressions one can proceed in the same manner. One takes control by imagining the sounds coming from a radio and then turning down the volume, altering the sound quality, etc. Olfactory impressions that become 'implanted' in the nose can be counteracted by spreading a little oil or other substance around the outside of the nostrils to override the scent or by seeking out other, more pleasant odours in one's imagination, which one then uses to suppress the unpleasant odour.

Trust your own powers!

The advice for coping with stress load is in accordance with the advice from the participants of the Network project to others who are to support the bereaved following traumatic death. The network members pointed out that it is important to trust one's common sense and knowledge of the grief-stricken as a basis for the support one provides. In addition, they specified the significance of taking care of oneself and one's own family, particularly during the initial chaotic weeks and days following the death. Their experience was that it was easy at this time, like the bereaved, to forget to get enough sleep, food and 'time outs' during the initial period.

Network members also recommended (according to need) taking periodic breaks where one provides less support, breaks that the bereaved are informed about. This can be accomplished by organizing the resources of the network members surrounding the bereaved family and allocating tasks where possible. Several found that one or more counselling sessions with a professional gave them the necessary confidence in their own personal resources. Beyond that, knowledge of the reactions of the bereaved, their need for support and help and not least processes between the parties contributes a sense of security, so that the social network can do its very best – without burning itself out.

Finally, we would specify that although support from professionals can be useful, it must never become a hindrance to the network's trusting itself and its own capacity to provide meaningful support on the basis of its own, independent assessments. The objective of support for network members is to give them confidence in their abilities, to give them the necessary courage to be there for the bereaved, close at hand. We do not want to reach a point where the network sits and waits for the municipal team to arrive before they dare offer support, out of the fear of doing something wrong. To the contrary, we support the statement of a close friend in the Network project: 'I believe that even if one does not do everything right the most important thing is to do something.'

Main themes

What do we know about the strains involved in supporting crisis-stricken people?

- Supporting crisis-stricken people over time is a source of strain for professional assistance workers.
- Professional frames of reference, experience, debriefing and knowledge are important in terms of managing the stress load.
- Networks lack experience and a professional frame of reference as volunteer helpers.
- Networks experience strain and uncertainty when they support those bereaved by a sudden death.
- Networks are at risk of over-involvement, compassion fatigue and burnout.

There is an increased risk of compassion fatigue and burnout in a support network when one:

- often finds oneself in complex situations involving large professional and human challenges – which can be impossible to solve or cure
- uses oneself as a tool for making a meaningful contribution to other human beings
- becomes seriously involved with crisis-stricken people with an ideal of being a strong and resourceful individual
- is exposed to powerful visual or auditory impressions that cannot be processed
- has a large capacity for empathy in relation to the needs of others and a large capacity to set aside one's own needs
- often experiences a sense of powerlessness and helplessness
- has few and poor routines for taking care of oneself (sleep, rest, pleasurable activities, etc.).

What are the signs of burnout?

- extreme fatigue and exhaustion, muscular pains, headaches
- digestive problems, poor appetite, nausea

- sleep disorders (problems falling asleep, waking up early or nightmares)
- increased vulnerability, despair, depression
- irritability, unstable and constant state of alertness
- rigidity and negativity
- excessive smoking, abuse of alcohol or medication
- state of anxiety and depression.

Support networks can be supported through:

- The support networks' network. These people:
  - share impressions, gain acceptance and support for use of time, reflect upon one's own initiatives through others' experiences, vent uncertainty, discuss the need for breaks, allocate tasks immediately following the death as a form of relief for one another and acquire inspiration with regard to providing support over time.
- Municipal crisis teams/assistance workers offer:
  - individual support counselling sessions, guidance and information, organizational help and crisis management courses in the local community.
- The bereaved and peer organizations:
  - include the desired network in the grief process, communicate what one is struggling with and one's support needs and give feedback on the support.
- Self-mastery advice helps one to:
  - contribute to open communication with the bereaved, adapt goals and requirements for oneself, gain support and guidance from others, not allow the support relation to become all-consuming, take care of one's own family and social relations, possibly take breaks from time to time and provide less support – of which the bereaved are informed.

Have faith in your own common sense and knowledge of the bereaved!

Projects mentioned in the book

In this book reference is made to a number of Norwegian studies carried out by the authors. In order to enable the reader to understand the context for the results of the studies, we will discuss the focus and sources of the studies. Those wishing further information on the methodological background should see the publications listed below each project. The projects discussed are:

- The Support and Care project (the encounter of the traumatic bereaved with social networks) – Project Manager: Dyregrov, K.
- The Network project (the encounter of social networks with the traumatic bereaved) – Project Manager: Dyregrov, K.
- Young Suicide Bereavement project (young bereaved by suicide and their situation and support needs) – Project Manager: Dyregrov, K.
- The Children and Cancer project (children and young people after parent's death by cancer/with cancer-afflicted parent) – Project Manager: Dyregrov, K.
- Intimacy and sexuality after the death of a child (intimacy and sexuality of couples following the loss of an infant child) – Project Manager: Dyregrov, A.

The Support and Care project (The Bereavement study)[1]
Main issues addressed/purpose
How do the bereaved experience and cope with their situation following suicide, sudden infant death and child accidents? What are their assistance needs and what type of support do they receive and want?

1   Here only the one part of the main study is addressed. The Community study (*Kommunestudien*), which explored the services of the public assistance scheme in relation to the same groups, comprised the other half of the study. This study is not addressed here.

Recruitment and sample characteristics

The sample was composed from a total of 300 families that had lost a child under the age of 30 by suicide (168), or had lost a child by sudden infant death, or had lost a child under the age of 18 by an accident (132) in Norway between July 1997 and December 1998. These families were located and contacted through the Norwegian police records (STRASAK). Parents and siblings age 15 and older were sent a written invitation to take part in a questionnaire survey and later, an interview survey. A total of 232 parents, representing 53 per cent of the deceased, responded to the questionnaire in the spring of 1999 and 69 of these were interviewed in depth in the course of the autumn of 1999. The parents' ages varied from 23 to 73 years. The bereaved by suicide were the eldest (M = 51.0, SD = 8.0), followed by the bereaved by accident (M = 40.0, SD = 8.5), while the sudden infant death parents comprised the youngest age group (M = 30.0, SD = 5.7). 56 per cent came from rural areas and 44 per cent from cities. In terms of education, 21 per cent had completed primary school, 47 per cent had completed secondary school, and 32 per cent had completed higher education (university or college). Most of the parents (70 per cent) had a full-time or part-time job outside of the home. The average age of the deceased was 22 years in the suicide group (11–29 years), 11 for the accident group (0–18 years) and 2.5 months for sudden infant death (0–1 years). The distribution of women and men was 77/52 for the bereaved by suicide, 19/16 for the bereaved by sudden infant death and 43/25 for the bereaved by accidents. The study took place 6 to 23 months after the respective deaths (M = 15 months, SD = 4.9).

Forty families (20 suicides, 10 sudden infant deaths and 10 child accidents) were selected to take part in an in-depth interview through use of a combination of theoretical and random selection methods. The characteristics of this sub-sample closely resembled the questionnaire sample. In addition, 90 siblings filled out the questionnaire and 20 siblings were interviewed.

Data sources and data collection

The data sources were standardized questionnaires and questionnaires of our own design, along with in-depth individual or couple interviews. The following standardized questionnaires were used for bereaved parents: Impact of Event Scale (IES) (Horowitz, Wilner and Alvarez, 1979), General Health Questionnaire – 28-question version (GHQ) (Goldberg and Williams, 1988) and Inventory of Complicated Grief (ICG) (Prigerson et al., 1995). For siblings we used: Impact of Event Scale (IES), Hogan Sibling Inventory of Bereavement (HSIB) (Hogan, 1990) (cf. p. 255) and the Rosenberg self-esteem scale (RSS)

(Hagborg, 1993). A comprehensive questionnaire, developed at the Center for Crisis Psychology, mapped the type of help they had received from social networks, level of satisfaction with the assistance, changes in their relationship to social networks, any lack of support, etc. In addition to the standardized questions (222 variables), three questions opened for qualitative descriptions of the care and support, what they were lacking, possible barriers to accepting help and what the ideal kind of support would entail.

A theme guide was used for the interviews. The main themes in the interview guide were: 1) relation to the deceased, 2) support before the death, 3) assistance and support following the death, 4) the individual's own grief mastery and 5) thoughts about an ideal assistance programme. The themes were connected with assistance and support for the public healthcare service, members of the clergy, police, volunteer organizations ('the public sphere') and the private sphere, comprising family, friends, neighbours and colleagues.

The in-depth interviews were carried out in the homes of the bereaved. Parents and siblings were in part interviewed individually, in part together (according to their own wishes). There was an emphasis on spending time on a 'let's get to know each other session' before the interview, which also contained thoroughly standardized information about the project for reasons pertaining to anonymity and the rights of informants. The researcher's presence in the homes lasted from three to eight hours, while the interviews lasted from two to three hours. On the average, the interview time was about two-and-a-half hours per couple/person. All interviews were tape recorded and transcribed. Data collection was terminated in November 1999.

Approvals and financing

The project obtained name and address lists from the Norwegian police records (STRASAK), where all sudden deaths in Norway are to be registered. Access was granted subsequent to extensive evaluations (a one-and-a-half-year-long application process) where the project's significance along with the ethical, juridical and medical aspects were assessed. Approvals were granted by the Attorney General, the Ministry of Law and Justice, the Norwegian Data Inspectorate, the Regional Committee for Medical Research Ethics at the University of Bergen and the Council for Professional Secrecy and Research at the University of Oslo.

The project received funding from the Norwegian Foundation for Health and Rehabilitation (three-year ordinary project and subsequently in the form of a three-year PhD project).

Publications

Dyregrov, K. (2001) Søsken etter selvmord ('Siblings after suicide'). In A. Dyregrov, G. Lorentzen and K. Raaheim (eds) *Et liv for barn. Utfordringer, omsorg og hjelpetiltak ('A life for children. Challenges, care and support, and help measures')* (p.14–158). Bergen: Fagbokforlaget.

Dyregrov, K. (2002) Assistance from local authorities versus survivors' needs for support after suicide. *Death Studies*, 26, 647–669.

Dyregrov, K. (2003) *The loss of child by suicide, SIDS, and accidents: Consequences, needs and provisions of help*. Doctoral thesis. HEMIL. Faculty of Psychology, University of Bergen.

Dyregrov, K. (2003–2004) Micro-sociological analysis of social support following traumatic bereavement: Unhelpful and avoidant responses from the community. *OMEGA – Journal of Death and Dying*, 48, 1, 23–44.

Dyregrov, K. (2004) Bereaved parents' experience of research participation. *Social Science and Medicine*, 58, 31–400.

Dyregrov, K. (2004) Strategies of professional assistance after traumatic deaths: Empowerment or disempowerment? *Scandinavian Journal of Psychology*, 45, 1–18.

Dyregrov, K. (2004) Søsken etter selvmord – 'de glemte sørgende' ('Siblings after suicide – "the forgotten bereaved"'). *Barn*, 3, 69–85.

Dyregrov, K. (2004) Hvilken hjelp ønsker etterlatte ved selvmord? ('What kind of help do bereaved by suicide want?'). *Suicidologi*, 9, 8–11.2.

Dyregrov, K. (2004) 'Hvordan er det å miste et barn?' – Et doktorgradsarbeid ('"What is it like to lose a child" – A doctoral work'). *Omsorg*, 4, 54–58.

Dyregrov, K. (2005) Do professionals disempower bereaved people? Grief and psychosocial intervention. *Bereavement Care*, 24, 1, 7–11.

Dyregrov, K. (2005) Umyndiggjør fagfolk sørgende and kriserammede? ('Do professionals disempower bereaved persons?'). *Tidsskrift for Den norske lægeforening*, 13–14, 125, 75–77.

Dyregrov, K. and Dyregrov, A. (2005) Helping the family following suicide. In B. Monroe and F. Kraus (eds) *Brief Interventions with Bereaved Children* (pp.201–215). Oxford: Oxford University Press.

Dyregrov, K. and Dyregrov, A. (2005) Siblings after suicide – 'the forgotten bereaved'. *Suicide and Life Threatening Behaviour*, 35, 6, 14–24.

Dyregrov, K., Nordanger, D. and Dyregrov, A. (2000) *Omsorg for etterlatte etter selvmord ('Support and care for the bereaved by suicide')*. The Bereavement Study. Report. Bergen: Center for Crisis Psychology.

Dyregrov, K., Nordanger, D. and Dyregrov, A. (2000) *Omsorg for etterlatte ved brå, uventet død. Evaluering av behov, tilbud og tiltak ('Support and care for the bereaved by sudden, unexpected death. An evaluation of needs, programmes and measures')*. Report. Bergen: Center for Crisis Psychology.

Dyregrov, K., Nordanger, D. and Dyregrov, A. (2003) Predictors of psychosocial distress after suicide, SidS and accidents. *Death Studies*, 2, 143–165.

Nordanger, D., Dyregrov, K. and Dyregrov, A. (2000) *Omsorg etter krybbedød og barneulykker ('Care and support after sudden infant death and child accidents')*. The Bereavement study. Report. Bergen: Center for Crisis Psychology.

The Network project

Main issues addressed/purpose

How do social networks experience supporting the bereaved following a sudden death? What challenges do they encounter and how can these challenges be resolved? The objective was to acquire knowledge about an unexplored field and subsequently to relate this to the Support and Care study in an upcoming book project on the encounter between the bereaved by sudden death and social networks (this book).

Recruitment and sample characteristics

The members of the Unexpected Child Death Society of Norway (LUB) and the Norwegian Organization for Suicide Survivors (LEVE) found on the membership lists of the organizations' respective magazines were sent a memo. The memo contained extensive information about the project and a request that they as bereaved individuals assist the project applicant to come into contact with their respective networks. They were otherwise informed that the researcher wished to interview families, friends, neighbours and colleagues in focus groups. In addition, the network members were asked to fill out a questionnaire. The bereaved distributed the memo to their support networks, upon which those who wished to take part sent their contact details to the researcher. A total of 101 (of 110) people filled out the questionnaire, resulting in a response rate of 92 per cent. The questionnaire sample was somewhat larger than the interview sample.

Based on criteria pertaining to variation, the researcher created focus groups for in-depth interviews. Interviewees comprised 21 groups of network members – ten groups that had supported parents who had lost a child by sudden infant death, and 11 groups who had supported the bereaved by suicide. In all, this comprised 70 interviewees, 55 women and 15 men. The LUB-groups comprised 20 women and three men, while the LEVE-groups comprised 35 women and 12 men. The 70 informants came from 12 different counties from throughout all of Norway and represented cities (42) and rural areas (28). The participants had a broad educational and professional background and the majority (two-thirds) lived less than ten kilometres away from the bereaved.

Data sources and data collection

The focus group interview and questionnaire of our own design for the network members who had given support following a suicide and sudden infant death provided the basis for the data sources. Twenty-one group interviews were carried out by the researcher. The network members helped out in organizing the interviews where they lived, either in their homes (12), at the researcher's hotel (6), at their workplace (2) or at the researcher's office (1). Slightly more than half of the groups consisted of network members who had supported the same bereaved family, while in the other groups the members had supported different families. The number of participants in each group varied from two to seven network members. The duration of the interviews varied from between one-and-a-half to four hours, with an average of three hours. In all, the interview material comprised 63 hours of interviews. All interviews were tape recorded and transcribed.

The interviews were based on an interview guide with the following themes: who took the initiative for support, the motivation for helping, the type of help they had contributed, frequency and duration, satisfaction with the effort, positive experiences from the relation, changes in relation to the bereaved, various difficulties in providing support.

A questionnaire developed at the Center for Crisis Psychology outlined the same themes as the in-depth interview with an eye towards acquiring quantifiable information. In addition, four questions opened up for qualitative descriptions of: impact on the support person, the most important support given, improvement potentials and advice to others in the same situation. The data collection was carried out from December 2003 to March 2004.

Approvals and financing
The project was approved by LUB and recommended by the Norwegian Social Science Data Services (NSD) and the Regional Committee for Medical Research Ethics (UiB). The project was financed by the Unexpected Child Death Society of Norway.

Publications
Dyregrov, K. (2005) Vondt, vanskelig og utrolig givende! Ny forskning om støtteprosessen mellom sosiale nettverk and foreldre som mister barn ('Painful, difficult and incredibly rewarding! Recent findings on the support process between social networks and parents who lose children'). *Oss foreldre imellom*, 4, 46–49.

Dyregrov, K. (2006) Experiences of social networks supporting traumatically bereaved. *Omega – Journal of Death and Dying*, 52, 4, 337–356.

The Young Suicide Bereavement project
Main issues addressed / purpose
How do young people bereaved by suicide experience their situation and what are their needs for care and support? What constitutes good support and

assistance and what do they find that they can do to alleviate some of the difficulties particular to their situation? The intention of the project was to inform and contribute new knowledge in potential support communities regarding how they can best support young people in their grief processing.

Recruitment and sample characteristics

The recruitment to the interview sample was carried out through LEVE's youth gatherings in the first phase (youth gatherings all over Norway) by the project 'Reinforced care and support scheme for young bereaved by suicide'. The majority of those who attended the youth gatherings for the project both filled out the questionnaire and took part in interviews (90 per cent participation rate). Thirty-two young bereaved, ten boys and 22 girls, filled out the questionnaire and took part in qualitative group interviews. The informants were 13–24 years of age (M = 18). Eight were attending primary school, 16 secondary school, and eight attended college or university. They represented all the health regions of Norway and approximately two-thirds lived in cities (69 per cent), while 31 per cent lived in rural areas. The interviewees had lost a mother/father (6), brother/sister (22) or other close relatives/friends (4). The age of the deceased varied from 12 to 56 years of age, with an average of around 27 years of age. The time since the deaths varied from one month to seven years (M = 3 years). Five young people (16 per cent) were present when the person who had committed suicide was found.

Data sources and data collection

The data collection was carried out after the youth gatherings, at which time the young people filled out the questionnaire and took part in focus group interviews. A total of 11 group interviews, with two to four young people per group, were carried out in connection with a gathering, at the researcher's office or in the young person's home. An interview guide ensured that certain themes were systematically addressed. There was a focus on the types of experiences the young people had had with assistance and support – from the public assistance scheme, the school and the social network. Further, one explored whether the young people would have liked to have received a different type of help: What kind of help/support would have been beneficial? Who would they have wanted assistance from? How would they prefer to be approached? When is it important to be approached/receive assistance? How large should the scope of the assistance be and for what duration of time? What quality/competence had they wanted? How would they have liked the contents of the support to have been? All interviews were tape recorded and transcribed.

A four-page questionnaire ('The assistance form' created at the Center for Crisis Psychology) focused on the young people's experiences with help and support from the public assistance scheme, the school and the social network. In addition, long-term traumatic reactions were recorded using the Impact of Event Scale (IES-15), self-esteem using the Rosenberg Self-Esteem Scale (RSS) and grief reactions and personal growth using the Hogan Sibling Inventory of Bereavement (HSIB).

Approvals and financing

The project was approved by LEVE (Norwegian Organization for Suicide Survivors) and recommended by the Norwegian Social Science Data Services (NSD) and the Regional Committee for Medical Research Ethics (UiB).

The project was financed by the Norwegian Foundation for Health and Rehabilitation.

Publications

Dyregrov, K. (2006) Hvordan ønsker unge selvmordsetterlatte å bli møtt av psykologer? – en brukerundersøkelse ('How do the young bereaved by suicide wish to be met by psychologists? A user study'). *Tidsskrift for Norsk Psykologforening* 43, 787–794.

Dyregrov, K. (2006) Skolens viktige rolle etter selvmord. Ny forskning om unge etterlattes ønsker for hjelp og støtte ('The important role of the school following a suicide. Recent findings on young bereaved persons' wishes for help and support'). *Bedre Skole,* 1, 46–51.

Dyregrov, K. (2006) *Støtte til unge etterlatte. Styrket omsorgsapparat for unge etterlatte ved selvmord ('Supporting the young bereaved. A reinforced care and support scheme for the young bereaved by suicide').* Report. Bergen: Center for Crisis Psychology.

Dyregrov, K. (in press) Hva sliter unge etterlatte etter selvmord med? ('What are the struggles of the young bereaved by suicide?'). *Tidsskrift for Norsk Psykologforening.*

The Children and Cancer project

Main problems addressed/purpose

What are children and young people's reactions to a mother's/father's cancer diagnosis and death and what are the potential psychosocial consequences? What are their assistance needs in relation to professionals, the school and the support network? To what extent do they experience that the help they want is available and how do they manage to utilize it? In addition, an objective was to obtain knowledge about how young people manage to cope with the difficult situation and to summarize their evaluations of a psychopedagogical course concept at the Montebello Centre (MBS).

Recruitment and sample characteristics

The sample was recruited from 107 children who took part in a rehabilitation course at MBS in the summer of 2005. Those who took part in the project questionnaire were 78 children and young people in the age group 6–18 years. The average age was 11 years (SD = 3.42). There were 58 children: 32 girls (55 per cent) and 26 boys (45 per cent) from courses where the mother or father had cancer (next-of-kin groups). These constituted 74 per cent of the sample. The remaining 26 per cent (20 children) were children and young people who had lost a parent by cancer (bereavement groups). Of these, ten were girls (50 per cent) and ten boys (50 per cent). The overall gender distribution in both groups was 42 girls (54 per cent) and 36 boys (46 per cent). They came from all of the health regions of Norway.

A sub-sample of 11 children and young people in the age group of 10–18 years (five boys and six girls) were interviewed. A theoretical sample was created from all those who volunteered to do a focus group interview (the number reporting for the project by far exceeded its capacity). The breadth and variation in terms of gender, domicile, age, experiential background, type of cancer and duration of the illness formed the basis for the selection. For the young bereaved, the time after the death was an important variable. The selection resulted in four groups of children/young people with two to three people in each: two next-of-kin peer groups and two young bereaved groups. The average age for these was 13 years old. Five children had mothers who had a serious form of cancer. Six of the children had lost one of their parents (two mothers and four fathers).

Data sources and data collection

The questionnaire and the focus group interview constituted the data sources. The questionnaires contained three pages of standardized and open questions in order to evaluate thematic and satisfaction-related aspects of the Montebello courses, and the need for and existing assistance programmes in the respective domiciles. The questionnaires were filled out at the Montebello Centre upon termination of the courses.

A theme guide was used to ensure that all themes from the questionnaire were addressed in depth in the focus groups. The main themes were: 1) Why was the family at the MB Centre? 2) How has the illness/death affected the child's life in general (food, sleep, school, friends, etc.)? 3) How have things changed at home? 4) What kind of help and support has the family received? 5) How has the school responded? 6) Has the family/child received the necessary assistance? 7) Have they received advice about professional assistance, schools and networks of friends who will support other young people in the same situation? 8) What is the most important thing the child has personally been able to do to alleviate the situation (process the loss)?

Two groups were interviewed immediately after the termination of the course at the MB Centre, the remainder within a two-month period. Two interviews were done at the MB Centre, one at a child's home and one in the Norwegian Cancer Society's local premises. All interviews were tape recorded and transcribed. The interviews lasted from one-and-a-half to three hours (an average of two hours). The data collection took place in the course of 2005.

Approvals and financing

The pilot project was approved by the board of the Montebello Centre and the Norwegian Cancer Society, and recommended by the Norwegian Social Science Data Services and the Regional Committee for Medical Research Ethics (UiB).

The project was financed by the Norwegian Cancer Society and the Montebello Centre.

Publications
Dyregrov, K. (2005) 'På tynn is' – Barn and unges situasjon når foreldre rammes av kreft. Resultat fra et Pilotprosjekt ('"On thin ice" – Children and young people's situation when parents are afflicted with cancer. Results from a pilot project'). Report. Bergen: Center for Crisis Psychology.

Intimacy and sexuality after the death of a child
Main issues addressed / purpose
The objective of the study was to produce knowledge of and understanding for parents' experience of intimate relations after the loss of a child by addressing the following: How do parents experience intimacy and sexuality after the death of a child? Are there gender differences? How do parents cope with any difficulties and what advice can they give to others? The goal was to provide a better basis from which to counsel parents and for possible necessary measures towards assisting those experiencing difficulties.

Recruitment and sample characteristics
The participants of the project were recruited through support/peer organizations by way of an inquiry regarding participation in the project directed to those members who had lost a child. A total of 1027 questionnaires were sent out, from the Norwegian organizations 'Vi som har et barn for lite'

('Those of us who lack a child') (652) and the Unexpected Child Death Society of Norway (375), respectively. In all, 321 parents agreed to take part in the questionnaire study.[2] Of these, 63 per cent were women and 37 per cent men. The parents were between the ages of 22 and 61 with an average age of 38.4 years (SD = 7.3). The women were on average slightly younger (37.6 years old) than the men (39.6 years old). A total of 93 per cent of the parents were married or living together, 4 per cent were divorced and the remainder were single or widows/widowers. The duration of the period of cohabitation was on average 13.5 years (SD = 7.5) for those who had partners. Of those with partners 93 per cent reported that the partner was the mother/father of the deceased child. The child's age at the time of death was on average 16.4 months (SD = 38.0), but varied from 0 months (stillbirths and deaths immediately following the birth) to 18 years of age.

A total of 105 people in the target group wished to be contacted for a follow-up interview. Ten parents were selected to participate in the interview. The characteristics of this sub-sample were very similar to the main sample. Five interviews were carried out with parent couples that had lost children by sudden infant death, three by stillbirths and two by accidents.

Data sources and data collection

Questionnaires and in-depth interviews of couples constituted the basis for data acquisition. A separately developed form (CfCP-form) contained a number of questions about intimacy and sexuality. This included how the parents had experienced intimacy and sexuality after the death, problems in this area, differences in the partners' views of intimacy and sexuality, and any advice they may have received in this area. The questionnaire alternated between multiple choice questions and open questions that asked for the participants' evaluations and written comments on the subject. In addition, a standardized form was used, 'Dyadic Adjustment Scale' (DAS) to plot adaptation in couples' relationships (Spanier, 1976).

A semi-structured interview guide was developed to plot out the various aspects covered by the questionnaires, while it also provided the opportunity for the informants to expand upon and comment in depth on topics in connection with intimacy and sexuality. The interviews were carried out in the homes

---

2   An unknown number of the recipients were support members and not parents who had lost
     a child and therefore it is not possible to ascertain the response rate in relation to the
     project's target group.

of the parents and lasted from two to three hours. All interviews were tape recorded and transcribed.

The questionnaire study was carried out in the autumn of 2005, while the interviews were done in January and February 2006.

Approvals and financing
The study was recommended by the Regional Committee for Medical Research Ethics (UiB) and the Norwegian Social Science Data Services (NSD). The project was financed by the Unexpected Child Death Society of Norway.

Publications
Dyregrov, A. (2007) *Nærhet and seksualitet etter et barns dødsfall ('Intimacy and sexuality after the death of a child')*. Report. Bergen: Center for Crisis Psychology.

References

Albrecht, T.L. and Goldsmith, D.J. (2003) Social support, social networks, and health. In T.L. Thompson, A.M. Dorsey, K.I. Miller and R. Parrot (eds) *Handbook of Health Communication* (pp.263–284). Mahwah, NJ: Erlbaum.

Amaya-Jackson, L., Davidson, J.R., Hughes, D.C., Swartz, M., Reynolds, V., George, L.K. and Blazer, D.G. (1999) Functional impairment and utilization of services associated with posttraumatic stress in the community. *Journal of Traumatic Stress*, 12, 709–724.

Bartone, P.T., Ursano, R.J., Wright, K.M. and Ingraham, L.H. (1989) The impact of a military air disaster on the health of assistance workers. *The Journal of Nervous and Mental Disease*, 177, 317–328.

Bateson, G. (1972) *Steps to an Ecology of Mind.* New York: Chandler Publishing Company.

Benson, H. (1975) *The Relaxation Response.* New York: Avon.

Berah, E.F., Jones, H.J. and Valent, P. (1984) The experience of a mental health team involved in the early phase of a disaster. *Australian and New Zealand Journal of Psychiatry*, 18, 354–358.

Berkman, L.F., Glass, T., Brisette, I. and Seeman, T.E. (2000) From sociological integration to health: Durkheim in the new millennium. *Social Science and Medicine*, 51, 843–857.

Bisson, J.I, Ehlers, A., Matthews, R., Pilling, S., Richards, D. and Turner, S. (2007) Psychological treatments for chronic post-traumatic stress disorder: Systematic review and meta-analysis. *British Journal of Psychiatry*, 190, 97–104.

Bohanek, J.G., Marin, K.A., Fivush, R. and Duke, M.P. (2006) Family narrative interaction and children's sense of self. *Family Process*, 45, 39–54.

Bonanno, G.A. and Kaltman, S. (2001) The varieties of grief experience. *Clinical Psychology Review*, 21, 705–734.

Boscarino, J.A., Adams, R.E. and Figley, C.R. (2005) A prospective cohort study of the effectiveness of employer-sponsored crisis interventions after a major disaster. *International Journal of Mental Health*, 7, 9–22.

Brabant, S., Forsyth, C. and McFarlain, G. (1995) Life after the death of a child: Initial and long-term support from others. *Omega*, 31, 67–85.

Bradley, R., Greene, J., Russ, E., Dutra, L. and Westen, D. (2005) A multidimensional meta-analysis of psychotherapy for PTSD. *American Journal of Psychiatry*, 162, 214–227.

Brent, D.A., Perper, J.A., Moritz, G., Liotus, L., Schweers, J., Roth, C., Balach, L. and Allman, C. (1993) Psychiatric impact of the loss of an adolescent sibling to suicide. *Journal of Affective Disorders*, 28, 249–256.

Breslau, N., Davis, G.C., Andreski, P., Peterson, E.L. and Schultz, L.R. (1997) Sex differences in posttraumatic stress disorder. *Archives of General Psychiatry*, 54, 1044–1048.

Brewin, C., Andrews, B. and Valentine, J.D. (2000) Meta-analysis of risk factors for posttraumatic stress disorder in trauma-exposed adults. *Journal of Consulting and Clinical Psychology*, 68, 748–766.

Briggs, C.L. (1986) *Learning How to Ask: A Sociolinguistic Appraisal of the Role of the Interview in Social Science Research*. Cambridge, MA: Cambridge University Press.

Brottveit, Å. (2003) Helt naturlig? Sorg and dødsritualer i et krysskulturelt perspektiv ('Completely natural? Grief and death rituals from a cross-cultural perspective'). In K. Bugge, O. Sandvik and H. Eriksen (eds) *Sorg* ('*Grief*'). Bergen: Fagbokforlaget.

Burleson, B.R. (2003) Emotional support skill. In J.O. Greene and B.R. Burleson (eds) *Handbook of Communication and Social Interaction Skills* (pp.551–594). Mahwah, NJ: Erlbaum.

Burleson, B.R. and Goldsmith, D.J. (1998) How comforting messages work: Some mechanisms through which messages may alleviate emotional distress. In P.A. Anderson and L.K. Guerrero (eds) *Handbook of Communication and Emotion: Research, Theory, Applications, and Contexts* (pp.245–280). Orlando, FL: Academic Press.

Calhoun, L.G, Abernathy, C.B. and Selby, J.W. (1986) The rule of bereavement: Are suicidal deaths different? *Journal of Community Psychology*, 14, 213–218.

Childhood Bereavement Network (2008) http://childhoodbereavementnetwork.org.uk/haad_about_bereavement_childhood_cr. htm (last accessed April 2008).

Clark, S. (2001) Bereavement after suicide – how far have we come and where do we go from here? *Crisis*, 22, 3, 102–108.

Cleiren, M. and Diekstra, R. (1995) After the loss: Bereavement after suicide and other types of death. In B. Mishara (ed.) *The Impact of Suicide* (pp.7–39). New York: Springer.

Cohen, S. (1988) Psychosocial models of the role of social support in the etiology of physical disease. *Health Psychology*, 7, 269–297.

Cohen, S. and Wills, T.A. (1985) Stress, social support, and the buffering hypothesis. *Psychological Bulletin*, 98, 2, 310–357.

Cook, J.A. (1988) Dad's double binds. *Journal of Contemporary Ethnography*, 17, 285–308.

Cruse Bereavement Care (2008) www.crusebereavementcare.org (last accessed April 2008).

Cutrona, C.E. and Suhr, J.A. (1992) Controllability of stressful events and satisfaction with spouse support behaviors. *Communication Research*, 19, 154–174.

Cutrona, C.E. and Suhr, J.A. (1994) Social support communication in the context of marriage: An analysis of couples' supportive interactions. In B.R. Burleson, T.L. Albrecht and I.G. Sarason (eds) *Communication of Social Support: Messages, Interactions, Relationships, and Community* (pp.113–135). Thousand Oaks, CA: Sage.

Dakof, G.A. and Taylor, S.E. (1990) Victims' perceptions of social support: What is helpful from whom? *Journal of Personality and Social Psychology*, 58, 80–89.

Davidowitz, M. and Myrick, R.D. (1984) Responding to the bereaved: An analysis of 'helping' statements. *Death Education*, 8, 1–10.

Davies, B. (1995) Sibling bereavement research: State of the art. In I.B. Corless, B.B. Germino and M.A. Pittman (eds) *A Challenge for Living. Dying, Death, and Bereavement* (pp.173–201). London: Jones and Bartlett Publishers.

De Groot, M.H., De Keijser, J. and Neeleman, J. (2006) Grief shortly after suicide and natural death: A comparative study among spouses and first-degree relatives. *Suicide and Life Threatening Behaviour*, 36, 418–431.

Demi, A.S. and Howell, C. (1991) Hiding and healing: Resolving the suicide of a parent or sibling. *Archives of Psychiatric Nursing*, 5, 6, 350–356.

Department for Education and Skills (DfES) and Department of Health (DoH) (2005) *National Healthy School Status: A Guide for Schools* www.healthyschools.gov.uk/ (last accessed April 2008).

Dijkstra, I.C. (2000) *Living with Loss: Parents Grieving for the Death of Their Child.* Dissertation paper. Utrecht University, Faculty of Social Sciences, Department of Clinical Psychology, The Netherlands.

Dunkel-Schetter, C., Blasband, D., Feinstein, L. and Herbert, T. (1992) Elements of supportive interactions: When are attempts to help effective? In S. Spacapan and S. Oskamp (eds) *Helping and Being Helped: Naturalistic Studies* (pp.83–114). Newbury Park, CA: Sage.

Dunne, E.J., McIntosh, J.L. and Dunne-Maxim, K. (eds) (1987) *Suicide and Its Aftermath: Understanding and Counselling the Survivors.* New York: Norton.

Dyregrov, A. (1988) *Parental Reactions to the Death of an Infant Child.* Doctoral dissertation. Department of Pediatrics, University of Bergen.

Dyregrov, A. (1989) Retningslinjer for hjelp til familier etter barns død ('Guidelines to help families following the death of a child'). *Tidsskrift for Den norske lægeforening,* 109, 3408–3411.

Dyregrov, A. (2000) Lederskap i krise and omstilling ('Management in crisis and readjustment'). In S. Einarsen and A. Skogstad (eds) *Det gode arbeidsmiljø* ('*The Good Working Environment*'). Bergen: Fagbokforlaget.

Dyregrov, A. (2001a) Telling the truth or hiding the facts. An evaluation of current strategies for assisting children following adverse events. *Association for Child Psychology and Psychiatry Occasional Papers,* 17, 25–38.

Dyregrov, A. (2002a) *Katastrofepsykologi* ('*Disaster Psychology*'). Bergen: Fagbokforlaget.

Dyregrov, A. (2004) Educational consequences of loss and trauma. *Educational and Child Psychology,* 21, 77–84.

Dyregrov, A. (2006a) Komplisert sorg: teori and behandling ('Complicated grief: Theory and treatment'). *Tidsskrift for Norsk Psykologforening,* 43, 779–786.

Dyregrov, A. (2006b) *Små barns sorg. Informasjon and veiledning til foreldre and andre voksne* ('*The grief of young children. Information and guidance for parents and other adults*'). Parent counselling programme. Oslo: Norwegian Directorate for Children, Youth and Family Affairs.

Dyregrov, A. (2007) *Nærhet and seksualitet etter et barns dødsfall* ('*Intimacy and sexuality after the death of a child*'). Report. Bergen: Center for Crisis Psychology.

Dyregrov, A. (2008) *Small Children's Grief.* London: Jessica Kingsley Publishers.

Dyregrov, A. and Dyregrov. K. (1999) Long-term impact of sudden infant death: A twelve to fifteen year follow-up. *Death Studies,* 23, 635–661.

Dyregrov, A., Dyregrov, K. and Nordanger, D. (2002) Praktisk organisering av psykososialt støttearbeid: Hvordan kan vi unngå de viktigste feilene? ('Practical organization of psychosocial assistance: How can we avoid the most significant mistakes?') *The Scandinavian Journal of Trauma and Emergency Medicine,* 10, 11–13.

Dyregrov, A. and Matthiesen, S.B. (1987) Anxiety and vulnerability in parents following the death of an infant. *Scandinavian Journal of Psychology,* 28, 16–25.

Dyregrov, A. and Mitchell, J.T. (1992) Psychological effects of working with traumatized children. *Journal of Traumatic Stress,* 5, 5–17.

Dyregrov, A. and Solomon, R.M. (1991) Mental health professionals in disasters. An exploratory study. *Disaster Management,* 3, 123–128.

Dyregrov, K. (2001b) Søsken etter selvmord ('Siblings after suicide'). In A. Dyregrov, G. Lorentzen and K. Raaheim (eds) *Et liv for barn. Utfordringer, omsorg and hjelpetiltak* ('*A life for children. Challenges, care and support, and help measures*') (pp.14–158). Bergen: Fagbokforlaget.

Dyregrov, K. (2002b) Assistance from local authorities versus survivors' needs for support after suicide. *Death Studies*, 26, 647–669.

Dyregrov, K. (2003) *The loss of a child by suicide, SIDS, and accidents: Consequences, needs and provisions of help*. Doctoral thesis. HEMIL, Faculty of Psychology, University of Bergen.

Dyregrov, K. (2003–2004) Micro-sociological analysis of social support following traumatic bereavement: Unhelpful and avoidant responses from the community. *OMEGA – Journal of Death and Dying*, 48, 23–44.

Dyregrov, K. (2004a) Hvilken hjelp ønsker etterlatte ved selvmord? ('What kind of help do bereaved by suicide want?'). *Suicidologi*, 9, 8–11.

Dyregrov, K. (2004b) Strategies of professional assistance after traumatic deaths: Empowerment or disempowerment? *Scandinavian Journal of Psychology*, 45, 179–187.

Dyregrov, K. (2005a) '*På tynn is' – Barn and unges situasjon når foreldre rammes av kreft. Resultat fra et Pilotprosjekt* ('"*On thin ice" – Children and young people's situation when parents are afflicted with cancer. Results from a pilot project*'). Report. Bergen: Center for Crisis Psychology.

Dyregrov, K. (2005b) Vondt, vanskelig and utrolig givende! Ny forskning om støtteprosessen mellom sosiale nettverk and foreldre som mister barn. ('Painful, difficult and incredibly rewarding! Recent findings on the support process between social networks and parents who lose children'). *Oss foreldre imellom*, 4, 46–49.

Dyregrov, K. (2006a) Hvordan ønsker unge selvmordsetterlate å bli møtt av psykologer? – en brukerundersøkelse ('How do the young bereaved by suicide wish to be met by psychologists? A user study'). *Tidsskrift for Norsk Psykologforening*, 43, 787–794.

Dyregrov, K. (2006b) *Støtte til unge etterlatte. Styrket omsorgsapparat for unge etterlatte ved selvmord* ('*Supporting the young bereaved. A reinforced care and support scheme for the young bereaved by suicide*'). Report. Bergen: Center for Crisis Psychology.

Dyregrov, K. (2006c) Experiences of social networks supporting traumatically bereaved. *OMEGA – Journal of Death and Dying*, 52, 4, 337–356.

Dyregrov, K. (2006d) Skolens viktige rolle etter selvmord. Ny forskning om unge etterlattes ønsker for hjelp and støtte ('The important role of the school following a suicide. Recent findings on young bereaved persons' wishes for help and support'). *Bedre Skole*, 1, 46–51.

Dyregrov, K. and Dyregrov, A. (2005a) Helping the family following suicide. In B. Monroe and F. Kraus (eds) *Brief Interventions with Bereaved Children* (pp.201–215). Oxford: Oxford University Press.

Dyregrov, K. and Dyregrov, A. (2005b) Siblings after suicide – 'the forgotten bereaved'. *Suicide and Life Threatening Behaviour*, 35, 6, 714–724.

Dyregrov, K., Dyregrov, A. and Nordanger, D. (1999) Omsorg for etterlatte etter selvmord – 'Kommunestudien'. ('Support and care after sudden unexpected deaths – "The Community Study"'). *Tidsskrift for Den norske lægeforening*, 27, 119, 4010–4015.

Dyregrov, K., Nordanger, D. and Dyregrov, A. (2000a) *Omsorg for etterlatte ved brå, uventet død. Evaluering av behov, tilbud og tiltak* ('*Support and care for the bereaved by sudden, unexpected death. An evaluation of needs, programmes and measures*'). Report. Bergen: Center for Crisis Psychology.

Dyregrov, K., Nordanger, D. and Dyregrov, A. (2000b) *Omsorg for etterlatte etter selvmord. Etterlattestudien ('Support and care for the bereaved by suicide – the Bereavement Study')*. Report. Bergen: Center for Crisis Psychology.

Dyregrov, K., Nordanger, D. and Dyregrov, A. (2003) Predictors of psychosocial distress after suicide, SIDS and accidents. *Death Studies, 27*, 143–165.

Field, N.P., Gao, B. and Paderna, L. (2006) Continuing bonds in bereavement: An attachment theory based perspective. *Death Studies, 29*, 277–299.

Figley, C.R. (1995) *Compassion Fatigue: Coping with Secondary Traumatic Stress Disorder in Those who Treat the Traumatized.* New York: Brunner/Mazel.

Figley, C.R., Bride, B.E. and Mazza, N. (1997) *Death and Trauma. The Traumatology of Grieving.* Washington, DC: Taylor and Francis.

Giddens, A. (1991) *Modernity and Self-identity.* Cambridge: Polity Press.

Goffman, E. (1967) *Interaction Ritual.* Middlesex: Penguin Books Ltd.

Goldberg, D. and Williams, P. (1988) *User's Guide to the General Health Questionnaire.* Windsor: NFER-Nelson.

Goldschmidt, O. and Weller, L. (2000) 'Talking emotions': Gender differences in a variety of conversational contexts. *Symbolic Interaction, 23*, 117–134.

Goldsmith, D.J. (2002) Managing conflicting goals in supportive interaction: An integrative theoretical framework. *Communication Research, 19*, 264–286.

Goldsmith, D.J. (2004) *Communicating Social Support.* Cambridge: Cambridge University Press.

Goldsmith, D.J. and Fitch, K. (1997) The normative context of advice as social support. *Human Communication Research, 23*, 454–476.

Gottlieb, B.H. (1992) Quandaries in translating support concepts to intervention. In H.O.F. Veiel and U. Baumann (eds) *The Meaning and Measurement of Social Support* (pp.293–309). New York: Hemisphere.

Greene, J.O. and Burleson, B.R. (eds) (2003) *Handbook of Communication and Social Interaction Skills.* New Jersey: Lawrence Erlbaum Associates.

Habermas, J. (1984) *The Theory of Communicative Action: Reason and the Rationalization of Society* (T. McCarthy, Trans., Vol. 1). Boston, MA: Beacon Press.

Hagborg, W.J. (1993) The Rosenberg self-esteem scale and Harter's self-perception profile for adolescents: A concurrent validity study. *Psychology in the Schools, 30*, 132–136.

Harley, K. and Reese, E. (1999) Origins of autobiographical memory. *Developmental Psychology, 35*, 1338–1348.

Harris, T.O. (1992) Some reflections on the process of social support and the nature of unsupportive behaviors. In H.O.F. Veiel and U. Baumann (eds) *The Meaning and Measurement of Social Support* (pp.171–190). New York: Hemisphere.

Health Development Agency (2004) Promoting Emotional Health and Wellbeing through the National Healthy School Standard. www.wiredforhealth.gov.uk/PDF/139641_HDA_Complete.pdf (England only) (last accessed April 2008).

Heltne, U. and Dyregrov, A. (2006) *Ungdommers erfaringer med hjelpeapparatet ('Young people's experiences with public assistance schemes')*. Report. Bergen: Center for Crisis Psychology.

Hogan, N. (1990) Hogan sibling inventory of bereavement. In J. Touliatos, B. Perlmutter and M. Straus (eds) *Handbook of Family Measurement Techniques.* Newbury Park, CA: Sage.

Horowitz, M., Wilner, N. and Alvarez, W. (1979) Impact of event scale: A measure of subjective stress. *Psychosomatic Medicine, 41*, 209–218.

House, J.S. and Kahn, R.L. (1985) Measures and concepts of social support. In S. Cohen and S.L. Syme (eds) *Social Support and Health* (pp.83–108). Orlando, FL: Academic Press.

Jacobs, S.C. (1999) *Traumatic Grief: Diagnosis, Treatment, and Prevention*. Philadelphia, PA: Brunner/Mazel.

Janoff-Bulman, R. (1992) *Shattered Assumptions. Towards a New Psychology of Trauma*. New York: The Free Press.

Johnson, T.P. (1991) Mental health, social relations, and social selection: A longitudinal analysis. *Journal of Health and Social Behavior*, 32, 408–423.

Johnston, S.J. (1993) Traumatic stress reactions in the crew of the Herald of Free Enterprise. In J.P. Wilson and B. Raphael (eds) *The International Handbook of Traumatic Stress Syndromes*. New York: Plenum Press.

Jordan, J.R. (2001) Is suicide bereavement different? A reassessment of the literature. *Suicide and Life-Threatening Behavior*, 31, 91–102.

Joseph, S. and Williams, R. (2005) Understanding posttraumatic stress: Theory, reflections, context and future. *Behavioural and Cognitive Psychotherapy*, 33, 423–441.

Kamm, S. and Vandenberg, B. (2001) Grief communication, grief reactions and marital satisfaction in bereaved parents. *Death Studies*, 25, 569–582.

Leffler, C.T. and Dembert, M.L. (1998) Posttraumatic stress symptoms among U.S. navy divers recovering TWA flight 800. *The Journal of Nervous and Mental Disease*, 186, 574–577.

Lehman, D.R., Ellard, J.H. and Wortman, C.B. (1986) Social support for the bereaved: Recipients' and providers' perspective on what is helpful. *Journal of Consulting and Clinical Psychology*, 54, 438–445.

Li, J., Precht, D.H., Mortensen, P.B. and Olsen, J. (2003) Mortality in parents after death of a child in Denmark: A nationwide follow-up study. *The Lancet*, 361, 9355, 363–367.

LOV 1982–11–19–66. Lov om helsetjenesten i kommunene (Norwegian Act of November 1982 No. 66 relating to municipal health services). www.lovdata.no/cgi-wift/wiftldles?doc=/usr/www/lovdata/all/nl-19821119-066.html&emne=lov+om+helsetjenesten+i+kommunen*&& (last accessed April 2008).

LOV 2000–06–23 nr. 56. Lov om helsemessig and sosial beredskap (Norwegian Act of 23 June 2000 No. 56 relating to health and psychosocial follow up after crisis and catastrophes). www.lovdata.no/cgi-wift/wiftldles?doc=/usr/www/lovdata/all/nl-20000623-056.html&emne=lov+om+helsemessig+og+sosial+beredskap*&& (last accessed April 2008).

Luckmann, T. (1995) Interaction planning and intersubjective adjustment of perspectives by communicative genres. In E.N. Goody (ed.) *Social Intelligence and Interaction* (p.179). Cambridge: Cambridge University Press.

Marmar, C.R., Weiss, D.S., Metzler, T.J., Ronfeldt, H.M. and Foreman, C. (1996) Stress responses of emergency services personnel to the Loma Prieta earthquake interstate 880 freeway collapse and control traumatic incidents. *Journal of Traumatic Stress*, 9, 1, 63–85.

Maslach, C. and Leiter, M.P. (1997) *The Truth about Burnout*. San Francisco, CA: Jossey Bass Inc.

McCarroll, J.E., Fullerton, C.S., Ursano, R.J. and Hermsen, J.M. (1996) Posttraumatic stress symptoms following forensic dental identification: Mt. Carmel, Waco, Texas. *American Journal of Psychiatry*, 153, 778–752.

McCarroll, J.E., Ursano, R.J. and Fullerton, C.S. (1993) Symptoms of posttraumatic stress disorder following recovery of war dead. *American Journal of Psychiatry*, 150, 1875–1877.

McCarroll, J.E., Ursano, R.J., Fullerton, C.S., Liu, X. and Lundy, A. (2001) Effects of exposure to death in a war mortuary on posttraumatic stress disorder symptoms of intrusion and avoidance. *The Journal of Nervous and Mental Disease*, 189, 44–48.

McMenamy, J.M., Jordan, J.R. and Mitchell, A. (in press) What do suicide survivors tell us they need? Results of a pilot study. *Suicide and Life Threatening Behaviour*.

Millar, F.E. and Rogers, L.E. (1976) A relational approach to interpersonal communication. In R.R. Millers (ed.) *Explorations in Interpersonal Communication*. Beverly Hills, CA: Sage.

Murphy, S.A. (2000) The use of research findings in bereavement programs: A case study. *Death Studies*, 24, 585–602.

Murphy, S.A., Braun, T., Tillery, L., Cain, K.C., Johnson, L.C. and Beaton, R.D. (1999) PTSD among bereaved parents following the violent deaths of their 12- to 28-year-old children: A longitudinal prospective analysis. *Journal of Traumatic Stress*, 12, 2, 273–291.

Murphy, S.A., Johnson, L.C. and Lohan, J. (2002) The aftermath of the violent death of a child: An integration of the assessments of parents' mental distress and PTSD during the first 5 years of bereavement. *Journal of Loss and Trauma*, 7, 203–222.

Murphy, S.A., Johnson, L.C., Wu, L., Fan, J.J. and Lohan, J. (2003) Bereaved parents' outcomes 4 to 60 months after their children's death by accident, suicide, or homicide: A comparative study demonstrating differences. *Death Studies*, 27, 39–61.

Nadeau, J.W. (1997) *Families Making Sense of Death*. Thousand Oaks, CA: Sage Publications Ltd.

Neimeyer, R.A. (1999) Narrative strategies in grief therapy. *Journal of Constructivist Psychology*, 12, 65–85.

Neimeyer, R.A. (2000) Searching for the meaning: Grief therapy and the process of reconstruction. *Death Studies*, 24, 541–558.

Neimeyer, R.A. (2001) The language of loss: Grief therapy as a process of meaning reconstruction. In R.A. Neimeyer (ed.) *Meaning Reconstruction and the Experience of Loss* (pp.261–292). Washington, DC: American Psychological Association.

Neimeyer, R.A., Baldwin, S.A. and Gillies, J. (2006) Continuing bonds and reconstructing meaning: Mitigating complications in bereavement. *Death Studies* 30, 715–738.

Nordanger, D., Dyregrov, K. and Dyregrov, A. (1998) Omsorg etter krybbedød og barneulykker. *Tilbudet i norske kommuner* ('Care and support after sudden infant death and child accidents. Assistance schemes in Norwegian communities'). Report. Bergen: Center for Crisis Psychology.

Nordanger, D., Dyregrov, K. and Dyregrov, A. (2000) Omsorg etter krybbedød og barneulykker. *Etterlattestudien* ('Care and support after sudden infant death and child accidents. The Bereavement Study'). Report. Bergen: Center for Crisis Psychology.

Nordanger, D., Dyregrov, K. and Dyregrov, A. (2003) Betydningen av skriftlige rutiner for omsorgen etter krybbedød og barneulykker ('The effect of written routines on bereavement care and support following sudden infant death and accidental child death'). *Tidsskrift for Den norske lægeforening*, 123, 933–935.

Oliver, L. (1999) Effects of a child's death on the marital relationship: a review. *Omega – Journal of Death and Dying*, 39, 197–227.

Parkes, C.M. (1998) Traditional models and theories of grief. *Bereavement Care*, 17, 2, 21–23.

Pfeffer, C.R., Martins, P., Mann, J., Sunkenberg, R.N. Ice, A., Damore, J.P., Gallo, C., Karpenos, I. and Jiang, H. (1997) Child survivors of suicide: Psychosocial characteristics. *Journal of the American Academy of Child and Adolescent Psychiatry*, 36, 1, 65–74.

Prigerson, H.G. and Jacobs, S.C. (2001) Diagnostic criteria for traumatic grief: A rationale, consensus criteria, and preliminary empirical test. Part II. Theory, methodology and ethical issues. In M.S. Stroebe, R.O. Hansson, W. Stroebe and H. Schut (eds) *Handbook of Bereavement Research: Consequences, Coping, and Care* (pp.614–646). Washington, DC: American Psychological Association.

Prigerson, H.G., Bierhals, A.J., Kasl, S.V., Reynolds, C.F., Shear, M.K., Day, N., Beery, L.C, Newsom, J.T. and Jacobs, S. (1997) Traumatic grief as a risk factor for mental and physical morbidity. *American Journal of Psychiatry*, 154, 616–623.

Prigerson, H.G., Maciejewski, P.K., Reynolds, C.F., Bierhals, A.J., Newsom, J.T., Fasiczka, A., Frank, E. and Miller, M. (1995) Inventory of complicated grief: A scale to measure maladaptive symptoms of loss. *Psychiatry Research*, 59, 65–79.

Prigerson, H.G., Shear, M.K., Jacobs, S.C, Kasl, S.V., Maciejewski, P.K., Silverman, G.K., Narayan, M. and Bremner, J.D. (2000) Grief and its relation to PTSD. In D. Nutt and J.R.T. Davidson (eds) *Post Traumatic Stress Disorders: Diagnosis, Management and Treatment* (pp.163–186). New York: Martin Dunitz Publishers.

Provini, C., Everett, J.R. and Pfeffer, C.R. (2000) Adults mourning suicide: Self-reported concerns about bereavement, needs for assistance, and help-seeking behavior. *Death Studies*, 24, 1–9.

Raphael, B., Singh, B., Bradbury, L. and Lambert, F. (1983–1984) Who helps the helpers? The effect of a disaster on the rescue workers. *Omega*, 14, 9–20.

Reed, M.D. (1993) Sudden death and bereavement outcomes: The impact of resources on grief symptomatology and detachment. *Suicide and Life-Threatening Behavior*, 23, 204–220.

Reed, M.D. (1998) Predicting grief symptomatology among the suddenly bereaved. *Suicide and Life-Threatening Behavior*, 28, 3, 285–300.

Reusch, J. and Bateson, G. (1951) Communication and human relations: An interdisciplinary approach. In J. Reusch and G. Bateson (eds) *Communication: The Social Matrix of Psychiatry*. New York: Norton.

Riches, G. and Dawson, P. (1996a) Making stories and taking stories: Methodological reflections on researching grief and marital tension following the death of a child. *British Journal of Guidance and Counselling*, 24, 3, 357–365.

Riches, G. and Dawson, P. (1996b) Communities of feeling: The culture of bereaved parents. *Mortality*, 1, 2.

Riches, G. and Dawson, P. (1996c) 'An intimate loneliness': Evaluating the impact of a child's death on parent self-identity and marital relationships. *Journal of Family Therapy*, 18, 1–22.

Rothschild, B. and Rand, M. (2006) *Help for the Helper. Self-care Strategies for Managing Burnout and Stress*. New York: Norton.

Samuelsson, M., Rådestad, I. and Segesten, K. (2001) A waste of life: Fathers' experience of losing a child before birth. *Birth*, 28, 124–130.

SANDS (2008) www.uk-sands.org/publications/support-and-information-leaflets.html (last accessed April 2008).

Sarason, B.R., Sarason, I.G. and Gurung, R.A.R. (1997) Close personal relationships and health outcomes: A key to the role of social support. In S. Duck (ed.) *Handbook of Personal Relationships. Theory, Research and Interventions* (pp.547–573). New York: Wiley and Sons.

Sarason, B.R., Sarason, I.G. and Pierce, G.R. (eds) (1990) *Social Support: An Interactional View*. New York: John Wiley and Sons.

Sarason, I.G., Sarason, B.R. and Shearin, E. (1986) Social support as an individual difference variable: Its stability, origins, and relational aspects. *Journal of Personality and Social Psychology*, 50, 4, 845–855.

Schaefer, C., Quesenberry, C.P. and Wi, S. (1995) Mortality following conjugal bereavement and the effects of a shared environment. *American Journal of Epidemiology*, 141, 1142–1152.

Schwab, R. (1998) A child's death and divorce: Dispelling the myth. *Death Studies*, 22, 445–468.

Schwarzer, R. and Leppin, A. (1989) Social support and health: A meta-analysis. *Psychology and Health: An International Journal*, 3, 1–15.

Scott, P.A. and Schwenk, T.L. (2000) Physical activity and mental health: Current concepts. Review article. *Sports Medicine*, 29, 167–180.

Sèguin, M., Lesage, A. and Kiely, M.C. (1995) Parental bereavement after suicide and accident: A comparative study. *Suicide and Life-Threatening Behavior*, 25, 4, 489–490.

Shear, K., Frank, E., Houck, P.R. and Reynolds, C.F. (2005) Treatment of complicated grief. *Journal of the American Medical Association*, 293, 2601–2608.

Sherkat, D.E. and Reed, M.D. (1992) The effects of religion and social support on self-esteem and depression among the suddenly bereaved. *Social Indicators Research*, 26, 259–275.

Spanier, G.B. (1976) Measuring dyadic adjustment: New scales for assessing the quality of marriage and similar dyads. *Journal of Marriage and the Family*, 38, 15–28.

Stamm, B.H. (1995) *Secondary Traumatic Stress: Self-care Issues for Clinicians, Researchers, and Educators*. Baltimore, MD: Sidran Press.

Stewart, A.E. (1999) Complicated bereavement and posttraumatic stress disorder following fatal car crashes: Recommendations for death notification practice. *Death Studies* 23, 289–321.

Stroebe, M.S. (1998) New directions in bereavement research: Exploration of gender differences. *Palliative Medicine*, 12, 5–12.

Stroebe, M.S. and Schut, H. (1999) The dual process model of coping with bereavement: Rationale and description. *Death Studies*, 23, 197–224.

Stroebe, M.S. and Schut, H. (2001) Models of coping with bereavement: A review. In M.S. Stroebe, R.O. Hansson, W. Stroebe and H. Schut (eds) *Handbook of Bereavement Research* (pp.375–403). Baltimore, MD: United Book Press, Inc.

Stroebe, M.S., Schut, H. and Stroebe, W. (2005) Attachment in coping with bereavement. A theoretical integration. *Review of General Psychology*, 9, 48–66.

Stroebe, W., Zech, E., Stroebe, M.S. and Abakoumkin, G. (2005) Does social support help in bereavement? *Journal of Social and Clinical Psychology*, 24, 7, 1030–1050.

Tedeschi, R.G. and Calhoun, L.G. (1995) *Trauma and Transformation. Growing in the Aftermath of Suffering*. London: Sage Publications.

Tedeschi, R.G., Park, C.L. and Calhoun, L.G. (1998) *Posttraumatic Growth: Positive Changes in the Aftermath of Crisis*. Mahwah, NJ: Erlbaum.

Thoits, P.A. (1995) Stress, coping, and social support processes: Where are we? What next? *Journal of Health and Social Behavior* (Extra issue), 53–79.

Thompson, K.E. and Range, L.M. (1992) Bereavement following suicide and other deaths: Why support attempts fail. *Omega*, 26, 61–70.

Thuen, F. (1997a) Received social support from informal networks and professionals in bereavement. *Psychology, Health and Medicine*, 2, 1, 51–59.

Thuen, F. (1997b) Social support after the loss of an infant child: A long-term perspective. *Scandinavian Journal of Psychology*, 38, 103–110.

Ursano, R.J., Fullerton, C.S., Tzu-Cheg, K. and Bhartiya, V.R. (1995) Longitudinal assessment of posttraumatic stress disorder and depression after exposure to traumatic death. *The Journal of Nervous and Mental Disease*, 183, 36–42.

Van Dongen, C.J. (1993) Social context of post suicide bereavement. *Death Studies* 17, 125–141.

Wagner, K.G. and Calhoun, L.G. (1991–1992) Perceptions of social support by suicide survivors and their social networks. *Omega*, 24, 61–73.

Watzlawick, P., Beavin Bavelas, J. and Jackson, D.D. (1967) *Pragmatics of Human Communication*. New York: Norton.

Wertheimer, A. (1999) *A Special Scar. The Experiences of People Bereaved by Suicide*. First edition. London: Routledge.

Wertsch, J.V. (1988) *Culture, Communication and Cognition. Vygotskian Perspectives*. New York: Cambridge University Press.

Williams, M.B. and Poijula, S. (eds) (2002) *The PTSD Workbook*. Oakland, CA: New Harbinger Publications, Inc.

Wilson, A. and Clark, S. (2005) South Australian Suicide Postvention Project. Report to Mental Health Services. Department of Health. Department of General Practice, University of Adelaide, Australia.

Winje, D. (1997) *Psychological adjustment after severe trauma. A longitudinal study of adults' and children's posttraumatic reactions and coping after the bus accident in Måbødalen, Norway, 1988*. Doctoral thesis. Institute of Clinical Psychology. Faculty of Psychology. University of Bergen.

Worden, J.W., Davies, B. and McCown, D. (1999) Comparing parent loss with sibling loss. *Death Studies*, 23, 1–15.

Wortman, C.B. and Silver, R.C. (2001) The myths of coping with loss revisited. In M.S. Stroebe, R.O. Hansson, W. Stroebe and H. Schut (eds) *Handbook of Bereavement Research* (pp.405–429). Baltimore, MD: United Book Press, Inc.

Yule, W. (ed.) (1999) *Post-Traumatic Stress Disorders. Concepts and Therapy*. London: John Wiley and Sons.

Subject Index

Author Index